RACE, SLAVERY, AND LIB NINETEENTH-CENTURY LITERATURE

Moving boldly between literary analysis and political theory, contemporary and antebellum US culture, Arthur Riss invites readers to rethink prevailing accounts of the relationship between slavery, liberalism, and literary representation. Situating Nathaniel Hawthorne, Harriet Beecher Stowe, and Frederick Douglass at the centre of antebellum debates over the personhood of the slave, this book examines how a nation dedicated to the proposition that "all men are created equal" formulates arguments both for and against race-based slavery. This revisionary argument promises to be unsettling for literary critics, political philosophers, historians of US slavery, as well as those interested in the link between literature and human rights.

ARTHUR RISS is Assistant Professor of English at Salem State College, Salem, Massachusetts.

CAMBRIDGE STUDIES IN AMERICAN LITERATURE AND CULTURE

Recent books in this series

149. JENNIFER ASHTON
From Modernism to Postmodernism: American Poetry and Theory in the Twentieth Century

148. MAURICE S. LEE
Slavery, Philosophy, and American Literature, 1830–1860

147. CINDY WEINSTEIN
Family, Kinship and Sympathy in Nineteenth-Century American Literature

146. ELIZABETH HEWITT
Correspondence and American Literature, 1770–1865

145. ANNA BRICKHOUSE
Transamerican Literary Relations and the Nineteenth-Century Public Sphere

144. ELIZA RICHARDS
Gender and the Poetics of Reception in Poe's Circle

143. JENNIE A. KASSANOFF
Edith Wharton and the Politics of Race

142. JOHN MCWILLIAMS
New England's Crises and Cultural Memory: Literature, Politics, History, Religion, 1620–1860

141. SUSAN M. GRIFFIN
Anti-Catholicism and Nineteenth-Century Fiction

RACE, SLAVERY, AND LIBERALISM IN NINETEENTH-CENTURY AMERICAN LITERATURE

ARTHUR RISS

CAMBRIDGE
UNIVERSITY PRESS

CAMBRIDGE UNIVERSITY PRESS
Cambridge, New York, Melbourne, Madrid, Cape Town, Singapore, São Paulo, Delhi

Cambridge University Press
The Edinburgh Building, Cambridge CB2 8RU, UK

Published in the United States of America by Cambridge University Press, New York

www.cambridge.org
Information on this title: www.cambridge.org/9780521120203

First published 2006
Third printing 2008
This digitally printed version 2009

A catalogue record for this publication is available from the British Library

Library of Congress Cataloguing in Publication data

Riss, Arthur, 1961–
Race, slavery, and liberalism in nineteenth-century American literature / Arthur Riss.
p. cm. – (Cambridge studies in American literature and culture)
Includes bibliographical references and index.
ISBN-13: 978-0-521-85674-4
ISBN-10: 0-521-85674-4
1. American literature – 19th century – History and criticism. 2. Slavery in literature.
3. Race in literature. 4. Liberalism in literature. 5. African Americans in literature. 6. Stowe, Harriet Beecher, 1811–1896 – Criticism and interpretation. 7. Hawthorne, Nathaniel, 1804–1864 – Criticism and interpretation. 8. Politics and literature – United States – History – 19th century. 9. United States – Politics and government–1783–1865. I. Title. II. Series: Cambridge studies in American literature and culture; 150.

PS217.S55R57 2006
810.9'3552–dc22
2005034534

ISBN 978-0-521-85674-4 hardback
ISBN 978-0-521-12020-3 paperback

Contents

Acknowledgements — *page* vii

Introduction: the figure a "person" makes: on the aesthetics of liberalism — 1

1 Slaves and persons — 27

2 Family values and racial essentialism in *Uncle Tom's Cabin* — 58

3 Eva's hair and the sentiments of race — 84

4 A is for Anything: US liberalism and the making of *The Scarlet Letter* — 111

5 The art of discrimination: *The Marble Faun*, "Chiefly About War Matters," and the aesthetics of anti-black racism — 136

6 Freedom, ethics, and the necessity of persons: Frederick Douglass and the scene of resistance — 164

Notes — 186

Index — 235

Acknowledgements

There is neither time nor space enough to list all of those who read, listened to, and/or commented on parts of this project in its various incarnations. I am glad, however, to have this opportunity to acknowledge some of the people who have substantially helped me think and live through this project. This book began at the University of California, Berkeley under the guidance of Mitch Breitwieser and Steve Knapp. They, in very different ways, have instructed and inspired me. Joe Cambray, Leonard Cassuto, Gregg Crane, Simone Davis, Frances Ferguson, Greg Forter, Mia Fuller, Robert Gunn, Allen Kurzweil, Nancy Schultz, Franny Nudelman, Jeff Peterson, Marilyn Reizbaum, Peter Walker, Ted Williams, and Brenda Wineapple offered crucial advice and direction at crucial moments. I appreciate the support (financial and institutional) I received from the University of California, Berkeley, the Mabelle McLeod Lewis Foundation, and Salem State College. I also want to thank the anonymous readers for Cambridge University Press for their careful and constructive critiques. Thanks are also due to Ray Ryan, Maartje Scheltens, and Liz Davey at Cambridge University Press for their patience and help in transforming typescript into print.

Mary Cappello and Jean Walton have offered me both personal and intellectual sustenance from the moment I met them. Their questions have made this a better book and me a better thinker (I am tempted to say "person"). I am very grateful that Lisa Guerin and Daniel Kim, two incredibly insightful and generous readers, tried, at very different times, to get "inside" my argument. Louis Suarez-Potts and Tony Corbeill have lived with this project as long as I have. Without them this book would not have been finished. I hope they know how much their abiding presence means to me. I feel lucky to have parents so dedicated to learning and so engaged in my work. And I will never forget that my sisters, Suzie and Wendy, were always willing to read my words, improve my prose, and then read more.

Nina jokes and says I owe everything to her . . . I have to agree. But I probably owe her more.

This book is for Natasha and Kolya: whence came their spirit I do not know.

Publication credits:

A version of Chapter 2 previously appeared in *American Quarterly*, 46:4 (December 1994): 513–544; a version of Chapter 5 previously appeared in *ELH* 71:1 (spring 2004): 251–287. I am grateful to the Johns Hopkins University Press for permission to reprint.

Introduction – the figure a "person" makes: on the aesthetics of liberalism

It is often asserted that the egalitarian rhetoric of the American Revolution, a rhetoric crystallized by the Declaration of Independence's claim that "all men are created equal," necessarily doomed US slavery. The values of the Declaration, as Winthrop Jordan has stated, are logically and morally incompatible with the institution of slavery and thus inexorably "require the complete abolition of slavery."[1] According to this account, the only reason the birth of America and the death of race-based slavery was not immediate is that this nation's founding principles failed to be "taken at face value," their obvious meaning misunderstood, distorted, or disavowed (p. 341).

Given the assumption that slavery obviously distorts the ideals of America, it is not surprising that the history of the United States is often imagined in terms of the progressive revelation of the clear and explicit meaning of this declaration. In his magisterial study of US citizenship, Rogers Smith, for example, has explored the extent to which an ascriptive political tradition, one that establishes political identities on the basis of race, gender, and religion, has competed with this nation's liberal tradition and worked to block the expression of the Declaration's ideals of freedom and equality.[2] Similarly, Garry Wills has argued that Lincoln's genius was to promote the Declaration of Independence rather than the more ambivalent Constitution as this nation's foundational document. Lincoln did so, according to Wills, because "[p]ut the claims of the Declaration as mildly as possible, and it still cannot be reconciled with slavery."[3]

In contrast to such accounts, this project begins by challenging the assumption that the Declaration of Independence possesses an obvious anti-slavery meaning. Rather than invoke statements like the clause "all men are created equal" as, according to one commentator, "plain words," words inherently antagonistic to race-based slavery, words that simply need to be expressed, this book focuses on how the self-evident meaning of these words has changed, shifting, for example, from the 1780s when only white propertied males were regarded as "men" to the 1990s when the word is understood as obviously comprehending (among others) women of all races.[4] That is, rather than argue that abolitionists simply needed to "apply to blacks, *in an immediate and literal fashion*, the dictum that 'all men are created equal,'" this project explores how the literal meaning of these words has itself been the subject of dispute.[5]

Indeed, modern confidence in the obvious and transparent anti-slavery meaning of the Declaration's most famous clause deserves comment not only because these words have come to be identified as the quintessence of the American ideological project, but also because such confidence seems to erase the historical problem that during the antebellum period these words legitimated arguments both for and against slavery.[6] For example, Abraham Lincoln, who strongly opposed slavery, and Chief Justice Taney, who in the Dred Scott Decision [1857] declared that slavery was constitutional and that the Negro "had no rights which the white man was bound to respect," both invoked the clause "all men are created equal" to prove their incompatible conclusions about the legitimacy of slavery.[7] If for Lincoln these words obviously condemn slavery as an incontrovertible violation of basic American values, for Taney these words are "too clear for dispute" and "conclusive": they establish that the Founders could not have intended the Negro to be included in the national community and that the race "formed no part of the people" (Dred Scott v. Sandford, 60 US (19 How.) 410).[8]

In part, it may seem clear why this phrase could be invoked in fundamentally opposing ways: during the antebellum period the question of the obvious and immediate meaning of the term Man was itself in dispute. Some, for example, considered it manifest that the Negro was a different species, one naturally and irrevocably inferior to the Anglo-Saxon race.[9] Contesting the anthropological and biological theorists of the Enlightenment, who asserted that mankind had a monogenetic origin and that racial differences were due to environmental factors, the most influential ethnologists of the antebellum era argued that nothing short of the separate creation of the races (polygenesis) could account for the diversity of Man and the stability of differentiating characteristics and concluded that only Caucasians were authentic progeny of Adam.[10] The scientists of the internationally respected American School of Ethnology, in fact, were committed to the anthropometric cataloging of the types of mankind – carefully measuring, among other things, skull size, facial angle, lips, length of the leg, size of the foot, shape of nostrils, distance between navel and penis, and the texture of hair of the Negro – precisely because it was assumed that such surface differences could reveal deeper truths about the absolute differences between White and Black.[11] By fusing the somatic and the semiotic, these researchers linked the visible markers of racial difference to cognitive, cultural, and moral characteristics, proving that race is destiny, a set of attributes that are immutable, innate to the species, the result neither of circumstance nor degeneration.[12]

While the American School of Ethnology was making ostensibly objective, empirical arguments about the Negro as a separate species, religious thinkers, troubled by the fact that the logic of polygenesis undermined the Mosaic account of creation found in Genesis, turned to the Bible as the clearest defense of slavery and as the best evidence of why the Negro race was divinely marked as essentially and eternally different.[13] Josiah Priest, for example, cited Biblical text to prove that Ham was a Black man and that the curse of Ham revealed how God had deliberately separated the Negro from the rest of mankind. In particular, Priest claimed that God had given the race overdeveloped sexual organs and had subjected the Negro to uncontrollable fits of sexual passion to place the race permanently beyond the reach of civilization.[14]

Given such scientific and religious proof that the Negro was not and could never be a (white) Man, it is not surprising that apologists for slavery rarely felt compelled to avoid the language of the Declaration of Independence. Although some did abandon the Declaration, most notoriously perhaps George Fitzhugh – the period's most ardent opponent of liberty – , more often than not pro-slavery advocates asserted their unswerving allegiance to the principles of the Revolution. Thus, Moncure Conway found it "self-evident" that "the Negro was not a Man within the meaning of the Declaration Independence" and concluded, as Senator Albert Gallatin Brown of Mississippi did, that "[n]owhere in this broad union but in the slaveholding states is there a living, breathing exemplification of the beautiful statement, that all men are equal."[15] According to such a line of argument, the notion of "men" obviously referred to only the *white* man. As one Southern planter put it, the Declaration is perfectly consistent with race-based slavery as long as these words are properly understood, that is, understood in the way they were obviously intended:

> . . .[slavery] does not appear to be consistent with the letter of one article in the Declaration of Independence; but however the expressions in the article may be apparently unlimited, it is certain they were designed to be understood in a

restricted sense: For it cannot be conceived that they were designed to declare that children, idiots, lunatics, or criminals should enjoy equal privileges of Society with the rest of the Community.[16]

To read "men" as all human creatures struck many during the antebellum period as a patent absurdity, a clear case of how an individual's perspective can distort one's interpretation. If such interpretative excess is allowed, Senator John Pettit of Indiana warned, these words are rendered "a self-evident lie."[17]

Of course, others during the antebellum period, such as Theodore Weld, Lydia Maria Child, William Lloyd Garrison, Wendell Phillips, and Frederick Douglass, cited these same words to affirm that it was self-evident that the word "men" included the Negro (although they differed about whether these words referred to women). Such thinkers ridiculed the fact that "we must have books to prove what is palpable even to brute creation – to wit: the negro is a man!"[18]

The former slave Solomon Northup deftly condenses antebellum debates over what the word Man obviously means in his sketch of an argument between Samuel Bass (a white carpenter) and Northup's master Edwin Epps:

'Look here, Epps,' continued his companion [Bass]; 'you can't laugh me down in that way. Some men are witty, and some ain't so witty as they think they are. Now let me ask you a question. *Are all men created free and equal as the Declaration of Independence hold they are?' Yes,' responded Epps, 'but all men, niggers, and monkeys ain't* (emphasis added).'[19]

Although parodied by Northup, Epps' assertion effectively recapitulates how the most famous clause of the Declaration of Independence has reproduced rather than resolved the problem of slavery. As this scene makes clear, even though this clause may be invoked as ending once and for all any question about the legitimacy of slavery, it ultimately crystallizes rather than ends the debate.

If, as Frederick Douglass stated, the "manhood of the Negro" is the "elementary" question on which the "whole defence [sic] of the slave system" hinges, then one could say that the legitimacy of US slavery was so intensely debated by antebellum culture precisely because the answer to this elementary question was itself under debate.[20] Indeed, since those on both sides of the antebellum debate on slavery summoned the notion of Man as if it were an immediate, transparent, and literal referent – the only plausible means to end debate – the historical battle over slavery can be understood as a battle to persuade others that a particular interpretation of Man is self-evident. Carried out not only in the scientific, but also in political, legal, and religious arenas, and, as I will argue, in literary discourse, the question of whether the Negro counted as a Man preoccupied antebellum culture.[21]

If one accepts that many during the antebellum period simply excluded the Negro from the category of Man and thus did not axiomatically recognize race-based slavery as fundamentally unjust and un-American, the question then becomes why it was not obvious during the antebellum period that the Negro is a Man. Why was antebellum culture so intensely debating an issue whose answer we know to be self-evident? It is this disparity between the antebellum controversy and our modern certainty about the meaning of this nation's foundational claim "all men are created equal" that initiates this project.

Conventionally, it is asserted that antebellum culture either could not or did not apprehend the true meaning of this clause to the extent that knowledge of this identity category was perverted by racial prejudice and irrationality, swayed by politics and self-interest, or misled by ignorance and historical exigencies. Thus, to cite a notorious example, the *Dred Scott* decision is now universally repudiated because Taney's ruling is characterized as grossly political, "twisted," and "infected" by contemporary racist beliefs.[22] Or, as I will discuss more fully in Chapter One, if Southern defenders of slavery are now conventionally understood as fundamentally hypocritical, as disavowing something that they know to be true (the fact that slavery misidentifies human beings as things), such a line of argument implicitly relies on the notion of Man as absolute and fixed, contrasting those who apprehend the plain and straightforward meaning of the word Man to those who distort or are unable to recognize it. It is precisely this assumption, however, that the history of race-based slavery challenges and this project sets out to interrogate.

To claim that racism or hypocrisy has disfigured the meaning of Man is to assume that there is some bedrock meaning to this term that then is interpreted (either rightly, i.e. objectively and rationally, or wrongly, i.e. in terms of self-interest, contingency, or irrationality). To argue, for example, that race-consciousness represses or twists this identity is to attribute to Man a fixed, immanent meaning, a meaning that racial categories block, a meaning upon which a racist interpretation is forcibly imposed and with which racialist premises inevitably interfere.[23] The assumption that such race-consciousness covers up the true meaning of Man for all intents and purposes assumes that the notion of Man possesses a solidity prior to and despite any historically conditioned interpretation, positing this identity category as something that can be viewed from various vantage points but which can only really be recognized if and when such parenthetical perspectives have been exorcised. Indeed, it is because such an approach presupposes that the true meaning of the conceptual category Man stands before and independent of any interpretation that we now conventionally regard a racist interpretation as a self-evidently false interpretation rather than as a competing one.

Such an approach assumes, in short, that the notion of Man, properly understood, is the self-evident point of departure for emancipatory thought. To do so is to forget how profoundly the concept to which we appeal has historically been contested and to erase that it is precisely the question of what the conceptual category Man literally and plainly means that antebellum culture put into dispute. It is to allow the clause "all men are created equal" to become a touchstone, something with a universal, neutral, and transparent meaning rather than one embedded in context and indebted to political struggle. Our certainty about what a Man is, in essence, has incited us to anachronistically redescribe the historical distance between antebellum and modern accounts of the Man as an absolute difference between understanding and misunderstanding, between mystification and demystification. The goal of this project is to put the notion of Man into history and to examine how significantly our understanding of US slavery and of the US liberal tradition is altered once the notion of Man is approached as a fundamentally contextual rather than absolute category of knowledge.

It is this abiding drive to summon Man as if this identity were intrinsically sufficient to determine liberal ethics that underwrites my use of the word "person" (rather than Man) to name the conceptual category at the heart of debates over slavery. In particular, since we now (at least theoretically) regard this conceptual category as independent of gender (among other identity markers), I will from now on deliberately eschew the term "man" when discussing the conceptual category at the center of liberal theory.

By abandoning a term that now strikes us as egregiously limited by its masculinist premise and substituting a more comprehensive term, I seek to foreground the function that this foundational conceptual category has served not only in debates over slavery, but also in liberal thought in general. If the term Man strikes a contemporary audience as inadequately exhaustive, the "person" more forcefully captures the sense of political innocence attributed to the identity summoned to end political debate, the identity that remains after irrational, biased, local, and contingent criteria (such as race) are removed. Simultaneously a legal and ethical concept, the "person" names the object comprehended to be the only true candidate for representation and liberation, a primal identity beyond and above the misrepresentations that politics and history have imposed upon it.

Similarly, I am using the term "person" rather than the term *human being* to suggest how the conceptual category grounding liberal thought has proven to be remarkably elastic, not necessarily restricted to or coterminous with the category of the human. The distance between "personhood" and "humanity," of course, is perhaps most evident in the scientific rhetoric of the American School of Ethnology. As the prominent Louisiana physician Samuel Cartwright explained when introducing his scientific classification of the Negro, the Negro is a peculiar kind of human being:

> It is not intended by the use of the term Prognathous to call in question the black man's humanity or the unity of the human races as a genus, but to prove that the species of the genus homo are not a unity, but a plurality, each essentially different from the others. . . not that the negro is a brute, or half-man and half brute, but a genuine human being, anatomically constructed, about the head and face, more like the monkey tribes and the lower order of animals than any other species of the genus man.[24]

Cartwright's statement clarifies the extent to which many pro-slavery thinkers recognized the Negro as a human being, but not as a "person," regarding the Negro as an essentially different species of human and therefore as ineligible for the legal rights and ethical regard inalienably guaranteed to "persons."[25]

If during the antebellum period "personhood" was at times resolutely allied with ascriptive ideologies of race, class, and gender and thus a strikingly exclusive category, one far more contracted than the notion of the human, today "personhood" is often invoked as a spectacularly inclusive category, one that extends well beyond the notion of the human. Thus, it has been argued that rights are possessed, according to legal theorists, by corporations, buildings, labor unions, and ships, and, according to deep ecologists, by animals, trees, and even rocks, and, according to futurists like Hans Moravec and Ray Kurzweil, by artificial intelligence and computer programs.[26]

It is this tension between a transcendental and a historical understanding of the privileged referent in liberal theory (the "person") that US slavery powerfully foregrounds. The horrors of slavery seem to tempt us to invoke the notion of the "person" as an irrepressible identity, an identity that in and of itself makes the injustice of slavery obvious. But the historical debates over slavery simultaneously reveal that this ostensibly neutral identity category is deeply political. To emphasize the historically contested nature of the "person," I have put this conceptual category under quotation. These marks are designed to accent how this term is a site of struggle and to provoke uncertainty about the way that the term is traditionally deployed.[27] I am not arguing that "persons" do not exist or that the category is never settled. Rather I am interested in how this identity in itself settles nothing. This conceptual category, one could say, does not exist in the way liberal thought imagines and hopes it does. My aim is to defamiliarize liberalism's production of and dependence on the "person" as an irreducible center, as an identity immunized from history.[28]

This book places the foundation on which liberals conventionally establish an understanding of the politics and history of slavery under investigation, regarding our certainty about the "person" as knowledge that, as Foucault would say, "is not made for understanding but for cutting."[29] Rather than take our knowledge about the "person" as immediate and *a priori*, I will argue that inasmuch as we have summoned the "person" as the primary instrument for studying slavery, we have disappeared this identity from the field of investigation, invoking it as the motor of, instead of a topic for, historical analysis.[30] The "person," however, is a historical consequence in need of the kind of explanation that it supposedly provides.

RACISM

To put the notion of the "person" into history is to suggest that modern confidence in the self-evident "personhood" of African-American slaves confuses the success of arguments for Negro "personhood" with the source of this argument's success, retroactively constructing a historical achievement (the "personification" of the US slave) as a transcendental fact (slaves always already are "persons") that inevitably will be expressed. Rather than trace how we have acquired more accurate knowledge of the "person," I am interested in the historical work needed to make the Negro into a "person." Having been achieved, this work – like the work needed to make propertyless Anglo-Saxon men, middle-class white women, and heathens into "persons" – is now conventionally understood as a process of removing the barriers (racism, sexism, anti-Catholicism etc.) that prevented our gaining epistemic clarity about an object ("personhood").

To understand such knowledge as always already existing and as simply unaccessed, however, is only possible to the extent that the battle over such knowledge is now over. Although it may seem reassuring to see "personhood" as an essential attribute of the oppressed, a pregiven identity that simply needs to be unveiled – liberated from prejudice, ethnocentrism, and irrationality – I am suggesting that "personhood" only becomes intrinsic and indisputably possessed retroactively. It is precisely because the work of "personifying" slaves has been completed that this work can be forgotten and so thoroughly erased.

It is only because we have now reached an undisputed consensus about the injustice of race-based slavery (everybody today almost reflexively asserts that slavery and racialized conceptions of the "person" are wrong) that we have imagined the "personhood" of the slave as something that would inevitably be expressed rather than as an identity that had to be asserted in the face of fierce national conflict. Our certainty that markers of difference (such as race, class, gender, religion, etc.) are inessential to determining an individual's worthiness for and access to liberal rights – our sense that such markers are "interesting accidents" to be consigned to the "wastebasket of the contingent" – has worked to obscure the extent to which antebellum culture debated this very question.[31]

My historicist account of the "person" should not be taken as analogous to the argument that Negroes were not "persons" in any absolute sense before they were represented as "persons." I am not interested in attacking the powerful and deeply affective humanistic belief that slaves are "persons." I am only asking whether questions about the incontestable reality of "personhood" are productive questions to ask. That is, instead of making truth statements about an autonomous reality from which to securely stage resistance to injustice – asking how "persons" could be reduced to slaves or claiming that slaves were not real "persons" – I focus on how such truth statements are articulated and become transparent. And similarly, rather than regret how the "person" has failed to function as a stable or objective foundation – a disappointment that would preserve a commitment to objectivity in an ostensible critique of objectivity – I am interested in interrogating the hope that the "person" transcends any context and thus can police political practices.

To examine the "personhood" of the Negro as a fact that needs to be produced as obvious is certainly not to excuse slavery or racism. But, it is to raise significant questions about how assertions that these practices are obviously immoral and unjust depend upon an ahistorical conception of the "person." Certainly many defenses of slavery, such as the one proposed by the editor of the *Richmond Examiner*, did depend upon racial difference to make slavery "safe" for America and to explain why US slavery is a "positive good":

> All argument drawn from principles invented and intended for the white man, like the aphorisms of our Declaration of Independence, are, when applied to the negro, illogical. They involve the assumption that the negro is the white man, only a little different in external appearance and education. But this assumption cannot be supported. Ethnology and anatomy, history and daily observation, all contradict that idea in a way about which there can be no mistake. . . . Again and again we repeat it, the negro is not the white man. Not with more safety do we assert that a hog is not a horse. Hay is good for horses, but not for hogs. Liberty is good for white men, but not for negroes.[32]

This argument clearly establishes an invidious hierarchy based upon race. To claim, however, that such assertions about racial identity distort and are artificially grafted onto an objective meaning of the "person" ultimately deflates the seriousness of slavery and racism, reducing each to mistakes that will inevitably be corrected.

"Racism" is by definition abhorrent. The problem is that not all practices that we classify as racist have universally been identified as abhorrent. Indeed, many practices that we now see as perverted by racism have historically been understood as simply reflecting the order of things. To have persuasively identified someone or some practice as racist signals the end of discussion – it is a trump card that presupposes a conclusion about what a "person" is – and thus this charge itself signals the ascendance of a particular account of the "person." By the time the term is convincingly applied to a specific behavior, the debate over what a "person" is has ended. The word racist, in short, is an effect of a set of assumptions about "personhood." Invocations of the term racism let us evade unsettling questions about the historical contingency of the "person," allowing us to mistake a historical symptom for a transhistorical cure. Again, this is not to say that race-based slavery or racism is not wrong; it is only to say that neither is wrong because of the way it misunderstands some inherent truth about the "person."[33] It is not to legitimate racism but to question the assumption that race is something added to the meaning of the "person" and that once this extraneous layer is subtracted, then "personhood" could be expressed.

This project thus seeks neither to uncover the ubiquitous racism informing antebellum debates over the Negro race's qualifications for citizenship (focusing on how figures such as Abraham Lincoln, Harriet Beecher Stowe, or Martin Delany imagined the "person" as essentially determined by race) nor to champion some for transcending such prevailing racialism (focusing on how figures such as Wendell Phillips, Frederick Douglass, or Lydia Maria Child argued for a color blind understanding of individuals). Both approaches are limited to the extent that each assumes that race is always already distinct from "personhood."[34] Such an assumption implicitly removes the "person" from history and attributes to this identity a universal content, one that simply needs to be accurately described. This focus is not to discount the era's vigorous debate over whether the Negro was capable of self-government, moral judgment, or abstract thought, but it is to subsume the impulse to reconstruct the different ways that antebellum culture attributed a specific content to the "person" within a discussion of how no matter what the content attributed to the "person," this content is imagined as intrinsic. As long as this content is imagined as immanent to the "person," an examination of how particular definitions of the "person" function in particular contexts is foreclosed. In contrast to arguments that approach the primary referent of liberal thought as possessing a meaning to be found and expressed, I examine how the "person" is continually under construction.

LIBERALISM

Since liberalism is a notoriously baggy term, my use of it requires specification. I am discussing liberalism not so much as a specific political doctrine, social program, or political party, but as a coherent metaphysical system, one that grounds its political, social, and legal institutions and practices on how well it defers to the authority of the "person." In my account, liberalism is an ensemble of discursive practices constituted and bounded by a particular account of the priority of the "person," a political philosophy that demands that all political and social institutions be derived from and sanctioned by the "person" rather than by some supernatural foundation. The primary innovation of liberalism is that it transposes a system of authority that defines rights vertically (as claims granted by some power above and beyond "persons") with one that holds a horizontal account of rights (the "person" itself is the source of rights and the claims of "persons" are defined in relation to the claims of other "persons"). One could say that liberalism marks a rupture in the way the problems of political philosophy must be framed: the problem of political authority is no longer debated in a divine or transcendent register; now it is cast in terms of the question "who is a 'person'?"

Thus, before the advent of liberalism, the right to rights was explicitly connected with one's affiliation to social and political organizations. In Ancient Greece and Ancient Rome, for example, the category of the "person" was an explicitly political identity, a social position explicitly rooted in one's birth and in the public sphere.[35] In such societies, all privileges were the privileges of the citizen. It is only within the contours of liberal political thought that the "person" leaves the political realm and becomes a natural and self-evident concept, the inviolate origin that a system of rights must express. With the ascendance of liberalism the "person" becomes the inert and pre-given ground to which politics refers and to which politics must remain subordinate. The mark of a liberal society is that "personhood" is invoked as distinct from political issues of nationality and citizenship.[36] Liberalism inaugurates the belief that if certain groups or individuals are refused civil and political rights, they can still appeal for such rights on the basis of their inherent status as "persons." Liberals summon the "person" to restrain the vicissitudes of politics.

I approach liberalism, in short, as a theory of representation, one that seeks to safeguard the object of liberal representation (the "person") from the contingent act of representation. Indeed, since this book seeks to question both the solidity of the object of liberal representation (the "person") and the liberal assumption that the "person" always remains prior to and thus can never be reduced to its representation, it can be seen as a literary revision of Hanna Pitkin's classic account of the relationship between "the people" (the object of liberal representation) and the act of liberal representation.[37] In *The Concept of Representation*, Pitkin carefully details the intellectual history of and the philosophical assumptions behind the notion of representative government. According to Pitkin, a government shows itself to be truly

> representative not by demonstrating its control over its subjects but just the reverse, by demonstrating that its subjects have control over what it does. Every government's actions are attributed to its subjects formally, legally. But in a representative government this attribution has substantive content: the people really do act through their government, and are not merely passive recipients of its actions. A representative government must not merely be in control, not merely promote the public interest, but must also be responsive to the people (232)

Underlying Pitkin's account of the ideal form of political representation is not simply the valorizing of liberal representation's emphasis on the "people" as the only standard by which to judge representation, but more importantly, the acceptance of liberalism's paradigmatic assumption that the foundational referent of representation (the "People") is a pre-existing and stable referent. Pitkin assumes that what is expressed in the machinery and structures of liberal representation is a political subject or identity that exists independently of and prior to the process of representation. She defines a liberal government as a structure that expresses and conforms to the "People." Thus she judges the legitimacy of political structures by determining how well a particular government responds to "persons," asking how accurately it reflects this object.[38]

Rather than follow Pitkin's assumption that the source of political representation can be fully present, my account more closely resembles Derrida's reading of the Declaration of Independence.[39] According to Derrida, the Declaration of Independence may claim to re-present an already existing political subject (the People), but the document actually brings this object into existence. Although it cites the People as the only legitimate source of authority, the document produces what it imagines as prior to its declaration. As Derrida puts it,

> [t]he 'we' of the declaration speaks 'in the name of the people.' . . . But this people does not exist. They do not exist as an entity, it does not exist, before this declaration . . . it gives birth to itself, as free and independent subject. . . The signature invents the signer (10).

For Derrida, the structure of this declaration is necessarily tautological. As both "the producer and the guarantor of its own signature," the Declaration forges (in both senses of the word) the People of the United States (Declarations, 10).

Although Derrida never explicitly states it, he is discussing the mechanics of liberal political representation. The "People" occupy the ground from which liberal governments claim to derive their authority, legitimating liberal representation because they are imagined as governing the economy of liberal representation. But the "People" only emerge within and from the act of representation itself. Derrida and Pitkin posit an opposite relation between the presence of the "People" and representation. While Derrida sees the "People's" presence as an effect of representation, Pitkin sees the presence of the "People" as the precondition for representation. Derrida, in essence, inverts the temporal logic of liberal discourse, positing the "person" as an effect rather than the source of liberal politics and contesting the way in which liberalism assumes that the notion of the "person" comes *first* and *then* is represented in liberal discourse and liberal institutions.

Deeply influenced by such a post-structuralist account of the performative nature of representation, my argument questions how the "person" (the putative origin of liberal representation) is deployed in liberal thought as an identity that transcends rather than emanates from politics and perspective. If for Pitkin the "People" positively exist and their needs simply have to be adequately voiced, and if for Derrida the "People" is a negativity, a transcendental signified whose meaning is endlessly deferred, I, in contrast, examine arguments over race-based slavery to clarify how "personhood" is produced at particular historical moments. This project does not seek to make absolute claims about the "person" (i.e. that the person *has* no content – *is* a fundamentally raceless category – or *can* never be captured by language), but to avoid such unconditional statements about what the "person" is. To focus on particular historical instantiations of the "person" is to argue that representationalist declarations about the correspondence between "persons" and reality have historically accomplished less than we have hoped and been more contested than we imagine.

Thus, if traditionally the history of liberal rights in the United States has been presented as if it were a gradual recognition of previously misrecognized "persons," I emphasize the secondary meaning of the term recognition: liberal representation confers and ascribes the identity of the "person" upon a being. Liberalism does not come to see an identity eternally present and merely invisible or repressed, but produces the identity that it professes to merely register. This project, in short, approaches the "person" as an effect rather than the source of liberal representation.

By placing liberalism's primary referent into History, my book revises traditional accounts of the US liberal tradition. But it does so, for the most part, without directly engaging the extensive body of historical work on whether a liberal (individualistic) consensus or a republican (civic humanist) tradition has dominated the social and political discourse of the United States.[40] I do so because I am interested in what these conventionally opposed traditions share rather than in what separates them. In particular, I am interested in how both the classical liberal and republican discourses attribute a prescriptive force to the notion of the "person." The conventional conflict between liberal and republican traditions can be seen as occurring within what I am calling the framework of liberal theory: both the classical liberal and the civic republican designate the "person" as the only proper origin of social and political thought. Both traditions posit the "person" as foundational. They simply hold onto different accounts of the "person." The liberal and the republican traditions, according to this account, are both engaged in the quintessentially liberal debate over the meaning of the "person."

The conflict between the liberal and republican traditions, in other words, is itself motivated by competing visions of what a "person" is. For example, although liberal political thought is traditionally apprehended as privileging individual rights, private property, and government by consent at the expense of the republican concern with a virtuous, participatory citizenry dedicated to a common good, this opposition collapses if the model of the "person" on which liberal thought is predicated is imagined as a fundamentally communal rather than atomistic identity.[41] Similarly, the classic republican indictment of liberalism as an ideology with an inadequate social ethic and an impoverished sense of communal meaning is possible only because a competing communal model of the "person" is posited as foundational. That is, rather than challenge the longstanding claim that liberalism is a key term for understanding US culture, I seek to shift its centrality, exploring the way that it is precisely the prevalence of readings of US history in terms of the self-sufficient notion of the "person" (a strategy most manifest in accounts of US slavery) that ultimately testifies to the dominance of a liberal consensus.[42]

HAWTHORNE AND STOWE

It may seem counterintuitive that an argument about liberalism, race-based slavery, and "personhood" foregrounds literary texts, focusing primarily on revising traditional readings of the literary works of Nathaniel Hawthorne and Harriet Beecher Stowe. In part, I turn to literature because I am examining liberal thought as a theory of representation and literature thematizes the act of representation. Indeed, since literature – in a way law and politics cannot afford – raises fundamental questions about the act of representation and the construction of the object being represented, literary theory has developed a sophisticated vocabulary with which to analyze the act of representation itself, distinguishing, for example, between representation as resemblance, as substitution (making present again what is now absent), and as performative.[43]

Even more importantly, however, literature serves as a privileged site with which to examine liberalism because recent scholarship has persuasively demonstrated that literature, particularly sentimental literature, was crucial in the humanizing of the Black slave during the antebellum period. Literature worked to disseminate decisive knowledge about the "person," assuming a prominent office in arguments both for and against slavery. And certainly no text played a more central role in the cultural process of "personifying" slaves than Stowe's *Uncle Tom's Cabin*, a text whose social force in antebellum culture is perhaps most clearly condensed in Abraham Lincoln's (perhaps apocryphal but nonetheless telling) comment upon meeting Stowe in 1862: "So you're the little woman who wrote the book that started this great war."[44] *Uncle Tom's Cabin* thus is a logical focal point of my examination of how knowledge about the "personhood" of the slave was being produced during the antebellum period.[45]

Indeed, since *Uncle Tom's Cabin* so powerfully influenced the discussion of slavery, it is not surprising that it inspired numerous anti-*Uncle Tom's Cabin* novels, texts such as *Aunt Phillis's Cabin* (1852), *North and South* (1852), *Uncle Robin, in His Cabin in Virginia, and Tom without One in Boston* (1853), *Liberia; or My Peyton's Experiment* (1853), *The Lofty and the Lonely* (1853), *The Planter's Northern Bride* (1854), and *The Master's House* (1855). That pro-slavery advocates so quickly attempted both to counter and capture the cultural power of Stowe's novel suggests how centrally literature participated in adjudicating the "personhood" of the slave. The literary texture of this political debate consolidates the representational paradox underlying the antebellum debate over race-based slavery: these literary texts (whether pro- or anti-slavery) claim to be realistically representing the very object that they are ultimately helping to determine. It is precisely this process of positing the object of representation as prior to the act of representation at the same time that this object is being constituted that literature so powerfully foregrounds.

If the prominence of *Uncle Tom's Cabin* has acquired a certain degree of unavoidability in any argument about slavery, the centrality of Hawthorne may seem less clear-cut. Hawthorne, after all, has been notorious for his self-consciously literary indifference to political questions in general and the question of slavery, in particular.[46] I focus on Hawthorne, however, because this indifference bespeaks a competing truth about the evil of slavery. He was not completely silent about slavery. For Hawthorne, the "personhood" of the Negro slave is far from obvious, and consequently he is suspicious of what he sees as the extremism of anti-slavery reformers, offering numerous explanations of why doing nothing about slavery is the best solution. As he notoriously wrote in the campaign biography of his closest friend, the pro-slavery candidate Franklin Pierce, those devoted to the Union are wise enough to "look upon slavery as one of those evils which divine Providence does not leave to be remedied by human contrivances, but which, in its own good time, by some means impossible to be anticipated, but of the simplest and easiest operation, when all its uses shall have been fulfilled, it causes to vanish like a dream"?[47] Hawthorne later explained that these words were written not simply to conform with political expedience or friendship but "are my real sentiments, and I do not regret that they are on record."[48]

Critics have thus increasingly worked from the premise that Hawthorne's defense of the "peculiar institution" is not simply limited to his life as a political functionary, but also subtends the logic of his fiction.[49] Jonathan Arac, in the article that inspired much of this recent work, has argued that the *Life of Pierce* merely translates the logic of Hawthorne's romances (especially *The Scarlet Letter*) onto the idiom of politics, thereby subordinating any generic distinction between the literary and non-literary to a common commitment to a "politics of issueless patience," a politics that works to legitimate the status quo of slavery (Arac, 257). If Stowe galvanized an opposition to slavery, Hawthorne, in contrast, can be seen as a central figure in producing an opposing conservative knowledge about slavery and "personhood," one that legitimates the prevailing distinction between slaves and "persons."

This juxtaposing of Hawthorne and Stowe is, of course, not completely surprising; their opposition has come to frame some of the most influential modern readings of the American Renaissance (the hermeneutic center of US literary studies).[50] Critics regularly turn to this opposition to discuss the politics of canon formation, the difference between popular and elite writing, the relation between the aesthetic and the ideological, or the gender-inflected assumptions behind the American Renaissance. And, of course, most notably, Hawthorne and Stowe have been contrasted in terms of their opposing engagement with race-based slavery. It has become standard to contrast Stowe's commitment to ending US slavery to Hawthorne's highly stylized, aesthetic avoidance of the subject.[51]

This traditional opposition between Hawthorne's aestheticism and Stowe's activism, however, is ultimately less interesting than the fact that contemporary readings of Hawthorne and Stowe have been haunted by questions that foreground how much our approach to these authors depends upon the self-evidence of the notion of the "person." How could Hawthorne's fiction, it is often asked, consistently represent one person's bondage to another as the Unpardonable Sin, while he remained at best indifferent to and at worst an apologist for Negro slavery, an institution that depended upon the unlimited power of one man over another? It is assumed that since Hawthorne regularly deployed slavery as a metaphor for psychological bondage he should have been more concerned with "the literal enslavement of blacks" (Yellin, 88). It is assumed that he would have "unavoidably" made this connection and repudiated contemporaneous slavery were he not a racist (Yellin, 89). Critics are consistently disturbed by the way that Hawthorne, a vigorous defender of individual rights and the "sanctity of the human heart," nevertheless represents Negro slavery, an obvious violation of the human heart, as a problem beyond the realm of individuals to effect.

Similarly, it is asked: how could Harriet Beecher Stowe write this country's most powerful condemnation of Negro slavery and at the same time solidify rather than repudiate degrading racial stereotypes of the African-American? As one critic has succinctly stated the problem: "[b]ecause these stereotyped notions not only appear in *Uncle Tom's Cabin* but show up more frequently than perhaps Stowe had intended, it would seem that Stowe's attitude toward chattel slavery. . .was ambivalent."[52] Scholars remain troubled by the fact that Stowe's spectacularly influential repudiation of race-based slavery was not accompanied by a correspondingly powerful repudiation of racial essentialism and thus conclude that the text was not truly dedicated to human rights. As Richard Yarborough has explained, Stowe's "commitment to challenging the claim of black inferiority was frequently undermined by her own endorsement of racial stereotypes."[53] Any true opposition to slavery, it is assumed, must be coeval with an opposition to a racialized conception of the "person."

My focus on Hawthorne and Stowe proceeds beyond an account of how each participated in solidifying different versions of objective knowledge about Negro "personhood" during the antebellum period; it extends to an examination of how modern critics have read Hawthorne and Stowe. If, on the one hand, critics acknowledge that literature was a crucial apparatus for producing knowledge about the "person," it nonetheless appears that prevailing readings of these authors continue to depend upon a static notion of the "person." Critics, even in ostensibly historical accounts of the period, often set out to examine how Hawthorne and Stowe either succeed or fail to represent the "personhood" of the slave. By doing so, a particular understanding of the "person" is being treated as knowledge that is not being produced but is either being misrecognized or recognized, acknowledged or repressed.

Such accounts assume that an authentic "person" exists before its representation. In contrast, I foreground how these authors are producing authentic knowledge about the "person," approaching the "person" as an identity category that only emerges through (as opposed to before) its representation. Rather than treating the "person" as something stable, a fact simply "out there" waiting to be discovered and represented, I use Hawthorne and Stowe to examine the way in which this identity was being invented during the antebellum period. Thus, I neither use *Uncle Tom's Cabin,* as one critic has felicitously characterized it, to "hit Hawthorne over the head" nor do I set out to explain what led Hawthorne and Stowe to hold such internally contradictory views of race-based slavery.[54] Rather than championing Stowe for her opposition to slavery and condemning Hawthorne for his indifference to slavery or condemning both as racists, I seek to challenge presuppositions about the "person" on which such indictments rest.

In my account, Hawthorne and Stowe need to be regarded as two of the most powerful anti-slavery liberals of the antebellum period. Both staunchly opposed slavery. The crucial difference in their dramatically different anti-slavery positions, however, lies in their opposing accounts about what counts as slavery. For us, this difference has too often been subordinated to the *fact* that both sought to liberate a version of the "person" that looks nothing like what we *know* the "person" truly to be. My revisionary readings of Hawthorne and Stowe are directed not at revealing the historically variable interpretative forms that have been imposed on a static identity (the "person") but to explore how this ostensibly static identity itself emerges within specific modes of formalization. The texts of Hawthorne and Stowe offer compelling theoretical statements against slavery, and in doing so, exemplify how the process of producing "persons" is socially shaped, constrained, and stabilized.

Hawthorne and Stowe, in short, are hyper-canonical authors, figures around whom both the antebellum debates over the "person" and the rupture between modern and antebellum certainty about the "personhood" of the Negro slave powerfully converge. This project rereads Hawthorne and Stowe as writers who claim to be merely re-presenting "persons" but are instead crucially involved in constructing opposing accounts of the "person." To explore how each constructs antagonistic models of Negro "personhood," I will focus in particular on texts that foreground the problem of interpreting markers of personal identity (Hester's A in *The Scarlet Letter,* hair in *Uncle Tom's Cabin,* and the mysterious ears of the man/faun Donatello in *The Marble Faun*). These texts are invested in antebellum debates over "personhood." I am interested in how modern readings of these texts have erased this debate on both a historical and historiographical level.

The liberal impulse to decontextualize the "person" is evident in the way that established interpretations of literary texts and race-based slavery deploy rather than interrogate a model of the "person." In each case, a modern truth about the "person" is approached as being true all along, assumed to have been distorted by or repressed in the past rather than alternatively constructed. Indeed, by depending on the transparency of the "person," we empty the antebellum debate over slavery of its historical significance, erasing not only how crucially Hawthorne and Stowe but also we ourselves participate in the cultural problem that preoccupies liberal culture.

Given that this impulse to decontextualize the "person" has been reproduced in dominant narratives not only of US slavery but of US literary history, one might say that the United States has been constructed as the paradigmatic liberal nation simultaneously on a political and aesthetic level: the dominant style of reading US political and literary history has been structured around an analogous and quintessentially liberal denial of the historicity of the "person." Indeed, if, as Renan has asserted, a nation is made by what it has been collectively obliged to forget, then prevailing discussions of US slavery and of US literature exemplify corresponding moments in a national pedagogy: each mark how we have worked to forget that we are always engaged in a debate over the concept of the "person."

POLEMIC

Since this is a polemical work, I want to clarify some of the arguments I am not making. Although this project seeks to put pressure on the self-evidence of the concept traditionally mobilized to establish the absolute injustice of race-based slavery, this argument certainly is not intended as a challenge to the claim that racism and slavery are wrong. At issue is not the question of identifying what the "person" really is. Rather the goal of this project is to move away from identifying the "person" and toward the question of what effects a particular definition of the "person" has in a particular context. It asks whether a more effective form of human rights perhaps can be generated, not by invoking the "person" as a pre-political fact, but by arguing that particular practices produce particular effects (such as creating pain or a subaltern population) that violate the type of community we not only wish to establish, but are already in the process of establishing. I am asking the pragmatic question of whether a liberal dependence upon the "person" is either a historically useful or theoretically adequate means to oppose slavery.

Historically, since both those who defended and those who repudiated US slavery invoked the absoluteness of the "person" to legitimate their arguments for social justice, the "person" can be seen as registering rather than resolving the problem of slavery. Theoretically, invocations of the "person" as an absolute seem problematic to the extent that such invocations implicitly foreclose questions about the constitution of "personhood." Only if the conditions of the "person"'s emergence are separated from the substantial and the contingent can this identity category simultaneously be invoked as the irreducible ground of emancipatory politics and acknowledged as precisely what the debate over emancipation is ultimately all about. Only if the "person" is posited as an identity existing above and outside the limitations of context does one think it sufficient to assert that slavery violates the "personhood" of slaves. Indeed, as long as we approach "personhood" as fundamentally antecedent to and independent of how the notion of the "person" has historically been represented, the debate over slavery can only be imagined as a conflict between the enlightened and unenlightened – any questions about slavery as a battle over the concept of the "person" axiomatically foreclosed, rendered beyond question.

This project focuses on modern and antebellum accounts of slavery precisely because slavery has incited arguments (both pro and anti, both antebellum and contemporary) that are premised on the claim that the "person" possesses an ethical force that transcends the local, the historical, and the political. If from our perspective it is clear that the most effective arguments against US slavery, although advertising themselves as context-transcending, were profoundly marked by the prejudices and interests of their particular historical moment, what remains less clear is why scholars regard the contemporary understanding of the "person" (colorblind and gender-neutral identity) as neutral and unbiased. Why is it imagined that, because we have overcome prejudice, interest, and irrationality, we are finally qualified to isolate antebellum misrepresentations and able to fully recognize "personhood"?

Of course, even if it seems historically and theoretically awkward to invoke the term under dispute as the principal means to end such disputes, it may nonetheless seem ethically necessary. It may strike some as dangerous to abandon the metaphysical stability of the conceptual category of the "person." Such an argument seems to lead one down the slippery slope of moral and cultural relativism. That is, some might argue that if we cannot check a particular account of human rights against the intrinsic nature of the "person," it becomes impossible to irrefutably oppose basic violations of basic rights. If the guarantee of the "person" as an independent source of social justice disappears, human rights seem to be grounded on nothing more stable than a shifting, social foundation, on a specifically modern and particularly Western understanding of things. As Tzvetan Todorov declares: "I am simply saying that it is not possible, without inconsistency, to defend human rights with one hand and deconstruct the idea of humanity with the other."[55] And as the Marxist theorist Norman Geras has stated, "if truth is wholly relativized or internalized to particular discourses or language games or social practices, there is no injustice. . .Morally and politically, therefore, anything goes."[56] Or as Clifford Geertz has succinctly put the problem, "To suggest that 'hard rock' foundations . . . may not be available is to find oneself accused of disbelieving the existence of the physical world, thinking pushpin as good as poetry, regarding Hitler as just a fellow with unstandard tastes."[57] Anti-foundationalism has been accused of being "good news for tyrants" and charged with inevitably auguring the torture of innocents.[58]

Or, to put this anxiety in terms of this project, if the "person" is treated as contingent, as a notion embedded in context, it may appear that the pro-slavery argument threatens to become merely a competing, equally legitimate position, an argument against which there is nothing to say since the "person" does not in itself reveal the injustice and brutality of slavery. If the "person" does not exist as an absolute, it is imagined that one is left only with the quicksand of the accidental and the contingent.[59] Unless the notion of the "person" remains more than its representation, unless it can be grounded in a reality external and antecedent to representation, it is feared that the "person" becomes available for any use and open to the most oppressive appropriations.

The suspicion of relativism, although misplaced, is not surprising. To foreground how judgments about "person" are embedded in a particular cultural frame is to challenge the claim that such judgments emanate from nowhere and transcend any cultural framework. But to discuss truth claims as not independent of the personal, the communal, and the contextual is not to deny the possibility of making truth claims or to insist on the impossibility of determinate judgment; it is only to assert (along pragmatist lines) that such claims and judgments are enabled (rather than discredited) because one is situated in a particular context and possesses a particular perspective. Indeed, my argument can be seen as inverting the charge that unless the "person" remains a brute, neutral, and stubborn fact, the identity loses all ethical force.

The charge of moral relativism that may be directed against any effort to historicize the "person" assumes that the only principled, justified, and warranted arguments about human rights must be external to any particular context or point of view. It is grounded in the fear that when two incommensurable accounts of "person" confront each other, one is left with nothing on which to establish an ethical judgment unless the "person" remains an independent foundation for judgment, one that transcends rather than is constituted in context. But to acknowledge that judgments about human rights are formulated within a particular context does not lead us to abandon human rights or require us to suspend ethical judgments. For, as Hilary Putnam has rhetorically asked and Richard Rorty has repeated, "we should use somebody *else's* conceptual scheme?"[60] The basis for privileging some practices over others is not lost, rather is only possible because we ourselves are embedded in a context, invested in a particular point of view.

Once one approaches the notion of the "person" as embedded in a particular context, the possibility of human rights does not evaporate, but it is reimagined as a political problem. It becomes a problem that cannot be resolved by appealing to some notion of the "person" untainted by history but can only be resolved by foregrounding the consequences of any particular argument. One, in fact, could say that the conflation of contextualism with relativism is only possible to the extent that one remains (either overtly or covertly) within the grip of philosophical universalism: only if a historicist perspective is equated with transcending its context and finding a (transhistorical) privileged space where any and all interpretative claims become equally good or equally bad or equally arbitrary can the act of putting things in history become synonymous with saying that there are no norms, there is no truth, and there can be no ethics.

This project, in other words, does not abandon ethics but shifts the ground on which ethical assertions are made. If one approaches the "person" as the ultimate sign of context rather than a concept that transcends context, questions about the reality of the "person" are replaced by questions about who controls the terms that establish this conceptual category and what are the effects of such an account. The crucial question becomes not whether a historical definition of the "person" accurately reflects a transhistorical object (the "person") but who is permitted to participate in the act of defining this identity category and what are the consequences of a particular definition. And once the question shifts from whether the "person" is properly represented to how the "person" is being represented and for what ends, then ethical claims about the necessity of the universal "person" become less urgent because they are understood as less determining of a particular politics. The conviction that an authority independent from context underwrites a particular account of the "person" ultimately says nothing about the ethical nature of that account of the "person." We may hope that we can turn to a pre-political identity to determine a just politics, but that notion will always be political (in the sense of being indebted to a political position rather than the source of such a position).

Antebellum arguments over the "person" make clear that to invoke the "person" as an independent check on social and political practices is both insufficient and vulnerable to being appropriated for multiple purposes. To question whether independent foundations (such as the "person") are needed, in other words, is not synonymous with the claim that there *are* no foundations. It is only to question whether on-going debates over "personhood" have ever been resolved by an appeal to the "person" as it *really* is. It is to approach the notion of the "person" as an inevitably political question rather than as an answer that depends upon one finally escaping politics.

Although I am foregrounding the historicity of the "person," it is important to note that I am not arguing that the problem with invoking the "person" as an absolute category is that it misidentifies what the "person" truly is (i.e. a context-bound and contingent rather than metaphysical identity) or lamenting that it can never accurately represent the real "person" (some *pure* "person" that resists history, exceeds the context of its articulation, and reposes with an eternal sameness beneath the superficial fluctuations of any manifestation). Rather than argue or hope that a particular definition of the "person" more accurately reflects the "person" in itself and thus is intrinsically more just, this project seeks to explore how the "person" has been represented at particular historical moments in order to consider the effects of specific accounts. I seek to replace the theoretical question of what the "person" *is* with a more localized question – the question of what a particular representation of the "person" does in a particular historical debate about "personhood."

Thus, I approach the conceptual category of the "person" as the primary symptom of a social and political rupture, not to make a claim about the "person" (for example, that it is a fundamentally empty or endlessly revisable or tragically unknown category) but to make clear how little representationalist claims about the "person" ultimately resolve.

Our clarity about the "personhood" of the slave does not reveal the neutrality or objectivity of our conception but how completely arguments over "personhood" of the slave are no longer being waged. We have not transcended politics as much as the politics of slavery has been surpassed. Our confidence in the "person" is retroactive, available only after a political conflict has been converted by history into a necessity. As current arguments over abortion dramatically demonstrate, political and ethical debates put into question the notion of the "person" and this dispute will only end once a particular political/religious argument about the "person" achieves ascendancy. Indeed, such confidence in the absoluteness of the "person" is only possible if one forgets the historical moment when particular political questions about the "person" are most pressing.

Moreover, our certainty that the Negro is a "person" should not be taken to suggest that for us the "person" is now unproblematically available to resolve any and all political argument. Debates over this category have not disappeared but have shifted. For, as arguments over fetal "personhood," animal rights, and genetic engineering dramatically demonstrate, modern liberal culture continues to be riven by controversies over this identity category.[61] And what makes these debates continuous with debates over slavery is the logic they share: these debates recruit the very notion at the heart of such debates (the "person") as the primary means to solve all debate.[62] That we regularly turn to the "person" as if it could serve as the unequivocal arbiter of justice reveals the extent to which we depend upon the "person" as an identity category external to any specific juridical, social, historical, or cultural framework. Indeed, the fact that we still debate the notion of the "person" in multiple political spheres suggests that the concept that we summon to once and for all explain and establish liberal practice is more contingent and less definitive than we hope.

Such arguments signal how the "person" does not accomplish what liberal thought asks it to do: serve as the foundation for social justice. We do not universally repudiate race-based slavery because the truth of the "person" has finally become clear to us, but because the debates about "personhood" have changed, and the questions that trouble us (debates about abortion, embryonic stem cell research, animal rights, green politics, and cloning) are not the debates that unsettled antebellum liberal culture. The dispute of the "person," in short, has moved to new arenas.

The issue of slavery may be settled once and for all, but the political debates over the "person" are far from over.

The following pages call into question the liberal desire to keep the "person" as the ultimate trump card of human rights and questions whether an essentialist conception of the "person" is an unproblematic sign of regressive politics. Such an argument, however, as I have said, is not motivated by the claim that a contextualist account of the "person" is inevitably emancipatory or ethical. Rather than claim that by placing the "person" in history and foregrounding the ways in which this conceptual category has been contested will trigger in and of itself an authentically progressive political outcome, I seek to dissolve claims about any universal or necessary yoking of an account of the "person" to an indisputable political consequence. Any attempt to preemptively affiliate a particular politics to a particular conception "person" implicitly removes this conceptual category from history and is only compelling when the political tenor of such claims has been forgotten.

Although contextualizing the "person" may not be axiomatically progressive, it does raise significant questions about the way in which dominant readings of antebellum culture are implicated in mystifying the "person." To the extent that the impulse to maintain the "person" as the category that intrinsically establishes the injustice of slavery has been reproduced in the most influential accounts of US liberal culture, the ensuing chapters suspend the logic of liberal representation. They explore what happens when we read some of the central literary texts of antebellum culture without the guarantee of a transcendentally fixed and self-determining notion of the "person." That is, rather than deploy the "person" as an intrinsic or necessary category that can unlock the texts of Hawthorne, Stowe, and Douglass, these chapters seek to defamiliarize modern certainty about the "person" by foregrounding how these exemplary authors participated in antebellum debates over the "person." In these chapters, I am less intent on highlighting how we have gotten better at knowing "persons" than in exploring what it means that we *recognize* "persons" so differently.

CHAPTER 1

Slaves and persons

Since slavery systematically negates the fundamental ideals of liberal political theory – in particular the ideals of autonomy, individual consent, equality before the law, the protection of personal property, etc. – it has long stood as the archetypical antithesis of liberalism.[1] Indeed, ever since John Locke, who is conventionally considered the principal theorist of classic liberal theory, the institution of slavery has marked the historical and theoretical limits of liberalism, representing the tyranny against which liberalism is articulated and measured. Establishing this foundational opposition at the beginning of his *First Treatise of Government*, Locke stated, "Slavery is so vile and miserable an Estate of Man, and so directly opposite to the generous Temper and Courage of our Nation; that 'tis hardly to be conceived that an *Englishman*, much less a *Gentleman*, should plead for't."[2]

The general claim that slavery is the litmus test of liberalism, however, has not been as perspicuous and straightforward as one might expect. What might seem a singularly neat opposition has, in fact, proven remarkably untidy. Thus, Locke – despite championing liberty, demonizing slavery, and being an English Gentleman – not only "pled for" slavery and invested in the colonial slave trade, but also, as secretary to the Lords Proprietors of Carolina, helped write the *Fundamental Constitution of the Carolinas*, a piece of legislation that declared that "every freeman of Carolina shall have absolute power and authority over his negro slaves."[3] Locke's radical claims for individual freedom and universal rights, in other words, were played out in counterpoint to his explicit defense of an institution designed to withhold such rights from particular groups. This justification of both the inalienable liberty of persons and the unconditional servitude of slaves has left many wondering "[h]ow can it be that so great a defender of the inalienable rights of man was not at heart a determined enemy of slavery?"[4] This tension between advocating rights and defending slavery is typically seen as the "paradox at the center of the liberal project."[5]

Given that slavery is conventionally understood as the self-evident repudiation of liberal values, it is not surprising that most recent scholarship on the US liberal tradition has been preoccupied with the problem of explaining how the United States, the nation whose founding documents officially aligned the nation's political ambitions with the Enlightenment project of universal liberty and individual freedom, and where it has been claimed Locke's principles have become a "massive national cliché," managed to morally accommodate or legally sanction slavery for so much of its history.[6] That is, the paradox that haunts liberal theory in general seems to be strikingly manifest in the history of the nation understood as the paradigmatic expression of the liberal project. Indeed, the convergence of liberal ideals and the practice of slavery has been the "American Dilemma," the "central paradox of American history," "the most remarkable anomaly in the history of the country," and "the most flagrant violation" of this nation's self-declared liberal ideals.[7]

Since this nation's commitment to liberal principles has not prevented nor, at the very least, presented a significant conceptual barrier to the stark brutality of race-based slavery, one of the central preoccupations of US cultural studies has been to explain this "monstrous inconsistency" (*White over Black*, 289).[8] This contradiction has generated two lines of argument: the conjunction of slavery and liberalism, it has been argued, either registers how liberal ideals can be distorted in practice or it exposes the true ideological character of liberalism, revealing a fundamental social injustice endemic to liberalism.

Some have looked to ideas and circumstances external to liberal thought to explain the conjunction of race-based slavery and freedom, citing labor shortages and working-class unrest,[9] the proliferation of anti-liberal traditions in US political thought,[10] or plain moral hypocrisy.[11] According to such an account liberalism and slavery are always fundamentally contradictory formations, but this nation either actively denied or was somehow blinded from recognizing this blatant contradiction. In such arguments, the co-existence of the institution of slavery and liberal ideals stands as a tragic misprision of liberal political values, an error gradually unveiled in the process of US culture becoming itself, i.e. truly liberal.[12] That is, this contradiction would have been obvious immediately if the liberal principles articulated in this nation's founding documents had been "properly understood," if, as Judith Shklar has put it, American political theory had not "failed to understand itself."[13] By approaching the historical conjunction of American Slavery and American Freedom as illustrating the way this nation's liberal values have been misread, misapplied, or hypocritically ignored, such scholars posit liberalism and race-based slavery as eternally segregated ideological formations despite the fact that they have been deeply filiated in practice.

Other scholars, less sanguine about the inherent egalitarianism of liberal premises, have understood the affiliation of the most radical claims for universal freedom with the most extreme form of servitude not as a contradiction but as a symptom of the true character of liberalism.[14] According to this account, something internal to liberal thought enables chattel slavery. Indeed, the contradiction between liberal values and racial inequality is, in this argument, illusory, a superficial antagonism that masks the way in which such racist practices are a "logical concomitant" of liberal theory's fraudulent universalism.[15] That is, even though liberalism may deploy a rhetoric of universal rights and liberties, inequality penetrates liberal theory at a genetic level, generating the very inequalities it pretends to oppose. As Matthew Jacobson has concluded in his study of race and US liberal citizenship, racism "appears not anomalous to the workings of American democracy, but fundamental to it" or in the eloquent words of Richard Delgado, "liberal democracy and racial subordination go hand in hand, like the sun, moon, and stars."[16] According to such accounts, liberal theory cannot be rehabilitated because liberal theory is itself the source of social injustice.[17]

The historical conjunction of slavery and liberal thought, in other words, has incited many to approach liberalism as if it were an ideological construct that one is either *for* or *against*, something either to be preserved or repudiated *tout court*. But such an approach produces its own problems. Those devoted to exorcising slavery from the US liberal tradition too quickly dismiss the historical complicity of race-based slavery and liberal principles (principles of property, individual rights, and choice), while those who denounce liberalism as intrinsically oppressive, too quickly dismiss the fact that historically marginalized groups have powerfully appealed to abstract liberal rights to combat not only slavery but also gross racial, gender, and sexual inequalities.[18] If, in contrast, one focuses on the possibility that no figure axiomatically possesses the right to bear rights, the problematic shifts; no longer does one ask about the definitive nature of liberalism, rather one examines the contested status of the "person." And by so doing, the multiplicity of liberal thought becomes more understandable.

Thus, in this chapter, rather than try to determine whether liberalism is itself good or bad, I am interested in the way this impulse to determine the essence of liberalism itself reveals something crucial about the dynamics of liberal representation. This continuing investment in determining the essence of liberalism ends up mystifying the category of the "person." To focus on the paradoxes of liberalism, one might say, is an answer (an answer to the historically contested issue of who is a "person") masquerading as a question (the question of why were "persons" denied recognition). Indeed, as long as we identify race-based slavery either as fundamentally discordant or as congruous with liberalism, we continue to ask how liberalism expresses or represses "persons," taking the conceptual category of the "person" as a post-political given, rather than exploring how this identity is itself the subject of historical dispute.

US SLAVERY, US LIBERALISM

If traditional models for understanding the relationship between race-based slavery and the US liberal tradition tend to subordinate the maddening multiplicity of liberal practices to a fixed account of liberalism's essence, my account of liberalism neither apologizes for nor repudiates liberalism, but emphasizes how liberalism has enabled multiple political practices because liberalism is fundamentally a formal structure that has been and can be organized in terms of multiple notions of the "person." Thus, if conventionally those who celebrate the power of liberalism to overcome its historical limitations are opposed to those for whom the concrete history of liberal practice reveals the essential bankruptcy of liberal ideas, I seek to reframe the question in terms of the historical elasticity of the "person." What both the partisans and debunkers of liberalism, in fact, share is a belief in the solidity of the "person," each dependent upon this identity category to establish the ethics of liberalism.

In contrast, a revisionary account of the US liberal tradition approaches "personhood" as the term that we attach to whomever we designate as deserving liberal rights and protections. The "person" stands simply as the relay point of liberal thought, marking where liberal rights converge and designating what liberalism can secure as well as what it can legitimately refuse. Thus, the history of liberalism can be redescribed as a series of substitutions of this conceptual center, in terms of competing, not necessarily increasingly true, versions of the "person."[19] By approaching slavery in terms of the question of how the institution misunderstands and misrepresents what a "person" is, conventional liberal discussions of slavery have worked to remove the "person" from history and to bar an examination how the identity of the "person" itself has been contested.

If conventional accounts of the relationship between slavery and liberalism have obscured questions about the relationship between the notion of the "person" and the scope of liberal rights, I, in contrast, want to raise the possibility that liberalism has remained unstable precisely because the conceptual category of the "person" has been unstable. Once one focuses on the historical plasticity of the conceptual category of the "person" rather than on the question of what liberalism essentially is, it becomes possible to explore how liberalism has proven enigmatic because competing constructions of the "person" have animated liberal representation, creating a rupture that sometimes is evident during a particular historical moment and at other times only becomes evident at a later period.

That is, liberalism may take as its starting point the concept of the "person" and certainly legitimates its political structures and policies by claiming that they reflect the needs and nature of the "person," but the master referent of liberalism has not possessed an inevitable and immanent meaning. Liberalism has not always understood the "person" in identical terms. Thus, even though the category of the bearer of rights has at times been defined in terms of race, sex, class, and nationality, I want to suggest that liberalism can only be identified as a theory that is axiomatically linked to the masculinist, racist, classist, or nationalist principles if liberalism is understood as depending upon an eternally fixed notion of the "person."

In contrast, I approach liberalism as an ideology that puts the conceptual category of the "person" in debate even as it simultaneously declares the "person" to be a pre-political identity. Such an approach foregrounds how as often as some liberals have understood the conceptual category of the "person" in ways that we might consider racist, sexist, classist, and nativist, other liberals have argued that the "person" obviously exceeds the specificities of race, sex, ethnicity, nationality, or class. Indeed, to either unconditionally separate liberalism from ascriptive ideologies of race, class, and gender, or exclusively link liberalism to such dogmas, is to decontextualize the "person," designating it as an identity before and above representation rather than acknowledging the extent to which this identity has been precisely what liberals battle over.

To understand how powerfully liberal thought has depended upon the reification of the "person," I want to turn to what has become the paradigmatic antebellum debate over race-based slavery. But, rather than seeing this debate as an occasion to rehearse how race-based slavery is the most manifest scandal in this nation's history, I ask what it means that race-based slavery was not always understood as a self-evident national sin.

PERSONS AND SLAVERY

The Illinois Senate race of 1858 saw Abraham Lincoln and Stephen Douglas engaged in a sustained public discussion of slavery. Although certainly not the only debate over slavery, this debate stands, as David Potter has said, as "one of the most important intellectual discussions of the slavery question during three decades of almost uninterrupted controversy."[20] These debates can be seen as a crisis point in this nation's understanding of liberal ideals precisely because at this moment everyone did not axiomatically agree that the conjunction of US slavery and US freedom obviously and intolerably contradicted this nation's founding liberal principles. At the heart of Lincoln's and Douglas' dispute was the Kansas-Nebraska Act – the law that recast the question of slavery as an issue of popular sovereignty – and at the heart of their opposing positions lies the question of who counts as a "person."

Douglas, the author of the Kansas-Nebraska Act, unapologetically champions both the Act and race-based slavery. According to Douglas, since the Act mandates that the final decision about slavery be put into the hands of each territory's inhabitants rather than be handed down by the Federal government, this legislation offers the only truly liberal way to resolve the slavery question. Indeed, he argues that since the Act takes recourse in the will of the inhabitants of each territory, it powerfully promotes individual liberty. As he wrote in response to critics who argued that the bill opened the whole country to slavery, "Why do they not state the matter truly, and say that it opens the country to *freedom* by leaving the people *perfectly free* to do as they please?"[21]

The claim that the potential expansion of Negro slavery signifies the extension of individual liberty rather than the extension of slavery does not strike Douglas as absurd because he does not regard the Negro (whether slave or free) as one of "the people":

> I hold that this Government was made on the white basis, made by the white men, for the benefit of white men and their posterity forever, and should be administered by white men and none others. I do not believe that the Almighty made the negro capable of self-government. I am aware that all the Abolition lecturers that you will find travelling about through the country are in the habit of proclaiming and reading the Declaration of Independence, to prove that all men were created equal, and endowed by their Creator with certain inalienable rights . . . Now, I state to you my fellow citizens, in my opinion the Signers of the Declaration of Independence had no reference whatever to the negro, when they declared all men to have been created equal. The Signers of the Declaration were

white men, of European birth and European descent, and had no reference either to the negro or to savage Indians, or the Feejee [sic], or the Malay, or any other inferior or degraded race, when they spoke of the equality of men (598).

Douglas does not deny that the institution of slavery absolutely refuses the Negro slave the very freedoms that liberalism canonizes. Rather it is this refusal that Douglas defends as fundamentally American: the Negro is not denied rights because the Negro, unlike the European, does not possess any inalienable rights. The only rights that the Negro can possess are those positively granted by the state.[22]

Douglas can seamlessly incorporate race-based slavery within his vision of an ideal liberal polity simply by placing the Negro naturally and permanently outside this polity. Douglas may seem to be imposing a purely political qualification on the notion of who constitutes the People (one based on the Founders' intentions), but Douglas' argument is not simply one about the Negro's contingent civic status. It is about the Negro's ontological status as a non-person: the "Almighty [did not make] the negro capable of self-government," and thus the Negro is not simply a "degraded" race but an "inferior" one. Since the Negro is not, according to Douglas, a "person" and since the political structures of the United States reflect this fact, Douglas can claim – without contradicting his championing of liberal ideals – that the Kansas-Nebraska Act is not only wholly congruent with, but actually fulfills, the sacred promises of the Declaration of Independence.

Lincoln, in contrast, condemns the institution of slavery as an unconscionable violation of this nation's basic liberal ideals. He declares that he "can not but hate" the Kansas-Nebraska Act because it permits the "monstrous injustices" of slavery to be perpetuated and thus "enables the enemies of free institutions, with plausibility, to taunt us as hypocrites" (315). This nation is justly accused of hypocrisy, Lincoln declares, because the Kansas-Nebraska Act in particular and race-based slavery in general withhold from the Negro the "absolute" and "eternal" right to self-government, the very right that this nation was constituted to preserve (329). In other words, if Douglas reconciles US liberalism and US slavery on the grounds that the Negro is obviously not a "person," Lincoln renders this nation's founding principles and race-based slavery fundamentally irreconcilable on the grounds that the Negro slave is obviously a "person." Thus, whereas Douglas claims that race-based slavery epitomizes this nation's originary ideals, Lincoln claims that the United States must end slavery in order to fulfill its destiny and, in essence, become itself.

The Lincoln-Douglas debates epitomize how thoroughly any account of the relationship between liberalism and slavery pivots on the question of who counts as a "person." Indeed, even though Lincoln certainly denounces race-based slavery for undermining the "leading principle–sheet anchor of American republicanism," he recognizes how thoroughly his claim necessarily hinges on the answer to the question "who is a 'person'?" As Lincoln put it,

> if the negro *is* a man, is it not to that extent, a total destruction of self-government, to say that he too shall not govern *himself*? When the white man governs himself, and also governs *another* man, that is *more* than self-government–that is despotism. If the negro is a *man*, why then my ancient faith teaches me that "all men are created equal;" and that there can be no moral right in connection with one man making a slave of another.[23]

Although clearly intended as a rhetorical strategy since Lincoln asserts that the Negro slave is obviously a "person," Lincoln's use of the conditional suggests how completely this nation's "sacred principles" demand that the Negro be allowed to the right to self-government *if* and *only if* the Negro is a "man." Lincoln denounces race-based slavery, but he, just as much as Douglas, grounds his defense of liberty in the belief that *only* "persons" deserve the right to liberal rights. Non-persons, Lincoln states, can legitimately be enslaved: if the Negro were not a "man," Lincoln explains to his audience, "why in that case, he who is man may, as a matter of self-government, do just as he pleases with him" (328).

By implicitly legitimating the slavery of non-persons, even as he explicitly condemns the slavery of the Negro, Lincoln reveals the extent to which a justification of certain kinds of slavery is embedded, at least potentially, within liberal political theory's powerful defense of natural rights. One could say, in fact, that liberal theory is at best mute concerning the slavery of non-persons, and, at worst, an ideology that is not simply continuous with but actually provides a powerful means to legitimate slavery. The congeniality of liberalism and slavery becomes particularly clear in the way pro-slavery thinkers (such as Douglas) did not repudiate the liberal logic that Lincoln employs, but merely repeated this logic differently. Such thinkers did not disagree with the foundational liberal principle that all "persons" are entitled to liberal rights and protections; they simply challenged the claim that the Negro is a "person." Indeed, since Lincoln and Douglas dispute not whether "persons" can be slaves but whether Negroes are "persons," they speak at cross-purposes. Rather than serve as the means by which the legitimacy of slavery can finally be determined, the notion of the "person" is the fault-line along which the question of slavery fractures.

The debate between Lincoln and Douglas, in short, exemplifies the extent to which declaring "all men" created equal and possessed of certain inalienable rights is not identical to promising anyone the inalienable right to be regarded as a "Man." Indeed, one might say that by declaring "all men created equal" the Declaration of Independence inaugurated both the paradigmatic liberal nation and the paradigmatic interpretative problem of liberalism: the problem of determining exactly to whom this signifier self-evidently refers. In this sense, the promise of the Declaration of Independence is in effect an incomplete promise, a promise that demands no inevitable outcome to the extent that the foundational referent of liberal political theory has proven itself to be in question, the subject of rather than the solution to liberal debates.

RECOGNIZING PERSONS

The claim that as long as a Negro slave was not axiomatically categorized as a "person," race-based slavery could be innocently reconciled with this nation's sacred liberal ideals is, in some sense, a relatively uncontroversial claim, coinciding with what has been well established: the principal strategy deployed to make Negro slavery acceptable in a liberal nation was to declare that the Negro was not one of "the People." This assertion, in fact, parallels what we know about the history of human rights in general: one of the most effective ways to legitimate lethal social practices (what we now call human rights violations) has been to declare the subjects of such violence "non-persons." And collaterally, one of the most effective means to identify certain beings as objects of illegitimate violence has been to declare them "persons." Currently, the latter "positive" version of this strategy is particularly evident in the actions of anti-abortion activists attempting to undermine a woman's right to choose, and the former "negative" version of this logic is tragically manifest in the contemporary ethnic killings in Cambodia, Rwanda, Bosnia, Kosovo, and the Sudan. In this sense the notion of the "person" can legitimate the abuse of human rights as much as their protection.

To foreground what most likely strikes many as a false, unscrupulous, and political use of the "person," however, does not give an adequate sense of what we expect the conceptual category of the "person" to do. What is striking is that although few would dispute that the concept of the "person" has certainly been invoked to legitimate egregious violations of human rights, such an acknowledgment has not prevented us from continuing nevertheless to appeal to the "person" as the standard by which ethical behavior can be adjudicated. Even though it is patent that the "person" has been summoned to legitimate the most cynical, unemancipatory, and barbaric ends, we, in the face of such assaults on the obviousness of "personhood," persevere in mobilizing this identity category to foreground the limitations of previous iterations, citing it as if it were a neutral tool of analysis, hoping that if we can objectively identify what a "person" really is, we can achieve justice.

What is striking, in other words, is how clearly we see Lincoln and Douglas participating in a political struggle for control of the notion of the "person" and how consistently we have nonetheless continued to invoke the notion of the "person" as if it could function as the transparent means to resolve antebellum debates over slavery. Indeed, most influential readings of US slavery have been established on the assumption that the conceptual category of the "person" does possess an intrinsic meaning, one that will express itself once prejudice and the limits of historical circumstances have been overcome. In the following section, I want to present in some detail how profoundly this impulse to hold onto the "person" as a foundational concept can be identified as the governing characteristic of modern scholarship on US slavery. What prevailing interpretations of US slavery ironically demonstrate is that it is precisely those attentive to the history of understandings of the "person" that have participated in and sustained the idea that the "person" exceeds history, conjuring it as a post-political category.

PUTTING THE "PERSON" OUT OF PLAY

The publication of David Brion Davis' *The Problem of Slavery in Western Culture* (1966), the first volume of his magisterial discussion of slavery in the Western world, marked the beginning of efforts to understand why it took so long to generate an effective anti-slavery argument.[24] Not until the 1730s, Davis explains, did anti-slavery advocates begin to make the argument that since "all men were born free and equal, Negro slavery was a violation of the natural rights of man" (412). Davis not only traces how anti-slavery arguments were grounded on appeals to the absolute notion of the "person," but himself depends upon this notion to characterize the historical problem of slavery, declaring that the moral problem of slavery will inevitably be exposed because slavery always "ran aground on the simple and solid fact, which for centuries had been obscured by philosophy and law, that a slave was not a piece of property, nor a half-human instrument, but a man held down by force"(261). That is, if Davis, on one hand, examines the extent to which slavery has been justified by legal and philosophical claims that slaves are non-persons, he simultaneously appeals to the conceptual category of the "person" as a foundation on which to develop his study of these historically mistaken accounts of the slave. For Davis, the "person" is a "simple and stable fact" that can be summoned to understand and interpret how previous historical contexts have repressed and misapprehended what a slave truly is.

I am not arguing that Davis specifically uses the term "person" (he more frequently uses the term "man") but that he deploys this conceptual category in the sense I have been discussing: Davis appeals to an identity so stable that it can stand as the fulcrum for distinguishing false from accurate understandings of slavery, even as he acknowledges that the concept serves as the primary means for justifying slavery. This tactic of placing the identity category of the "person" simultaneously inside and outside of historical context is far from idiosyncratic. So embedded is the assumption that the notion of the "person" can serve as an axis of analysis even as it is the subject of study that it has become commonplace to assert that the horror of slavery devolves from the mistake of treating "persons" as things. That is, the dominant historical narratives about slavery place the "person" outside of analysis precisely at the very moment that such accounts are detailing how thoroughly slaves are being imagined as non-persons.

By examining how some resisted or were prevented (blinded or blocked) from apprehending the "personhood" of the Negro, such accounts conjure the "person" as an identity that is always more than its history. And to the degree that narratives about slavery have been generated by the problem of determining how and why the "personhood" of the slave was misrecognized, ignored, or actively withheld, they depend upon the notion of the "person" as a concept that simply exists and needs to be acknowledged. Indeed, this tendency runs so deep that it is manifest in multiple disciplines. For example, the philosopher Stanley Cavell argues in *The Claim of Reason*[25] that slave-owners' assertion that the slave is not a "person" "cannot really be meant" (373). Cavell points to specific actions of slave-owners (such as controlling the slave's religious practices – something that they did not do to horses or chairs) that, he argues, prove that slave-owners were actively "disowning" knowledge of the slave's personhood. According to Cavell, the slave-owner refuses to acknowledge that what he "really believes is not that slaves are not human beings, but that some human beings are slaves" (375). Cavell sees slavery as a system founded upon an untenable belief – the belief that "certain human beings can treat certain others whom they know, or all but know, to be human" as non-human – and thus he imagines slavery as inevitably causing its own collapse (377). As he concludes, the Civil War was "tragic because it was unnecessary, rather than tragic because necessary" (377).

But for Cavell to declare so confidently that slavery is founded upon a performative contradiction (slave-owners are attempting to disown knowledge that cannot be disowned), he must assume that knowledge about the "personhood" of the slave (he uses the term "human being" but the force of the term operates like the conceptual category of the "person") is beyond question, something that can be concealed but not contested. Unless he did, Cavell would have to entertain the possibility that the "personhood" of the slave is not secure, not knowledge that is always already owned, but knowledge that is itself under debate. One might ask why Cavell does not imagine that the "non-personhood" of the slave could in itself constitute certain knowledge. Why, in other words, is it inconceivable for slaveholders to *know* that slaves were not "persons"? And why couldn't such knowledge be believed? There was, after all, no shortage of respectable political, scientific, religious, and historical arguments available for establishing the legitimacy of race-based slavery and white supremacy. Cavell suggests that such arguments, however, remain little more than hypocritical rationalizations precisely because he understands such knowledge to announce itself no matter what people may believe or believe they believe.

Although it intervenes in a philosophical rather than a historiographical tradition, Cavell's argument can be seen as continuous with the classic work of historians such as Charles Sellers and W.J. Cash, who argued that antebellum slave-owners were horribly guilt-stricken about enslaving "persons" and violating this nation's sacred liberal ideals.[26] According to this tradition, slave-owners could not help but unconsciously give voice to their repressed anxieties about slavery. What is striking is that such guilt is assumed even though few Southerners spoke of guilt and almost all historians concede that very few Southerners felt so.[27] The absence of such evidence is telling. It suggests how deeply the positing of "guiltomania" among slaveholders or among US culture collectively (i.e. slavery as the National Sin) assumes that the notion of Negro "personhood" must always have been in effect – if not externally and explicitly in law and policy, then internally and implicitly in everyone's heart and mind – even if (or perhaps precisely because) any acknowledgment of such guilt is not manifestly detected. To assume that because we know that race-based slavery is wrong others at another time and in another context must have known (either pre-consciously, unconsciously, or subconsciously) that slavery is wrong suggests how thoroughly we imagine the conceptual category of the "person" as producing its meaning independent of any context, as possessing a meaning that can be appreciated or repressed, manifest or latent, but never absent.

The most influential discussions of US slavery, in fact, have been characterized by the premise that slavery attempts to repress the self-evident truth that a slave is a "person" – a being who could never be legitimately treated as if a thing.[28] For example, Eugene Genovese summons the concept of repression to explain legal efforts to treat the slave as both property and as "person." According to Genovese, "the South had discovered, as had every previous slave society, that it could not deny the slave's humanity, however many preposterous legal fictions it invented."[29] Again, although Genovese does not use the term "person," his argument depends upon a conceptual category that exceeds practice and context (he uses the term "humanity") in order to generate his claim about the immanent incoherence of slavery. For Genovese, the South may refuse or be unable to recognize the "personhood" of slaves, but neither slaveholders nor their apologists could ever successfully carry through on such a refusal.[30] To make such a claim Genovese depends upon a pre-political touchstone, an identity (he calls it humanity) that can be recognized or refused but which, in the end, remains prior to any end or content attributed to it.

Working from Judge Thomas Ruffin's notorious ruling in *State v. Mann* that the "power of the master must be absolute to render the submission of the slave perfect," scholars have typically argued that any limits on the absolute property rights of the master betrays an unconscious acknowledgment of the humanity of the slave and thus of the illegitimacy of slavery.[31] How, it is often asked, can slaveholders simultaneously recognize slaves as human beings and as property?[32] Recently, however, scholars such as Jenny Wahl, Thomas Morris, and William Wiethoff have compellingly argued that recognizing the humanity of the slave did not necessarily bring about the end of slavery but actually refined its efficiency and allowed the slave to be used more profitably.[33]

By emphasizing slaves as both property and human, judges explained why slaves were a uniquely valuable species of property, a figure who is neither simply human nor simply property.[34] For example, in *Summers v. Bean* (Va., 1856), a case that considered the appropriate remedy for a failed sale of slaves, Judge Richard Moncure, writing the majority opinion, criticized the only English case (*Pearne v. Lisle*) he found on point because that judge "rightly considered negroes as property; but seems not to have considered them as human beings, of greater peculiar value than 'a cherry-stone very finely engraved' or an 'extraordinary wrought piece of plate'."[35] According to Moncure, unless one considers the special status of the slave, their position as both property and human being, one cannot properly determine their value. That is, to recognize the humanity of the slave does not invalidate their sale; it merely evidences why monetary damages are not adequate relief for the loss of their services. Although he criticizes the English judge's insensitivity, Moncure betrays no anxiety about the legitimacy of slavery. Rather than inevitably foregrounding the logical contradiction at the heart of slavery, the recognition that the slave is "not in the condition of a horse or an ox" marks the extent to which the logic of slavery does not inevitably shatter when it hits the bedrock of the slave's resemblance to "persons."[36] To assume that the legitimacy of US slavery is inevitably undermined because it cannot help but recognize the humanity of the slave is to discount how invocations of the slave's similarity to "persons" could sustain just as powerfully as they could challenge slavery. The premise that the humanity of the slave remains a recalcitrant fact that can never be successfully incorporated into the logic slavery, in other words, places the notion of humanity beyond debate and outside of any context or narrative. To assert that Southern slave law reveals itself to be established, in the words of one historian, on "unresolved dichotomies," is to assume that no matter what the legal fictions that may be institutionalized or believed, the "person" remains aggressively irreducible to any such historically situated perspective.[37]

In recent literary discussions of US slavery, this practice of approaching slavery in terms of the irrepressible "personhood" of the Negro has been particularly evident and pointed. In *Constituting Americans*, for example, Priscilla Wald[38] deploys the notion of the uncanny in order to describe the way in which the personhood of the Negro, though "suppressed and repressed by official stories of We the People," repeatedly "resurfaces" and puts these national narratives under tremendous strain (4, 10). The United States, she argues, has been fundamentally "haunted" by the return of the repressed because this nation attempts to "legitimate a version of the official story of the nation" that is based on the denial of rights to groups of people who deserve such rights. As Wald sees it, this project is essentially anxiogenic because those "deprived of natural rights" manifest a significant "challenge to the conception of personhood articulated in the founding texts," incarnating "the alienability of natural rights" and thus pointing to the "power of government to violate its sacred trust" (19). Assuming that Negroes are "persons" who have been denied their natural rights, Wald claims their situation powerfully unveils this nation's promise of universal rights as a fundamentally false promise. And it is the attempt to repress this knowledge in this nation's official narratives that, according to Wald, occasions the "uncanniness of human beings excluded from personhood" (39).[39]

Translating this nation's classic paradox (the tension between slavery and freedom) into formalist terms, Wald claims that Negro slaves pose a significant "representational threat" to this nation's legitimating narrative. The source of her confidence in the inevitable expression of "personhood" is her belief that this nation's "ill-fitting" "conceptualization of personhood" can cover-up and distort but can never obliterate the fact that real "persons" are being excluded from the political community and being unjustly enslaved (10, 7). For Wald, Blacks and Native Americans are "human beings whom the law *would not* fully and equally represent," figures who reveal the "instability" and "the contingency" of official narratives about the person (23, emphasis added). Wald's narrative of a national unconscious deeply anxious over the exclusion of real "persons" from legal "personhood" begs the question of what a "person" is; it assumes that the answer is obvious and can never truly be contested or challenged. By identifying the "person" as the means by which the injustice of slavery is preeminently exposed rather than the identity that slavery puts into dispute, Wald, in the end, suggests that her interest is not, despite her title, in the process of constituting "persons" but in what remains beyond being constituted.[40]

Although grounded in the science of evolutionary biology rather than psychoanalysis, Leonard Cassuto's account of US race-based slavery complements Wald. In *The Inhuman Race*, Cassuto cites biological and neurological evidence of the ineluctable anthropomorphism of human perception to establish how difficult and unnatural it is to dehumanize others. Since we are hard-wired for "anthropomorphic perception," an "anxiety" inevitably "accompanies the attempt to turn a human being into something non-human" and this anxiety "produces tension and contradiction throughout a culture's belief system" (xvii). According to Cassuto, pro-slavery ideologues and slaveholders "contorted themselves in spectacular fashion to defend their position" and to evade "the reality" of Negro humanity (136, 139).[41] That is, one could say that Cassuto's argument is the flipside of Wald's: whereas Wald sees "personhood" as intrinsic to the object of repression, Cassuto sees "personhood" as something intrinsic to the perceiving subject. Behind both Cassuto and Wald's arguments is the assumption that the Negro is a "person" despite legal, scientific, and social pronouncements to the contrary, that this hard fact has been ignored, repressed, or misrepresented, and, most importantly, that this fact will inevitably be expressed either as the uncanny (Wald) or as the grotesque (Cassuto).

This emphasis on the "person" as the primary safeguard against the brutality of slavery suggests why the psychoanalytic language of repression has been so closely yoked to the political logic of emancipation. It often appears nowadays that a gothic rhetoric – a language of haunting and ghosts, of repression and return, of encryption and re-animation – has become the prevailing and privileged (if not the sole) language for formulating politically progressive arguments. The convergence of the psychoanalytic and the political register on the notions of the uncanny and repression culminates in a modern liberal focus on the absolute "personhood" of the slave and the inherent contradictions of slavery.[42] That it has become common to assert that oppressive social and political formations (such as slavery) silence "personhood" and that such "personhood" needs to be (or cannot help but be) brought to light marks how deeply we assume that the notion of the "person" is an impervious identity category, one that stands beyond the limits of the temporal and the contingent and thus in and of itself is sufficient for generating ethics. The gothic language of haunting, repression, and return invokes the "person" as if it were a theological category, the source of itself, an identity that can be repressed but never erased, distorted but never produced.

A theorist of slavery such as Orlando Patterson, in other words, follows this gothic logic when he characterizes slavery as a process of "social death," assuming that the slave was once "alive" and had been pronounced "socially dead" by society. By locating the injustice of slavery in such a wrongful death, Patterson never examines the possibility that the US slave, for example, was a qualitatively different order of being who needed to be brought to life (i.e. "personified") before it was possible to posit any rights as having been forfeited or to imagine the slave as the living dead.[43] It has, I would suggest, become difficult to reconstruct the historicity of the "person" precisely because having produced the slave as a self-evident "person," it is now difficult to imagine this *fact* as not always already present. The modern notion of the "person," in essence, readily passes as the source of history itself.

Assertions about the eternal stability of the slave's "personhood" may seem reassuring; they seem to securely ground condemnations of race-based slavery and guarantee the collapse of the institution. But such claims are in themselves symptomatic of the end of slavery, not its cause. We can sanguinely identify the real "person" existing beneath and outside any specific political understanding because for us a particular knowledge about the "personhood" of the slave has become indisputable. If this knowledge were in dispute, then absolute assertions about the "person" would in themselves replay the political debate not resolve it. Indeed, such assertions are tautological to the extent that we only know what blocks or what expresses "personhood" from a particular set of circumstances. When we use our knowledge about the "person" as if it provided a universal and pre-political standard with which to interpret political disputes about slavery, we not only erase the political disputes historically waged over the notion of the "person" but also inoculate our account of the "person" from politics and from examination.

THE PERSON FUNCTION AND THE LOGIC OF LIBERAL REPRESENTATION

The alchemical transformation of the "person" from what motivates, enacts, and fuels into what suspends, constrains, and resolves political debates, I have been arguing, is the distinguishing feature of modern scholarship on US slavery. But the only way for the "person" to explain history and politics at the same time that the concept has historically been the primary object of political conflict is if the concept of the "person" is posited, at some level, as a concept that precedes the contingent history of its representation.[44] If it seems both historically and theoretically unsatisfactory to invoke the term under dispute as the principal means to end such disputes, one wonders what provokes us to bestow upon the "person" such solidity. The short answer: we have done so, because we operate within a liberal paradigm of representation. The impulse to transcendentalize the "person" – to treat it as an unchanging constant to be set against a long history of conflicting articulations – is the primal fantasy of liberal thought. Scholars, in other words, are responding to an incitement built into the structure of liberal representation. The conceptual sleight of hand that has morphed the effect of historical dispute (the "person") into the indisputable and ahistorical source of historical change needs to be understood as the exemplary ideological and formal achievement of liberal representation.

The explicit function of the conceptual category of the "person" in liberal theory, as I have discussed in the introduction, is to orient, organize, and determine the structure of liberalism. Liberal theory takes the "person" as the privileged and primary object to be accurately reflected in the formal institutions and policies of the liberal state. The liberal state stakes its claim to be the most evolved political structure on the fact that it is the best system for translating the nature of the "person" into civil and social structures. By doing so, liberalism first and foremost advertises itself as a mimetic formation: it claims to represent most accurately the authentic "person." The liberal state legitimates itself by faithfully capturing the notion of the "person." It decides upon policy by evaluating how well a practice corresponds to this foundational identity. The liberal order of things is realism by other means. Its ideal is to develop a system of political and social representation that allows the needs and desires of the irreplaceable object of liberal discourse (the "person") to be formally mirrored in the structures of the liberal state. According to liberal theory, the "ought" of the political order must be wholly derived from the "is" of the "person." And, to the extent that liberal theory demands that the "person" provide in itself a self-evident answer to all political disputes, liberalism conjures the "person" as a conceptual category that determines rather than is determined by history.

In order for liberal theory to place the "person" at its referential origin and locate this concept as the source by which liberal political ideals are legitimated and from which liberal rights are derived, a particular knowledge about the "person" must be produced. As long as liberalism strives to be congruent with the "person," the "person" must be imagined as an identity that remains external to and independent of the contingency of circumstance, the pregiven ground upon which political judgments can be subjected and by which social practices and institutions can be restrained.

Liberal representation, in other words, demands a specific relation between the act and object of representation, inevitably hierarchizing these two elements: the reproductive apparatuses of the state that represent the "person" must remain subordinate and secondary to the object (the "person") that is being resembled. Indeed, because liberal theory legitimates its fundamental ideological principles and structures in terms of how well they describe, reflect, and reproduce the "person," the precondition for liberalism is that the conceptual category of the "person" be the natural and unmediated precursor of liberalism, a pre-existing and discovered entity to which liberalism faithfully defers. Indeed, unless the concept of the "person" exists beyond and before its interpretation and representation in liberal discourse, it loses its function as the source of liberal principles and its status as the indispensable referee of liberal practice. Liberal representation, in short, must understand the "person" as an irreducible and antecedent conceptual category in order to legitimate itself.

FOUNDATIONAL PERSONHOOD

I have been arguing that our fear that unless the "person" possesses an intrinsic meaning we will no longer be able to resolve political disputes, guarantee liberatory thought, and preserve an authentic ethical critique marks how deeply we remain within the liberal imaginary. This project seeks to abandon the liberal impulse to establish an accurate representation of what a "person" is. Unlike prevailing critiques of liberalism that tend to understand the identification of "persons" as the end of politics, this project seeks to relieve the "person" of its descriptive function (the "person" **is** socially constructed or transcendent, material or metaphysical, empty or substantive, perpetually open or fundamentally stable), or more accurately it seeks to identify such positivist claims as themselves political articulations.

Of course, to have such goals presupposes that liberal political theory forecloses questions about the "person" as a political category. But such a claim about the directives of liberal theory might strike some as discounting how self-consciously vigilant liberal theorists (especially contemporary ones) have been about the danger of appearing to define the "person" as a metaphysical identity, one irrespective of context and antecedent to history. Indeed, although it may seem perhaps legitimate to claim that classic liberals (such as Locke, Kant, and Mill) operate according to a realist logic, to brand contemporary liberalism with the charge of placing the "person" before politics, might seem to disregard the work of the most influential theorist of contemporary liberalism, John Rawls.[45] Given Rawls' self-conscious effort to establish a liberal theory that is not based upon a decontextualized theory of the "person," his work stands as an ideal illustration of how powerfully modern liberal thought continues to be driven by the impulse to remove the person from history and politics.

Rawls, especially in his work after *A Theory of Justice*, explicitly sets out to construct a liberal theory that is not grounded in any particular metaphysical or comprehensive doctrine and takes great pains in *Political Liberalism* to elaborate how his conception of the "person" and of justice looks only to the contingency of "public culture itself" and on "the shared fund of implicitly recognized basic ideas and principles."[46] According to Rawls, his theory emerges within a particular historical and cultural context rather than transcendentally or naturalistically, depending upon a "purely political conception of the person" rather than upon a theory of human nature, the relation of the mind and body, or the distinction between public and private (*Political Liberalism*, 29–35). Indeed, Rawls is so committed to grounding liberalism on no particular view of morality that he came to criticize *A Theory of Justice* for relying "on a premise the realization of which its principles of justice rule out."[47]

Despite this commitment to founding justice on nothing but the shared elements of the public life of a democratic culture, Rawls ends up relying on the conceptual category of the "person" as a notion that exceeds and counteracts social contingency, thereby placing the "person" outside and before politics. Rawls, in other words, may seek to legitimate his theory of justice on purely historical grounds (rather than on some external source such as nature, God, or the Truth) and may claim that the "person" that stands as the self-referential ground and source of justice is purely contextual, but, as we will see, the "person" whom Rawls describes as determining liberal principles (the figure whom he imagines in the Original Position) paradoxically ends up looking nothing like the "person" who is situated in the world. There are, in short, two "persons" in Rawls theory; one empirical and one a pre-political foundation, and it is the later "person" – the "person" who stands before context – whom Rawls ultimately privileges as the source of justice.

My critique of Rawls, thus, is not the conventional claim that his theory of justice depends upon an abstract or transcendental conception of "person." Numerous critics, as Rawls notes, have argued that his version of liberalism is "intrinsically faulty because it uses an individualistic, unsocial idea of human nature," but, as Rawls also notes, such interpretations are grounded in a misunderstanding of his account of the Original Position (OP)(*Political Liberalism*, xxix). He claims that the OP conceives of "the person as political" because in the OP (the hypothetical starting point of his theory of justice) individuals are to choose the principles of social justice behind a gradually disappearing "veil of ignorance" – that is, in the OP one begins as ignorant of "features relating to social position, native endowment, and historical accident, as well as to the contents of persons' determinate conceptions of the good" [what Rawls calls "comprehensive doctrines"] (*Political Liberalism*, 29, 79). Such a scenario, in which one is an disembodied identity – unaware of one's race, gender, social standing, talents, conceptions of the good etc – has "tempt[ed]," Rawls acknowledges, his critics to "think that a metaphysical doctrine of the person is presupposed" (*Political Liberalism,* 29). But Rawls emphasizes that the OP is simply a heuristic, a "device of representation" that carries with it "no specific metaphysical implications concerning the nature of the self" (such as that "the essential nature of persons is independent of and prior to their contingent attributes") any more than "our acting a part in a play, say of Macbeth or Lady Macbeth, commits us to thinking that we are really a king or queen. . ." (*Political Liberalism,* 27). For Rawls the OP is merely a thought experiment, a hypothetical choice situation that facilitates and clarifies the principles of justice and is unconcerned with statements about the nature of the "person."

Indeed, according to Rawls, the principles of justice are framed in terms of this thought experiment for purely pragmatic and contextual reasons: it simply serves as an effective mechanism for indexing the principles of justice. The strategy of abstracting from the particularity of any concrete position, Rawls argues, is merely a means to generate social cooperation (what Rawls calls an "overlapping consensus") given the diversity of comprehensive moral, philosophical, and religious visions in democratic political culture. To the extent that Rawls is only talking about a particular political tradition rather than any antecedent truth about human nature, the order of things, or God, his theory is, as Rorty characterizes it, "thoroughly historicist and antiuniversalist," committed not "to a philosophical account the human self, but only to a historico-sociological description of the way we live now".[48]

But when one examines Rawls' account of the OP, one begins to suspect that Rorty's faith in Rawls' historicism is misplaced. Although Rawls seeks to establish a theory in which historical beings determine the principles of justice for themselves and for their own purposes, Rawls, nonetheless, depends upon a distinction between the "person" who chooses and the "person" who exists in the world. The "person" behind the Veil of Ignorance, the figure who serves as the immediate source of the principles of justice, remains ignorant of and unimpeded by concrete knowledge and the particularities that define us and lead to the kind of social unrest that Rawls seeks to overcome. That is, in order to facilitate the possibility of agreement within pluralism, Rawls establishes a fundamental incommensurability between two types of "personhood," disconnecting the "person" at the foundation of his theory (the subject who chooses) from the "person" situated in history (the one subjected to history and to conflicting comprehensive doctrines).

The "person" who is represented and respected by Rawls ends up being situated prior to the ends it chooses and the attributes it possesses. This figure may be imaginary rather than actual, but to the extent that the "person" formulating the principles of justice is fundamentally abstract and therefore nothing like us (we are, Rawls acknowledges, fundamentally concrete and encumbered), it is for all intents and purposes irrelevant whether or not the OP is a fiction or not. In either case, the result is the same: the immediate source of the principles of justice is not self-referential (and thus historical) but a figure who exists before any particular context and thus is fundamentally distinct from the "person" whose rights and duties are ultimately being decided.

Rawls, of course, argues that such a "person" is necessary given the pluralism of modern democratic society; as he puts it, the OP is a means to help "us work out what we now think" by providing a "clear and uncluttered view of what justice requires" (*Political Liberalism* 26, 46). Such a divorce, according to Rawls, is necessary to filter out the knowledge and circumstances that are "irrelevant" from the point of view of justice (79). He argues that we can only think about justice if we "find some point of view, removed from and not distorted by the particular features and circumstances of the all-encompassing background framework" (23). The OP allows consensus without agreement. But to argue that the OP is a pragmatic means to discover justice is to reaffirm something that is already formulated not to explain the need for positing a crucial conceptual difference between those "abstract from and not. . . affected by the contingencies of the social world" – and those embedded in the world – i.e. "persons" with specific beliefs, values, talents, social identities, and commitments (*Political Liberalism*, 23).[49] Since the OP is purely heuristic and never really exists, the reason to construct it cannot be that it helps us find justice because, unless we already know what justice looks like, we cannot know what helps and what hinders its articulation.

Rawls, in short, presupposes the very thing that he establishes the OP to discover. For in order to know the aspects of "personhood" that interfere with justice and those that do not, Rawls must already know what justice is. It is only possible to anticipate what kind of "restrictions on information" facilitate the task of establishing social justice if we already have access to the very thing being sought (*Political Liberalism*, 27). A particular account of justice precedes the very framework designed to enable "persons" to derive the principles of justice and this presumption is then hidden by the ostensibly neutral constraints built into the OP. What is designed to find the shared norms that Rawls assumes stand behind democratic culture actually produces these shared norms. Of course, one might respond that what else could his starting point be but the historical reality of the way we live now. Indeed, since all the mechanisms (the OP, the veil of ignorance, the difference principle) Rawls devises are intended to suss out prevailing principles of justice, such assumptions are both inevitable and beside the point.[50] But such assumptions are not beside the point to the extent that the procedure that Rawls adopts is designed to move us beyond the impasse of existing debates. He is not getting us out of debate, however, he is determining which side of the debate (i.e. those who privilege identity as raceless, genderless, agnostic, etc) will win.

Rawls, in short, has rigged the hypothetical starting point of his theory. He has posited the "person" who is choosing the principles of justice as having always already bracketed whatever elements of identity might generate disagreement rather than agreement. Rawls already knows what justice looks like because he already knows the kind of "person" who makes the decisions about what counts as justice. Rawls may claim to be sensitive to the situatedness of "persons," but in the end the immediate source of Rawls' liberalism is not the historically contingent "person" at all, but a purely imaginary figure who operates under the specific constraints of the OP.[51] Since this "person" is independent from context in a way that Rawls acknowledges empirical "persons" never can be, Rawls' political liberalism ultimately orients itself in terms of a "person" who lives before politics and beyond revision.[52] This "person" is not self-determining but pre-determined, not the source of Rawls' system but its primary effect. Rawls, one might say, has relocated, not given up, the premise that the "person" precedes liberal thought. By imagining that he has found a tactic (the OP) by which we can come to know what we already are but are blocked from recognizing by being in the world, he subordinates the "person" made in history to the imaginary "person" who stands both at the center of his theory and beyond the limitations of any context.

Indeed, the extent to which Rawls' political conception of the "person" ultimately displaces politics altogether becomes particularly evident when he discusses slavery. In order to explain why abolitionists, whose opposition to slavery Rawls acknowledges was grounded on comprehensive moral and religious doctrine, did not violate the protocols of political liberalism, Rawls declares that for a "well-ordered society to come about" it may be "require[d] that comprehensive reasons be invoked" (*Political Liberalism*, 251, n. 41). In other words, liberalism's "ideal of public reason" is reconcilable with comprehensive claims about the Good if such appeals prefigure and point toward the day when such appeals are no longer a necessary part of public reason (*Political Liberalism*, 251). In order to make this assertion, Rawls assumes that the "personhood" of the slave is such a patently rational statement that it can be used to retroactively justify historical arguments that seem on the surface to fundamentally conflict with his definition of political liberalism as eschewing comprehensive doctrines. In making this claim it becomes clear that Rawls is not championing political liberalism for "removing from the political agenda the most divisive issues" nor simply assuming that our current social context and settled convictions are "just" for us, but assuming that our account of "personhood," justice, and slavery is always already reasonable (*Political Liberalism*, 157).

By rewriting abolitionists' allegiance to comprehensive doctrines as proto-liberal, Rawls manifests an anxiety that his account of political liberalism may leave no space to condemn slavery because it may seem to imply that the divisive issue of slavery should be taken "off the political agenda" (*Political Liberalism*, 151). It is not by accident that at the moment Rawls turns to slavery his claims for the contextual nature of his version of liberalism collapse. For Rawls to approach some claims about the "person" as always already unreasonable (and therefore as what must be superseded to achieve a "well-ordered" society), he builds his ostensibly historical argument on transhistorical grounds, beginning with the premise that slavery always distorts the "person." Rawls' liberalism, it turns out, is more teleological than he advertises: it removes a particular understanding of the "person" from history and places it within a narrative of unfolding reason. At the very moment when he confronts what it would mean to develop a theory of justice that is fundamentally contextual – one relying on nothing more than existing institutions, structures, and assumptions – Rawls proves himself a representative liberal. He pulls back from a purely political conception of the "person." But, then again, what else could he do as long as he continues to preserve some version of the "person" as the source rather than as an effect of a particular conception of justice.

This liberal impulse to identify the "person" as the independent ground for settling questions about ethics in general and the ethics of slavery in particular is not limited to thinkers who self-identify as liberal; it has also been reproduced in critiques of liberalism. For example, Saidiya Hartman's compelling account of the emancipation of Black slaves as a new form of subjection itself depends upon an absolutist notion of the "person." Focusing on how the "extension of humanity to the enslaved ironically reinscribe[d] their subjugated status" and arguing that emancipation "conferred sovereignty as it engendered subjection," Hartman seeks to counter the unequivocal championing of freedom that the transition from slavery to freedom, from thing to subject, has inspired.[53] In critiquing the sort of subjectivity achieved in liberal freedom, Hartman (deeply influenced, as I will discuss, by the work of Judith Butler) draws attention to the way that a slave's experience of self (of "innate capacities and inner feelings," of pleasure, pain, embodiment, love, responsibility etc) conflates subjectivity and subjugation (p. 26).

Such critique is premised on the assumption that in order to truly experience one's self that experience must remain before and outside the regulatory apparatuses of the state, of the law, of conscience, and of the concept of individuality itself.[54] Suspicious of the way that "the official acknowledgment of agency and humanity" ultimately recuperates "the object status and absolute subjugation" of the enslaved "in terms of personhood," Hartman seeks to recover the "sensibility," the "impulse," the "inexplicable, yet irrepressible" desire for freedom that exceeds any regime of power (62, 64). She searches for elements of sentience that exist apart from any regulatory matrix and locates the real self there because, as she puts it, "the contented bondsman" reveals how slavery (just like liberal freedom in general) elides the "difference between volition and violation" and makes "discipline a pleasure" (43).

By claiming that any identity constructed within structures of liberalism is *a priori* false, Hartman assumes that authentic "personhood" must go beyond politically contingent representations ("the desires and longings that exceed the frame of civil rights and political emancipation"), aspiring to retrieve the figure who exists behind such false representations and to gesture towards an "unrealized freedom" (13, 14). In foregrounding the "contented subjection" of liberal freedom, Hartman imagines an asymmetry between an idealized subjectivity and the subjugated subjectivity of the Negro (both slave and free) within the liberal state (49). Such critique is only possible to the extent that true "personhood" is imagined as expressed only at moments when it exceeds such oppressive frameworks and stands as its own independent ground. Hartman may set out to indict liberalism, but she ends up reproducing the quintessential logic of liberal representation: she preserves the "person" as the intrinsic source of social justice.

In some sense the liberal logic haunting Hartman's work is not surprising since it also haunts the work of the theorist who lies behind Hartman's argument: Judith Butler. Indeed, since Butler's explicitly political project (I will be focusing on *The Psychic Life of Power*)[55] seeks to analyze how fundamental categories of identity are cultural and social productions, her project shares much with my discussion of "personhood." It is for this reason that I will conclude my account of the dominance of the logic of liberal representation with a discussion of Butler's enormously powerful and influential argument.

Butler, following Foucault, studies the subject as a contingent identity category, one constantly being produced rather than a pre-existing form finally properly represented. She resists any appeal to an external substance to which power has no access. But to the extent that her goal is to identify how the subject can exceed and, in some sense, be independent from its origin in and through power, her work preserves traditional repressive conceptions of power. That is, Butler sees power as the condition of possibility for the subject – power simultaneously sustains and is sustained by subjects – but she ends up emphasizing subjugation (rather than the subjectification), asking how a subject can be anything but inevitably complicit with and organized by the dominant order.

Butler's project, in part, is to show how one does not need to enact change from a position of transcendence (a formulation she calls "naïve") because once constituted in and by power, the subject does not mechanically reproduce the terms of power (*PLP*, 17). As Butler puts it, "the iterability of the subject shows how agency may well consist in opposing and transforming the social terms by which it is spawned" (*PLP*, 29). If power is sustained by reiteration, it can also be subverted, deflected, parodied, and turned against dominant norms. Or as she says in *Excitable Speech*, "within political discourse, the very terms of resistance and insurgency are spawned in part by the powers they oppose."[56] But the claim that resistance is an inevitable component of any system of power (as well as of language) is not where Butler's project rests. She is not interested in simply describing the way we are constituted in and through power, but in trying to overcome this insight, to analyze how the (essentially negative) workings of power can be exposed. It is her sense of our vulnerability to power that motivates her account of resistance.

Indeed, the question that initiates her study – "how to take an oppositional relation to power that is, admittedly, implicated in the very power one opposes" – can only be formulated if Butler ultimately does not accept Foucault's emphasis on the positivity of power (*PLP*, 17). In Butler's account, power is simultaneously the condition of our being and what we need to exceed. Although Butler powerfully criticizes the impossible fantasy of a standpoint not sustained by and complicit with the forces "that have constituted it," she, nonetheless, seems to seek something that looks a lot like the pristine notion of resistance she repeatedly rejects, positing emancipation as the overcoming of our original subjection (*PLP*, 17). For Butler, it appears that resistance is universally good because power is fundamentally restrictive. Butler, in contrast to Foucault, imagines that one resists power rather than particular deployments of power relations, making the removal of power collateral with emancipation.[57]

Butler, of course, does not explicitly expect the subject to transcend context (what Butler calls the "insurmountability of the social"). But she preserves such an expectation in the way that she distinguishes an action that sustains from one that resists subjection, asking how the subject can eclipse the "conditions of its own emergence," be "enabled but not finally constrained by the prior working of power" (*PLP*, 14, 15). Indeed, since resistance threatens the "social existence" of the subject, putting the subject at "risk of death," one wonders what motivates Butler to privilege her account of resistance (*PLP*, 28–29). And, since, as Butler argues, power (like language) is always vulnerable to reappropriation and resignification, one wonders why Butler continues to imagine resistance as fundamentally distinct from power.

The only reason for such formulations of resistance appears to be that Butler posits an opposition to power as always already emancipatory. The social must be surmounted because there remains something in our being that power fundamentally misrecognizes. Butler never names this space (it is fundamentally unnamable), but nonetheless invokes it by assuming that subjectivity is an imposition upon this original state of being, something that "presses upon" us rather than simply is us (*PLP*, 3). Subjectivity expresses "a primary and inaugurative alienation" and "a primary violence" because a place before and external to power is hypothesized (*PLP*, 28). Butler, in other words, seems to simultaneously claim that there is no subject prior to our subjectification, but then imagines this subjectifying as a form of misrecognition. Her account, in short, is that a fundamental violence has been perpetrated, but one wonders, given her discursive account of identity, exactly how she can posit something existing to be misrecognized unless she imagines that our truest identity stands independent from and prior to the *limitations* of context and contingency. And it is here that one sees how deeply Butler's critique of liberal thought recapitulates the liberal notion of the "person." Rather than being insurmountable, the historical and the social, it turns out, mark both what we are not and what is suspect.

Or to put this another way, the very notion of the sovereign subject that she begins by moving beyond, in the end returns in mystified form as the latent motive of her project. Indeed, the embedding of psychic life makes conceptualizing agency more difficult only if agency remains within an Enlightenment understanding of the individual as the origin of its acts and ideas. Preoccupied by the liberal fantasy of the subject, Butler is unsettled by how the subject is subjugated by discourse. Her attachment to the humanist subject who can dominate the world becomes clear when she describes the problem facing any subject: a subject's "'voice' is from the start borrowed from elsewhere" and bound "to seek recognition of its own existence in categories, terms, and names that are not of its own making . . . in a discourse at once dominant and indifferent" (*PLP*, 198, 20). Although resistance is possible, the subject, according to Butler, cannot be the conscious agent of resistance precisely because the subject is primarily an effect of power.[58] Indeed, it is precisely because the subject cannot intentionally resist, that resistance seems to be given a life of its own. Thus, as Butler argues that neither the subject nor the body nor the unconscious is essentially resistant, she, nonetheless, keeps the idea of essential resistance. What Butler seeks to liberate, in short, is resistance *per se.*

That is, the category of resistance ends up "personified," looking a lot like the paradigmatic liberal identity: untouched by the political, historical, contextual, uncorrupted by any relation to the social. By identifying resistance as distinct from any disciplinary system, Butler ironically reintroduces the very insight that began her study (that there is no subject unimplicated in the disciplinary system it opposes) as the solution to the threat of power she has identified. If both Rawls and Butler preserve the conceptual category of the "person" at the very moment they seek to contextualize it (Rawls) and dissolve it (Butler), I want to briefly return to Lincoln's argument against race-based slavery, in order to explore what it would mean to read "personhood" differently.

RECONSTRUCTING LINCOLN AFTER THE PERSON

"I think," Lincoln declared in an 1857 speech *against* the Dred Scott decision that "the authors of that notable instrument [the Declaration of Independence] intended to include *all* men, but they did not intend to declare all men equal *in all respects.* They did not mean to say all were equal in color, size, intellect, moral development or social capacity"

(*Library of America*, 398). Although Lincoln, unlike Douglas, claims that the Negro slave is a "person," Lincoln, no less than Douglas, subscribes to the notion that the Negro has certain essential characteristics. He frames his argument against slavery in terms of the absolute difference between the races:

> There is a physical difference between the two [white and Black races], which in my judgment will probably forever forbid their living together on terms of respect, social and political equality, and inasmuch as it becomes a necessity that there must be a superiority somewhere, I, as well as Judge Douglas, am in favor of the race to which I belong having the superior position; but I hold that because of all this there is no reason at all furnished why the negro after all is not entitled to all that the declaration of independence holds out, which is, "life, liberty, and the pursuit of happiness" and I hold that he is as much entitled to that as the white man.[59]

Lincoln argues that even though the Negro is essentially and biologically different from the white race, the fundamental liberal rights that the Declaration of Independence promises to all "persons" nonetheless belong to the Negro as well as to the Anglo-Saxon. That is, Lincoln claims that Negroes are "persons," but he does so without claiming either that race is inessential or that any differences between the Negro and the white races must be subordinated to a universal notion of the "person."

I am not citing Lincoln's belief in racial essences either to accuse Lincoln of being as racist as Douglas (the project of identifying degrees of racism seems pointless since racism names practices that we axiomatically regard as retrograde) or to indict him for being insincere in his opposition to slavery (he clearly was committed to ending what he believed to be an immoral practice).[60] Rather, I cite Lincoln's belief in racial essences in order to foreground the central problem that scholars have confronted when studying many of the most powerful antebellum statements against race-based slavery: the fact that many of the most influential opponents of Negro slavery, most notoriously perhaps Lincoln, the African American separatist Martin Delany, and Harriet Beecher Stowe, believed *both* in the truth of essential differences between the races and in the evil of race-based slavery.[61] Such prominent anti-slavery advocates argued that slavery was unjust because Black slaves were "persons" at the same time that they configured the category of the "person" in fundamentally racial terms.

It is, of course, clear why so many have been troubled by the reaffirmation of racial essentialist thought in ostensibly progressive thinkers. It strikes us as perverse to claim "personhood" and to affirm absolute racial difference because such differences are precisely what rendered slavery *safe* for this liberal nation, justifying Negro slavery as the slavery of "non-persons." By condemning slavery without attacking the essentialist logic that crucially subtends the pro-slavery argument, this kind of anti-slavery argument seems to converge with and reinforce the ideological justification of slavery, transforming but not addressing the category (race) that organizes, legitimates, and allows such oppression to emerge in the first place.

Although such a repudiation of racial essentialism certainly is understandable, this repudiation makes the situation too easy. If one regards every instance of racial essentialism as *a priori* regressive, one too quickly dismisses not only the difference between Lincoln and Douglas but also the extent to which such essentialism worked to enable and energize the antebellum argument against slavery. Indeed, as Lincoln argues, only if we appreciate the essential racial difference of the races, do we become able to recognize the particular "personhood" of the Negro. If we demand that the Negro and the white race be identical, we will, Lincoln suggests, inevitably justify race-based slavery because we will be unable to see the Negro as anything but an inferior version of the Anglo-Saxon.

That is, we see Lincoln's yoking of racial essentialism and anti-slavery as an inadequate response because we posit racial essentialism as intrinsically regressive. We imagine that such a representation of the "person" distorts what a "person" *is.* In contrast, I am suggesting that Lincoln is not misrepresenting the "personhood" of the slave, but failing to conceptualize the figure of the "person" in the way we do. And we assume that a color blind conception of the "person" is progressive because we posit such a representation as reflecting the intrinsic meaning of the "person." Lincoln's opposition to slavery not only foregrounds the disjunction between prevailing antebellum and modern conceptions of the "person" (Lincoln, after all, did not articulate a marginal position) but, more importantly, marks how profoundly we presume that it is only by removing the concept of the "person" from context that we can guarantee social justice.

Arguments over civil rights during Reconstruction, however, make clear that color blindness does not necessarily produce what we would see as a progressive politics. For example, Radical Republicans argued that the racial categories that had been used before the war to subordinate Blacks could be used after the war to uplift them. Indeed, those who argued for a color blind understanding of justice and who asserted that using race, even for the goal of preventing or redressing discrimination, was inconsistent with equal protection regularly used a universalist rhetoric to oppose legislation designed to improve the condition of newly freed slaves.[62] That is, to the extent that a colorblind reading of the Constitution prevailed, many laws and programs designed to remedy slavery by addressing newly freed Black slaves exclusively were defeated in the name of equality.

Readings of Lincoln, in short, exemplify how an anachronistic certainty about the solidity of the "person" has allowed the political problem of the "person" to be erased. Rather than discussing Lincoln's anti-slavery argument as compromised by a distortion of the "person," Lincoln needs to be approached in terms of the question of what are the political consequences of the "person" that Lincoln deploys. Indeed, to the extent that his account works to delegitimate slavery, something crucial is lost by axiomatically discounting it as fundamentally unjust. Such a claim does not mean that Lincoln's position cannot be critiqued but it does imply that it does little good to critique Lincoln's argument by claiming that he is making a fundamental mistake about the nature of the "person." I am not, of course, seeking to justify Lincoln's hierarchizing of the Anglo-Saxon over the African or claiming that Lincoln's model of the "person" is ideal. But I am suggesting that any critique of Lincoln examine the effects his particular model of the "person" has, rather than presume he is obviously misrepresenting what a "person" is (i.e. adds race to the "person").

To simply conflate Lincoln's argument against slavery with racism is to remove the "person" from the realm of politics (in which one asks what this concept does) and to place it in the realm of truth (in which one simply states what a person is). To the extent that a particular account of the "person" is posited as an irreducible and sufficient resource for distinguishing the ethical from the unethical, the emancipatory from the regressive, a particular understanding of the "person" (ours) is inflated into a universal, treated as an inevitable guarantee of progressive politics and removed from interrogation. In my next two chapters, I turn to Stowe's *Uncle Tom's Cabin*, the antebellum text that most powerfully personified the Negro, to explore what happens to dominant interpretations of race-based slavery when one stops presuming that every instance of race-consciousness produces an identical ideological effect.

CHAPTER 2

Family values and racial essentialism in Uncle Tom's Cabin

When Harriet Beecher Stowe introduces her readers to Uncle Tom's cabin, she remarks that the "wall over the fireplace was adorned with some very brilliant Scriptural prints and a portrait of General Washington."[1] In their privileged position over the hearth, these domestic adornments, one sacred, and the other secular, prefigure the Christian virtue and the desire for personal liberty that Tom's life, and by extension his home, will come to embody. As George Shelby tells the slaves he manumits at the novel's conclusion, "Think of your freedom every time you see UNCLE TOM'S CABIN; and let it be a memorial to put you all in mind to follow in his steps, and be as honest and faithful and Christian as he was" (437). Of course, it was not unusual to find either Scriptural prints or a portrait of Washington in a typical nineteenth-century American home.[2] One might assume, therefore, that Stowe places these generic household icons in the cabin of a slave in order to demonstrate that the American slave and the American citizen are essentially similar. However, readers learn that there is a striking difference between the slave and the citizen. Tom's portrait of Washington is "drawn and colored in a manner which would certainly have astonished that hero" (20). Tom's Washington is Black.

The strange form of this presidential portrait is of more than passing significance. It suggests more than the fact that Tom yearns for, yet is denied the personal liberty that the figure of Washington represents. The portrait implies that Tom's attraction to Washington depends as much on Washington's physical appearance as upon his figurative effect. Indeed, even though Washington may seem the ideal symbol of Tom's desire for freedom and domestic tranquility, it is not sufficient for Tom merely to worship what this Founding Father represents.[3] Apparently, if Washington is to be Tom's hero, he must be Black like Tom.

Rather than seeing this "negrification" of Washington as Stowe's effort to expose the hypocrisy of distributing liberal rights according to race,

I will argue in this chapter that this moment exemplifies Stowe's belief that racial homogeneity can provide the only secure foundation for either a familial or a political community. Stowe projects onto Tom, "a full black" with "truly African features," her prejudice for having literal and figurative fathers be of the same race (21).[4] According to Stowe's account of political genealogy, even though Washington's whiteness certainly does not prevent him from literally fathering Black slaves, it does prevent him from serving as the symbolic national Father of Black slaves.[5] Stowe's blackening of Washington, in other words, foregrounds color as the empirical "fact" that marks the disjunction between the Father of this country and the inherited condition of Tom's race. And as *Uncle Tom's Cabin* unfolds, it becomes clearer that Stowe is interested not in denying the significance of racial differences, but in affirming the material importance of race in the formation of both personal and national families.

Stowe's patent interest in racial difference, of course, has long disturbed critics. Assuming that such racialism distorts "personhood," critics have demanded that such racial traits be segregated from any effort to "personify" slaves. In contrast to this tradition of attacking *Uncle Tom's Cabin* because the novel does not condemn a belief in racial essences as forcefully as it indicts slavery, I will argue that Stowe's commitment to racial difference is precisely what enables her "personification" of the Negro slave and her denunciation of slavery. The lesson of *Uncle Tom's Cabin* is that there must be two Washingtons. Stowe's argument against slavery depends upon a racialized nationalism.

Stowe's claims about the absoluteness of Negro "personhood," in other words, cannot be separated from her understanding of racial essentialism. Ultimately, rather than advocating individual rights irrespective of race, *Uncle Tom's Cabin* justifies liberal pluralism by means of racialism.[6] Such biological essentialism cannot be separated from Stowe's sentimental rescue of the Black slave. Therefore, rather than dismissing Stowe's blatant racialism as a curious but marginal nuance, or an embarrassing superannuated element that can be exorcised from the novel, I investigate such racialism as inseparable from Stowe's absolute claims about Negro "personhood." Stowe's "progressive" liberal politics has been misidentified because a transhistorical notion of the "person" has been deployed to adjudicate Stowe's argument against slavery. We have qualms about Stowe's representation of the "person" not because we oppose her efforts to condemn slavery but because we are offended by her understanding of the "person." And we have these qualms about her account of the "person" precisely because we have reproduced her absolutist claims about "personhood."

Until recently, critics, citing Stowe's obvious use of racial stereotypes, regularly condemned Stowe as a racist. They declared that Stowe's belief in inherent racial characteristics tainted, and perhaps even wholly negated, the sincerity and the ultimate value of *Uncle Tom's Cabin*'s manifest anti-slavery politics.[7] In probably the most scathing attack on the novel's racial stereotypes, J. C. Furnas in *Goodbye to Uncle Tom* (1956) argues that Stowe's books in general and *Uncle Tom's Cabin* in particular are intrinsically "racist propaganda" and that "their effect must always have been to instill or to strengthen racist ideas."[8] The stereotype that Furnas most objects to is the notion that the African race is inherently affectionate and peaceful. Such a sentimentalization of the "Negro," according to Furnas, has "sadly clogged the efforts of modern good will" and is responsible for "the wrongheadedness, distortions and wishful thinkings about Negroes . . . that still plague us today" (8). Furnas acknowledges that the popular use of the Uncle Tom epithet "is unfair to the figure that Mrs. Stowe created," but he nevertheless reproves Stowe for having so "persuasively formulated and thus frozen" an "apparently authoritative racist doctrine to plump out" her readers' "previously inchoate notions" (8). As Furnas melodramatically concludes, the "devil could have forged no shrewder weapon for the Negro's worst enemy" (51).

More recently, however, critical interest has turned away from such condemnations of Stowe's sentimental stereotyping of the Black slave and has moved towards a more favorable examination of the ways in which Stowe's use of domestic sentimentality worked to secure social authority for women. This revisionist account of *Uncle Tom's Cabin* has effectively recast the tenor of investigations into the novel: positive characterizations of Stowe's gender politics have subsumed anxieties about her racial politics. Although such a feminist characterization of Stowe's domestic sentimentality has allowed *Uncle Tom's Cabin* to be effectively incorporated into the canon, this identification of the novel's sentimental power has "muted" the issue of race precisely because it seems motivated by a fundamental discomfort with the novel's racial theory. Indeed, Stowe has been redeemed to the extent that Stowe's sentimentalism has been persuasively represented as fundamentally extraneous to, rather than mutually supporting of, her racial politics.[9]

When critics do register their uneasiness about Stowe's representation of race, they tend to treat Stowe's racialism as a perplexing anomaly, an unfortunate historical residue that obscures the political and social work of *Uncle Tom's Cabin.* Gillian Brown, for example, has noted the "troubling contradictions of *Uncle Tom's Cabin*: the novel's simultaneous advancement of domestic feminism, anti-slavery, and racism." Unlike Furnas, who has no trouble condemning the novel, Brown has "difficulty in accounting for. . .the disconcerting fact that Stowe's sentimentalism forwards both abolitionism and racism."[10] Brown's difficulty stems from the widely-held assumption that racial essentialism is a dangerously reactionary formation that simply should not dovetail with the progressive politics of abolition and sentimentality. Expressing a similar logic, Brook Thomas has argued that Stowe's "racial and gender essentialism" are "self-contradictory" ideological positions profoundly at odds with Stowe's powerful condemnation of slavery.[11] But, in emphasizing Stowe's essentialism, Thomas acknowledges that he "neglect[s] one of the most effective ways in which Stowe elicits sympathy for blacks"–her effort to show "how character is shaped by existing economic systems" and "perpetuated through cultural, not hereditary, transmission." It is only reluctantly, therefore, that Thomas confesses, "I accuse Stowe of essentialism" (130–131, 130).

The reactions of Brown and Thomas are representative of the widespread sentiment among the novel's critics that Stowe's admirable anti-slavery position should be accompanied by and derive from an equally praiseworthy liberal stance against racial essences.[12] This framework indeed has been elaborated in much current criticism, manifesting itself, for example, in Timothy Powell's recent effort to "resolve" this tension.[13] Powell recognizes that Stowe's "essentialist view of race and class is highly problematic in terms of Stowe's ideological commitment to both abolition and the women's movement" (122). Indeed, Powell sees the tension between Stowe's progressive politics and her racial essentialism as so foundational and so vexing that his solution is to "steer" away from this irresolvable problem, identifying this sidestep strategy as the best way to avoid "becoming caught up in [an] endless, mutually destructive cycle," "an internecine war between white feminists [who champion the novel] and African American critics [who have condemned Stowe's racial essentialism]" (126). Powell, in short, accepts that there is a "racist subtext" to Stowe's novel and concludes that only if we stop "focusing (once again)" on such racial essentialism can we "construct a more radically inclusive vision" of America and move "toward reincorporating" African Americans into "America" (127). Rather than interrogate the premises of Stowe's racial essentialism, Powell asks us, one might say, to simply "get over it" and focus on issues that can be more constructively managed.

Powell's frustration with Stowe's limited politics is symptomatic of the way that most contemporary critics repudiate any account of "natural" identities as reactionary and destructive. Given that, in the present day, the essences being attributed to African-Americans often authorize an invidious social hierarchy, this rejection of racial essences makes some sense. But, the assertion that Stowe's anti-slavery politics and racial essentialism are "self-contradictory" is both theoretically imprecise and historically inadequate.

Theoretically, this line of argument depends upon the contemporary liberal belief that racialism intrinsically supports an oppressive social hierarchy and thus too quickly conflates racialism with racism. Indeed, this typically liberal judgment against any attribution of an essential identity based on one's biological or physical nature ultimately removes the notion of the "person" from debate. It imputes a fixed essence to any account of the "person" that depends upon racial essences; it relies on the "fact" that essentialism possesses a self-evidently pernicious ideological character because it misrepresents "personhood." Rather than abandoning transhistorical claims, the anti-essentialist notion of the "person" driving this critique of Stowe's racial politics reinscribes the fundamental premise of essentialism: it reifies the "person" and occludes the historical contexts in which this notion emerges just as profoundly as an explicitly essentialist account would.

Historically, this tendency to axiomatically condemn essentialism becomes suspect once Stowe's account of the relationship between racial essences and "personhood" is situated within an antebellum context. The fact that Stowe believed in racial essences means little in and of itself since the assumption that race crucially formed personal and national identity thoroughly pervaded antebellum culture.[14] Rather than reflexively condemn all instances of such biologism, Stowe's particular version of racial essentialism must be recovered. For when it is, it becomes clear that Stowe advocates the abolition of slavery not by discrediting racialism, but by advocating a stronger sense of biological racialism. One cannot forget that the most effective way Stowe elicits sympathy for "Negroes" is by giving them an essentially Christian character.

This is not to say that the widespread popular and scientific belief in the innate inferiority of the Negro was not central to many defenses of slavery and repudiations of abolition, but it is to question the assumption that essentialist conceptions of the Negro were always in the service of a pro-slavery position. Indeed, to the extent that a modern liberal prejudice against essentialism guides interpretations of *Uncle Tom's Cabin,* discussions of Stowe's work will continue to regard her simultaneous embrace of racialism and anti-slavery, her concomitant efforts to segregate the races and to secure equal rights for Negroes, as logical contradictions, rather than as reciprocal historical effects affiliated by their common dependence upon Stowe's fundamental commitment to biological essentialism. Stowe can persuade her readers to hate slavery only because she can rely on the fact that they could be convinced to love particular racial stereotypes. As long as this connection between racialism and the anti-slavery impulse is minimized, the way in which *Uncle Tom's Cabin* works to grant "personhood" to Black slaves will continue to be interpreted as an example of the extension of abstract liberal values to previously excluded groups, rather than as a materialist critique and rewriting of prevailing antebellum conceptions of the Negro. In *Uncle Tom's Cabin*, rather than deny or transcend the "grossly biological" nature of the African (as a modern liberal would), Stowe sets out to redescribe this "grossly biological" nature in positive terms. That is, I want to examine how Stowe is constructing a notion of the "person" rather than foreground how Stowe misidentifies the "personhood" of the African American.

THE CHRISTIAN RACE

Stowe regretted that the ever-increasing size of *The Key to Uncle Tom's Cabin* had forced her to "omit one whole department–that of the characteristics and developments of the colored race in various countries and circumstances," but, despite this omission, Stowe's writing makes clear that she believes in essential racial characteristics.[15] For example, it is only because Stowe believes so deeply in the permanence of race that she declares "that the half-breeds often inherit, to a great degree, the traits of their white ancestors"; similarly, she is careful to specify the proportion of Blackness in the exemplary free Blacks she lists at the conclusion of *Uncle Tom's Cabin* (*Key*, 17). Personal characteristics, according to Stowe, are transmitted through biology rather than culture and environment. That Stowe is a racialist, in short, requires elaboration rather than demonstration.

For Stowe, the most significant personal characteristic of Africans is their essential affinity for Christianity.[16] Negroes, as Tom most clearly demonstrates, have "a natural genius for religion"; "in their gentleness, their lowly docility of heart, their aptitude to repose on a superior mind and rest on a higher power, their child-like simplicity of affection and facility of forgiveness. . .they will exhibit the highest form of the peculiarly *Christian life*" (*Uncle Tom's Cabin*, 183, 178, original emphasis).[17] Of "all races of the earth," Stowe repeatedly tells her readers, "none have received the Gospel with such eager docility" (*Uncle Tom's Cabin*, 393). Although the Negro's natural love of Christianity could have been attributed to cultural rather than genetic transmission, Stowe very carefully defines this distinctive feature as biological. Such religious behavior, acccording to Stowe, emanates from the fact that the "principle of reliance and unquestioning faith," the foundation of Christianity, is "more a native element" in the African race than any other, "more native" to the Negro because the race is "possessed of *a nervous system peculiarly susceptible and impressible*" (*Uncle Tom's Cabin*, 393; *Key to Uncle Tom's Cabin*, 45 emphasis added). Deeply indebted to Jonathan Edwards's account of the importance of the affections in religious conversion, Stowe believes that religious faith is essentially sensational, a matter of the heart. Since the African race is the race most open to sensations, Negroes constitutively possess the greatest sensitivity to the Word of God and are naturally great Christians: "the divine graces of love and faith, when in-breathed by the Holy Spirit, find in [the Negro's] natural temperament a more congenial atmosphere" (*Key*, 41). To be Christian is simply the natural expression of the African's inherently impressionable character.[18]

This racialist claim about the African's instinct for Christianity is clearly a powerful strategy to secure white sympathy for the Negro slave. Such "romantic racialism" opposes the charge of biologically-based racial inferiority not by denying biologism, but by arguing that the biological identity of the African has been misidentified.[19] In claiming that the Negro race is naturally a Christian race, Stowe appeals to her audience's belief that the Negro is a distinct race but then proceeds to define this biological uniqueness in terms of the moral values that her audience already privileges. Rather than repudiating racialism, Stowe seeks to intensify a particular brand of racialism.

Despite Stowe's undisguised racialist claims about the nature of Africans, many critics, uncomfortable with notions of racial essences, have tried to argue that Stowe ultimately emphasizes nurture rather than nature. Such attempts at a liberal redemption of Stowe's racial stereotypes, however, overlook the fact that such an environmentalist account of African character would undermine her anti-slavery argument. If Stowe maintained that the surroundings wholly constituted a slave's character, Southerners could then invoke her positive characterization of Tom to prove that slavery benefited the African. A predominantly environmental or social account of the effects of slavery upon the Negro character either would make it extremely difficult for Stowe to present a heroic slave, or would require her to de-emphasize the evils of slavery and to acknowledge that slavery can produce virtuous slaves.

Southern apologists for slavery, in fact, did commonly insist that the novel in general, and Tom in particular, provided proof of their contention that slavery was a "positive good" for the African. Even Thomas Wentworth Higginson, a staunch abolitionist, felt compelled to admit, "if it is the normal tendency of bondage to produce saints like Uncle Tom, let us offer ourselves at auction immediately."[20] Pro-slavery advocates, such as the novelist William Gilmore Simms, an ardent defender of all things Southern (or Southron, as he, appropriating the term from Walter Scott's *Waverley* novels, called it), stated the case even more strongly. He declared that Southerners could easily recognize Uncle Tom as a typical product of slavery:

> That such a negro should grow up under the institution of slavery, is perhaps sufficiently conclusive in behalf of the institution. The North has no such characters. We shall not deny Uncle Tom. His is a Southron all over. He could not have been other than a Southron. We have many Uncle Toms.[21]

Unless Tom's heroism exists despite, not because of, the Southern slave system, his actions would support rather than undermine Southern claims that

> SLAVERY MADE UNCLE TOM. Had not it been for slavery, he would have been a savage in Africa, a brutish slave to his fetishes, living in a jungle, perhaps; and had you stumbled upon him he would very likely have roasted you and picked your bones.[22]

Although Stowe's biological essentialism clearly could not silence Southern claims about the positive influence of slavery, its presence did work to anticipate and counter the pro-slavery claim that slavery substantially benefited the essentially immoral nature of the African. It did so, not by denying that the African possessed a racial essence, but by attributing to the Negro a positive essence.

Stowe's understanding of the priority of race in forming a Negro's character certainly would not have surprised her contemporaneous readers. Indeed, during the antebellum period it would have been more surprising had Stowe done anything other than attribute cultural differences to race. As one historian has stated: "although the United States shared in a general Western movement toward racialist thinking, American writers in the years from 1830 to 1850 led Europeans in expounding views of innate racial difference."[23] This impulse was expressed by an increasing interest in the science of ethnology, the study – in the words of Josiah Nott one of its leading thinkers – of "the whole mental and physical history of the various Types of Mankind. . . [of] the primitive organic structure of each race."[24] And, by the time *Uncle Tom's Cabin* was published, racial difference was considered a permanent and self-evident fact.

The tremendous amount of empirical evidence assembled by US ethnologists proving the stability of racial differences, in fact, established the American School of Ethnology at the forefront of the emerging science of race, a discipline that Ephraim Squier called in 1849 the "science of the age."[25] Based primarily on precise measurements of cranial size, capacity, and structure, but also quantifying everything from hair pilosity to types of body lice, ethnology (or "niggerology" as one of the leaders in the field termed the discipline) was driven by the Enlightenment imperative to find objective means to determine the endurance and significance of racial difference.[26] These scientists confirmed eternal biological peculiarities as well as identified intrinsic moral and intellectual differences between the races that suggested a separate creation for the white and Black races (polygenesis). The giant of the American ethnologists, Dr. Samuel G. Morton of Philadelphia, for example, had carefully collected and studied the skulls of the various races. In 1839 he published his masterpiece *Crania Americana* in which he set forth massive empirical evidence of the eternal differences of the races based on his research on these skulls and argued that permanent differences in their cranial capacities (which he determined by loading white pepper seeds into the skulls) proved the separate origins of the races.[27] The scientific rigor of Morton's work was almost universally acclaimed.[28]

Not only did the discipline of ethnology, supported by the anatomical "science" of craniometry, steadily produce extensive "scientific proof" of racial differences and support the theory that the races were of distinct origins, but also the period's most influential historians – Bancroft, Prescott, Motley, and Parkman – detailed the ways in which the historical differences between nations were eternal, a product of "blood" rather than environment.[29] Indeed, political scientists and ministers commonly explained the American love of liberty as an instinct inherited from primitive Teutonic tribes and averred that this nation's democratic institutions were more racial than historical in origin.[30] At its most extreme, such racialist thinking produced works such as Dr. Robert Knox's *Races of*

Men, designed to prove that "Race is everything. Literature, science, art, in a word, civilization, depend on it."[31]

Emerson's discussion of the English race in *English Traits*, is typical of the way in which antebellum intellectuals racialized what we would now consider cultural traits. Emerson does not think it possible to understand the English without taking account of their racial nature. Emerson begins his chapter "Race" by acknowledging that Knox's book *Races of Men* is "charged with pungent and unforgettable truths."[32] Although Emerson admits that he has doubts about the precise number of races, he declares that one must recognize that:

> It is race, is it not? that puts the hundred millions of India under the dominion of a remote island in the north of Europe. Race avails much, if that be true, which is alleged, that all Celts are Catholics, all Saxons are Protestants; that Celts love unity of power, and Saxons the representative principle. Race is a controlling influence in the Jew, who, for more than two millenniums, under every climate, has preserved the same character and employments. *Race in the Negro is of appalling importance.* The French in Canada, cut off from all intercourse with the parent people, have held their national traits. I chanced to read Tacitus "on the Manners of the Germans," not long since, in Missouri, and the heart of Illinois, and I found abundant points of resemblance between the Germans of the Hercynian forest, and our Hoosiers, Suckers, and Badgers of the American woods. (*English Traits*, 792, my emphasis)

Clearly Emerson regards race, which he calls "a symmetry that reaches as far as to the wit" because it forms both personal and national identity, as a formidable natural force (791).

But Emerson also makes clear that the material influence of race can be mitigated and perhaps even wholly transcended. Although race in the case of the Negro "is of appalling importance," Emerson notes that for the Hoosier, race merely marks "points of resemblance." Emerson's discussion of race exemplifies the tendency among antebellum intellectuals to regard race as wholly determinative when discussing the Negro, but as only influential when discussing the constitution of the Anglo-Saxon. Thus, Emerson states that the "Arabs of to-day are the Arabs of Pharaoh; but the Briton of today is a very different person from Cassibelaunus or Ossian" (792). "Civilization," Emerson claims, is the source of the changing character of the Anglo-Saxon. For even as "race works immortally to keep its own, it is resisted by other forces," chiefly by the counterforce of a civilized culture (*English Traits*, 792). Thus, "civilization," according to Emerson, "is a re-agent, and eats away the old traits, thereby carrying the Anglo-Saxon beyond the bounds of his biological nature by his culture" (792).

Given the power of culture, Emerson is interested in detailing the extent to which the English, unlike more "primitive races," have resisted, rather than been absolutely determined by, the effects of their racial nature. According to Emerson, the more advanced races mark the "limitations of the formidable doctrine of race," because they possess the civilization necessary to work as "counteracting forces to race" (793, 792). Since the ability to transcend race becomes the most reliable sign of Anglo-Saxon superiority, Emerson's analysis of the force of race simply reproduces the hierarchy of the races in terms of the ability to repudiate racial characteristics: the "civilized" Anglo-Saxons have risen above the "primitive" African race precisely because they have managed to challenge rather than simply reflect the "fixity or inconvertibleness" of their racial essence (793).[33] Emerson, in short, ends up making culture look like just another racial trait.

For Emerson if race is determining, civilization is lacking. Stowe, however, is more explicit in her racialism, arguing that what Emerson identifies as the Anglo-Saxon's ability to escape the influence of race is only an expression of the Anglo-Saxon's essential racial character. Rather than defying his racial nature, the Anglo-Saxon, in Stowe's account, reveals his most pronounced racial trait when he desires to transcend the force of materialist influences. What Emerson views as the Anglo-Saxon's cultural superiority, Stowe regards as the distinctive feature of this race's essential nature. Whereas Emerson identifies Man's greatest strength in the moments when culture subsumes race, Stowe consistently seeks to reinscribe Man within his biological limits, to affirm the abiding force of each race's invariable nature. As Stowe sees it, Emerson's transcendental liberalism is in the blood of the Anglo-Saxon man.

Stowe represents the Emersonian struggle against nature as representative of Anglo-Saxon "coldness." For example, Senator Bird betrays a typically Anglo-Saxon love for the transcendental realm of the "coldly and strictly logical" when, discussing the dangers of disobeying the Fugitive Slave Law, he counsels his wife about letting "feelings run away with our judgment" (*Uncle Tom's Cabin*, 77). As he explains to his wife, even though "your feelings are all quite right, dear, and interesting, and I love you for them," there are nevertheless "great public interests involved,–there is such a state of public agitation rising, that we must put aside our private feelings" (*Uncle Tom's Cabin*, 77). Though Senator Bird eventually abandons his claims for abstract "duty" when he comes face to face with Eliza, an actual fugitive slave, his sympathy reveals not his ability to go against his racial nature, but rather the tension between Anglo-Saxon coldness and the Christian ethic of compassion.

According to Stowe, it is precisely this instinct for cold abstraction that motivates the essential antagonism between the Anglo-Saxon and the African. As Stowe avers in the first sentence of the novel's preface, "Polite and refined society" in the United States has ignored, misunderstood, and degraded the Negro precisely because the Negro is an "exotic race, whose ancestors, born beneath a tropic sun, brought with them, and perpetuated to their descendants, a character . . . essentially unlike the hard and dominant Anglo-Saxon race" (*Uncle Tom's Cabin*, xvii). This opening gesture immediately signals Stowe's intention of reinterpreting the Anglo-Saxon's hostility towards the Negro as determined by each race's opposing essences rather than by the superiority or inferiority of each race's level of civilization or intellectual ability. The Negro's racial essence does not simply conflict with the racial essence of the "colder and more correct white race," it contradicts the talent for abstraction that the Anglo-Saxon regards as the *summun bonum* of civilization (*Uncle Tom's Cabin*, 161). As Stowe explains, "the Anglo-Saxon race – cool, logical, and practical – have yet to learn the doctrine of toleration for the peculiarities of other races" (*Key*, 46). Since the Anglo-Saxon mistakes his partial racial genius for a universal principle, he is unable to appreciate the native genius of the African.

By positing racial materialism at the foundation of the Anglo-Saxon and the African character, Stowe strikes at the hierarchy Emerson constructs between the literally higher and materially lower races. But in doing so, Stowe does not simply urge her readers to accept the natural order of racial differences. Instead she attempts to establish a new hierarchy founded on a particular account of Christian values, one that emphasizes the very virtues of docility and submission that the African "naturally" possesses and the Anglo-Saxon male "naturally" shuns. Such an account of the essential nature of the Anglo-Saxon, recalls William Ellery Channing's assertion that it is "one of the most remarkable events of history" that Christianity should ever have "struck root" among Europeans since they are a race "distinguished by qualities opposed to the spirit of Christianity."[34]

Though the Anglo-Saxon's racially-determined ability and desire to be logical and cold are not conducive to Christian morality, these traits do effectively collude to allow cruelty of slavery to be successfully excused. Stowe identifies the Anglo-Saxon's natural impulse "to generalize and to take enlarged views" as the primary reason that the slave system, despite its obvious brutality, has been able to be legitimated (*Uncle Tom's Cabin*, 128). According to Stowe, if the "unutterably horrible and cruel actions" of slave-owners and slave-traders had not been successfully refigured in terms of abstract relations – reimagined as relations which Stowe sarcastically declares "an American divine tells us has 'no evil but such as are inseparable from any other relations in social and domestic life' " – such actions could never have been tolerated (*Uncle Tom's Cabin*, 128). In other words, Stowe claims that the Anglo-Saxon's "natural" desire to transcend the literal and the material cannot be separated from the fact that "American state law *coolly* classes" human beings with "bundles, and bales, and boxes" (*Uncle Tom's Cabin*, 128 emphasis added). The Anglo-Saxon's racial nature and the "fiction of law" which legitimates slavery are mutually reinforcing; each is informed by a similar urge to deny the materiality of the literal and affirm figural abstractions (*Uncle Tom's Cabin*, 308). Stowe, in fact, sees the harshness of the American slave code as an expression of the Anglo-Saxon race's love of logic and abstraction:

> The French and the Spanish nations are, by constitution, more impulsive, passionate and poetic, than logical; hence it will be found that while there may be more instances of individual barbarity, as might be expected among impulsive and passionate people, there is in their slave-code more exhibition of humanity. The code of the State of Louisiana contains more human provisions, were there any means of enforcing them, than that of any other state in the Union (*Key*, 155).[35]

The reason, Stowe explains, why the slave code of the United States is not only "so accurately, elegantly, and scientifically arranged" but also "more atrocious than any ever before exhibited under the sun" is precisely because the "Anglo-Saxon race are a more coldly and strictly logical race, and have an unflinching courage to . . . work out an accursed principle, with mathematical accuracy, to it most accursed result." One of the principal goals of *Uncle Tom's Cabin*, therefore, is to reveal the disturbing fact that the natural impulses of the Anglo-Saxon perfectly conspire with the logic of a system "designed in the most precise and scientific manner to DESTROY THE IMMORTAL SOUL" (*Key*, 155).

RACIALIZING THE FAMILY

Although Stowe's biological essentialism is clearest in her strategy for representing the Negro character, such racialism also grounds her critique of the patriarchal nature of slavery. The notion of the family, as many critics have noted, stands at the heart of Stowe's moral indictment of slavery. In one of the most elegant and compelling discussions of *Uncle Tom's Cabin*, Philip Fisher has argued that the social power of the novel stems from Stowe's redescription of slavery as a series of offenses against the integrity of the family.[36] Fisher argues that Stowe makes "the separation of families" the "central psychological and social evil of slavery" (102). By doing so, Stowe is able to make the family into the bridge by which the reader can "cross over to the inner world" of the slave (119). Although the reader probably "had no experience of having a member of his family suddenly sold off to a distant plantation. . .the reader did almost certainly undergo traumatic, unexpected separation from someone, often a child, by death" (118–119). The sentimental novel, in Fisher's account, mobilizes the emotions an average reader held towards his or her own family in order to forge "experimental equations" between the reader and "novel objects of feelings," equations that encourage the reader to extend "full and complete humanity to classes of figures [such as children, prisoners, and slaves] from whom it [humanity] has been socially withheld" (98, 99).

Fisher's revisionary argument responds to standard complaints about the moral and political emptiness of sentimental literature by characterizing sentimentality not as a genre that exploits sympathy, but as an aesthetic strategy designed to initiate and energize a radically new form of social egalitarianism. But even as recent investigations of the progressive cultural work of sentimentality have focused with particular intensity on the genre's representations of the family, critics have tended to regard the family as a self-evident concept, one that could be forcefully invoked by sentimental authors precisely because it is always powerfully loved rather than fundamentally contested.[37] But, by assuming that the family exists as a substantively stable institution intrinsically opposed to slavery, critics ignore the fact that familial rhetoric provided the South with its most effective means of defending slavery.[38] Not only had slaves and slavery been integrated into Southern society under the auspices of the family, but also the notion of the family was instrumentally conjoined to the Southern legitimation of the slave system. Therefore, in order for Stowe to call slavery a crime against the family, she could not depend upon a monolithic view of this domestic institution, but needed to replace representations of the family that complemented defenses of slavery with a notion that opposed the putatively paternalistic character of slavery. Stowe could not simply place the family at the moral center of her novel; she had to establish and privilege a very particular configuration of the family. The cultural work of Stowe's novel is to persuade her readers that race-based slavery and the family are essentially antagonistic institutions.

SOUTHERN FAMILIES

Citing slavery's familial character, Southerners consistently considered slavery a "domestic question" and warned that any interference with the institution threatened "the safety of our families, our altars, and our firesides."[39] Southern slavery thoroughly appropriated the rhetoric of kinship relations: "Auntie," "Uncle," "Mammy" were the common forms of address that owners, or Fathers, used toward their slaves. This identification of the family and slavery provided the terms with which to defend slavery. For example, C.G. Memminger, later Secretary of the Treasury of the Confederacy, declared that because slavery is founded upon the household economy, it is merely an extension of the family. According to Memminger, in slavery:

> Domestic relations become those things which are most prized–each family recognizes its duty–and its members feel a responsibility for its discharge. The fifth commandment becomes the foundation of society. The state is looked to only as the ultimate head in its external relations while all internal duties, such as support, education, and the relative duties of individuals, are left to domestic regulation (1851).[40]

Memminger argues, in short, that Southerners "dignify the family" by advocating the domestic relations of slavery.

Implicit in Memminger's representation of slavery is an indictment of the North. The North and the South, Memminger argues, "work upon different principles."[41] The North, he claims, imagines the family as a refuge from the world precisely because Northern capitalism has isolated the family from the public realm and has segregated the duties of the family from the rest of society. The South, in contrast, has avoided such a harmful dichotomy by establishing the family as the underlying principle of its entire social and political structure. By affirming the familial character of slavery's social and economic organization, Southerners, like Memminger, were able to construct formidable arguments for slavery as a "positive good."[42]

This strategy of equating slavery with the family was articulated perhaps most powerfully by George Fitzhugh, the era's most rigorous philosopher of slavery. Fitzhugh rests his defense of slavery on the notion that slavery reproduces the structures and duties of the domestic household and thus promotes a system of civil society ethically superior to Northern "wage slavery."[43] Whereas the Northern laborer shares only an economic relation with his employer, the Southern slave is linked to his master by an organic bond, a bond that allows the slave to be both accepted into and protected by the master's household. Thus, as forcefully as Stowe condemns slavery for separating families, Fitzhugh praises slavery for supporting family values:

> Slavery protects the infants, the aged and the sick; nay takes far better care of them than of the healthy, the middle-aged and the strong. They are part of the family, and self-interest and domestic affection combine to shelter, shield, and foster them.[44]

As Fitzhugh put it, slavery "leaves but little of the world without the family."[45] For Fitzhugh, the social status of the slave differed only gradually rather than qualitatively from that of women, children, and other dependants. In Fitzhugh's social theory, therefore, slavery not only loses its morally anomalous character, but also becomes the model social system, one which, he declares, mankind is morally obligated to extend over all of society.[46] "Human law," Fitzhugh contends, could never "beget benevolence, affection, maternal and paternal love. . .it may abolish slavery, but it can never create between the capitalist and the laborer, between the employer and the employed, the kind and affectionate relations that usually exist between master and slave."[47]

Asserting that only within "the family circle" of slavery does "the law of love prevails," Fitzhugh sets out to reverse liberal political theory's valorization of an individual's natural right to liberty and autonomy: parodying the claims of the Declaration of Independence, he declares that "about nineteen out of every twenty individuals have 'a natural and inalienable right' to be taken care of and protected, to have guardians, trustees, husbands, or masters; in other words, they have a natural and inalienable right to be slaves" (*Cannibals All!*, 69). The power of Fitzhugh's defense of slavery does not derive from the limited claim that slavery benefits Black slaves, but rather from his radical attempt to overturn the foundations of the American liberal tradition by advocating the moral superiority of the paternalism of slavery. Not interested merely in finding the means to tolerate slavery, Fitzhugh aims to make all of society conform to the familial principles of slavery.

Since Fitzhugh's social theory depends upon the identity of slavery and the family, a corollary argument inevitably follows: the defense of slavery is inseparable from a devotion to the family. According to Fitzhugh, all those who attack slavery actually attack the family. The "tendency and terminus of all abolition," Fitzhugh warns, "is to the sovereignty of the individual" and this plan only becomes possible with "the breaking up of families and no government" (*Cannibals All!*, 194). As Fitzhugh sees it, abolition contemplates nothing less than "the total overthrow of the Family" (*Cannibals All!*, 198). Indeed, abolitionism epitomizes modern attacks on all forms of the family:

> All modern philosophy converges to a single point–the overthrow of all government, the substitution of the untrammelled 'Sovereignty of the Individual' for the Sovereignty of Society. . . . First domestic slavery, next religious institutions, then separate property, then political government, and *finally family government and family relations*, are to be swept away. This is the distinctly avowed programme of all able abolitionists (*Cannibals All!*, 190, emphasis added).

Since "the family is threatened," Fitzhugh declares that "all men North or South who love and revere it, should be up and a-doing," protecting slavery from the family-hating abolitionists (198).

Clearly, Fitzhugh imagines the family he wants to save as a patriarchical and hierarchical one:

> The father is the natural representative of his family . . . His feelings and affections, as well as his interests, are so blended and interwoven with theirs, that whatever affects them, beneficially or injuriously, in like manner affects him. He is the natural head or ruler of his family, and their natural and faithful representative. This is patriarchical government, the oldest, the best, and still the most common, and seemingly the most despotic form of government.[48]

But in order for Fitzhugh to represent plantation slavery as the family writ large, he must affirm a very particular representation of this patriarchy. In Fitzhugh's account of slavery, the master rules over quite an extended family: "besides wife and children, brothers and sister, *dogs, horses, birds and flowers – slaves, also, belong to the family circle* (*Cannibals All!*, 205, emphasis added). Fitzhugh's family is spectacularly encompassing because it is grounded in sociology rather than biology.[49]

For this reason, Fitzhugh deliberately separated his championing of slavery from arguments that legitimated slavery in terms of the biological character of the Black slave.[50] Fitzhugh is quite explicit: "He who justifies mere negro slavery, and condemns other forms of slavery does not think at all – no, not in the least. . . . Domestic slavery must be vindicated in the abstract . . . as a normal, natural and, in general, necessitous element of civilised society, without regard to race or colour."[51] Indeed, on one occasion he went so far as to assert that whites made the best slaves.[52] Although some commentators have been perplexed by Fitzhugh's rejection of racial inferiority as an adequate justification for the institution of slavery, Fitzhugh recognized that a slave system based on the biological peculiarity of the Negro would undermine any attempt to universalize the principles of slavery. Since he denies that the family is a genealogically specific unit, Fitzhugh's family can, theoretically, include anyone – Black or white, human or non-human, plant or animal. The plantation, according to Fitzhugh, is a family not because everyone is substantially related, but rather because everyone is part of the same domestic economy. The kinship of the plantation is familial but not necessarily consanguineous, sociological rather than inevitably genealogical.[53]

REAL FAMILIES

The cultural power of Stowe's attack on the Southern image of the plantation family lies in her claim that Southerners fundamentally misunderstand the nature of the domestic institution. Distinguishing her notion of the family from Southern domestic rhetoric, Stowe posits substantive blood relations as the only determining sign of a family. In *Uncle Tom's Cabin*, the only real families are biological families. Thus, slavery is dangerous precisely because it substitutes imaginary families for real families, attempting to replace actual, substantive kinship with metaphorical and inauthentic forms of kinship. According to Stowe, the difference between freedom and slavery is the difference between "real" and "pseudo" families. Figural families offer only fictional protection.

Stowe initiates this critique by attacking popular legends about the patriarchal nature of slavery. As she explains in the first chapter of *Uncle Tom's Cabin,* those who visit the South:

> might be tempted to dream the oft-fabled poetic legend of a patriarchal institution, and all that; but over and above the scene there broods a portentous shadow – the shadow of *law*. So long as the law considers all these human beings, with beating hearts and living affections only as so many *things* belonging to a master, – so long as the failure, or misfortune, or imprudence, or death of the kind owner, may cause them any day to exchange a life of kind protection and indulgence for one of hopeless misery and toil, – so long it is impossible to make anything beautiful or desirable in the best-regulated administration of slavery (*Uncle Tom's Cabin*, 8).

This popular account of slavery as a beneficial patriarchal institution morally offends Stowe, for such beliefs enable the crimes that slavery commits against "real" families to be concealed.[54] So easily rent, the bonds between master and slave reveal that slavery is a patriarchy manqué, an immaterial paternalism in which any familial bond can be easily dissolved.

It is no accident that one plot (the story of Eliza) of the novel is initiated by the sale of a slave child and the other (the story of Tom) by the sale of a slave father, or that the novel marks the end of slavery by reunifying a biologically-related family. Stowe devotes so much of *The Key to Uncle Tom's Cabin* to gathering evidence to prove that economic relations support the slave trade only because Southerners devoted commensurate energy to "proving" the security and stability of a plantation patriarchy. Because defenders of slavery contended that the sale of slaves and the separation of slave families occurred only in a "rare case for some crime," Stowe strategically emphasizes that slaves were commonly sold and families often separated purely for the sake of money. In doing so, Stowe intends to persuade her audience that it is impossible to regard a master's self-professed paternal relation to his slave as anything but a crass economic relation. For example, when Topsy replies to a question about her parents, "Never was born. . .never had no father nor mother. . ..I was raised by a speculator," she crystallizes how thoroughly slavery perverts the familial structure (*Uncle Tom's Cabin*, 240). Since slavery replaces the patriarch with the speculator, Stowe suggests that Topsy's wildness is to be expected: market relations are inherently unstable. The master's love of money will inevitably overwhelm his "love" of his putative children. In other words, rather than attacking the patriarchy, as many critics have argued, Stowe is attacking slavery for so poorly imitating a true and secure patriarchy. Stowe's account of the family is anti-patriarchal only insofar as it is an attack on counterfeit fathers.

Just as Stowe's indictment of the falsely patriarchal nature of slavery is not an indictment of patriarchs *per se*, her attack on the way in which slavemasters own slaves is not an attack on the idea of owning "persons" in itself. Stowe quite explicitly presents moments when persons are in rightful possession of others. For instance, just after he is reunited with his family, George Harris declares to his wife:

> O! Eliza, if these people only knew what a blessing it is for a man to feel that his wife and child belong to *him*. I've often wondered to see men that could call their wives and children *their own* fretting and worrying about anything else.
> (*Uncle Tom's Cabin*, 185, original emphasis).

In a novel about owning other human beings, such language cannot be inadvertent. According to Stowe, George is a legitimate owner of his family.

Similarly, when Legree claims to own Tom "body and soul," Tom defends himself not by repudiating the notion of ownership, but by insisting on the inadequacy of Legree's power to own: "No! no! no! my soul an't yours, Mas'r! You haven't bought it, – ye can't buy it! It's been bought and paid for by One that is able to keep it" (356). Completely indebted to a logic of ownership, Tom's exclamation makes clear that ownership in itself is not the source of slavery's immorality. Rather, according to Stowe, the problem with slavery is that it allows false patriarchs to become owners. Thus, although it may seem ironic that George equates freedom with the ability to own his family, and that Tom imagines freedom as his death ("The Lord's bought me, and is going to take me home"), this is only so if one assumes that slavery is substantially defined as the treatment of human beings as property (*Uncle Tom's Cabin*, 416). Such a definition of slavery, however, fails to give an adequate account of the institution represented in *Uncle Tom's Cabin.* The novel repeatedly shows that slaves are not incorrectly treated as property objects.[55] The ownership of others as property incompletely defines both the nature and the immorality of slavery. Stowe does not object to the principle of persons being owned, but to the way that slavery institutionalizes the wrong kind of ownership – a non-racial one.

THE BIOLOGY OF OWNERSHIP

Slavery, according to Stowe, makes it too easy for anyone to be legally nominated an owner. In response to this significant moral problem at the heart of the slave system, Stowe proposes that biology can serve as the only reliable social test for proper ownership. Whereas slavery offers "to the half-maniac drunkard, to the man notorious for hardness and cruelty, to the man sunk entirely below public opinion, to the bitter infidel and blasphemer" the power to own others, biological relations limit the category of the proper master (*Key*, 69). Given the inadequacy of the metaphorical family of the plantation, *Uncle Tom's Cabin* reimagines true families in terms of a biology of ownership; individuals can, according to this logic, only properly own their own flesh and blood. For Stowe, the substantive feelings that biology generates for other kin is the only guarantee of proper ownership. Throughout the novel, the bond of biology secures the only relations untainted by the pressures of the market or the contingency of circumstance. As many critics have noted, Stowe repeatedly represents the emotional bond of mothers and children as surpassing and prior to all the contingent vicissitudes of slavery, but what has not been sufficiently recognized is that this bond is exemplary rather than exhaustive of the force of biology. That is, even though the mother/child bond instantiates perhaps the most powerful representation of the kind of ownership entitled by biology, it is not the only example of a legitimate biological relation.

In contrast to such a genealogical account of the family, Christianity might seem to offer the promise of a universal family that transcends biological relations. But even the Christian universal family, Stowe reveals, is an inadequate temporal family. The seemingly ideal Quaker community – embodied in the utopian nurture of Rachel Halliday's kitchen – most clearly marks the limits of the universal family. Certainly the rhetoric of familial love is more justly used by the Quakers than by slavemasters, and surely the Quaker community is sincerely willing to accept into its egalitarian family circle both slaves and slavemasters, runaway slaves and slavecatchers. But it is important to note than no one accepts the "overflowing kindness" of the Quakers. When the runaway slaves Eliza, Harry, and George Harris are offered a home in this utopian community, George recognizes that even though "[t]his was indeed a home, – home – a word that George had never yet known a meaning for," this place is not his family's home (*Uncle Tom's Cabin*, 138). Even the reformed slavecatcher Tom Loker, though tempted to stay, feels he does not really belong among the Quakers. Thus, although the Quakers may welcome all, no one seems to want to join their family. The rejection of this invitation suggests how thoroughly biology circumscribes Stowe's representation of the true family.

The fact of miscegenation, however, seems to contradict seriously Stowe's utopian vision of the coincidence of the proper family with genealogical kinship. Clearly this apparent tension does not result from Stowe's blindness to the fact of miscegenation. She recognized that white masters often fathered many of their slaves and that such biological paternity did not guarantee a proper sense of obligation towards one's kin. In examples such as Cassy's tragic life story, Stowe forcefully represents the fact that white husbands and white fathers often did betray, abandon, and sell their Black "wives" and their Black children. Just as the speculator proves himself a false father, in the case of miscegenation the biological father shows himself to be a mock parent. Although it may seem paradoxical that Stowe simultaneously defends the biological family and condemns miscegenation, these bad biological fathers do not evidence an exception to Stowe's faith in biological racialism. Rather these ersatz fathers illustrate the extent to which Stowe's notion of the family is hyper-biological and hyper-racialist. Stowe argues for the integrity of the family not as a normative social unit that can be constructed and reconstructed in various ways among various individuals, but rather as a group that must be racially unified. Grounded not simply in the literal blood relations of a parent to a child (which are ultimately mysterious since plausible grounds can always be summoned to deny such relations) but in the physical signs of a racial essence, the family's inviolability, according to Stowe's idealized vision, can only be guaranteed if all involved share the same race.[56] Failures of the family, in short, are actually failures of race.

Families, according to Stowe, are constituted not by the fact that the children are related to the parents, but by the fact that the parents are biologically related to each other. Only members of the same racial family can produce true families. Rather than simply conflate the category of the family and the notion of race, Stowe imagines that ascriptions of race actually replace paternity as the ultimate mark of belonging to a family. Surpassing all juridical contracts and the mere fact of sexual relations, race serves as the only legitimate sign of the family.

RACIAL NATIONALISM

Stowe reproduces her notions of the family on the level of national identity. National solidarity is simply the extension of loving one's family, the familial bond modulating seamlessly into national citizenship. Feelings of nationality are merely an effect of possessing a shared race. Thus, one should not be surprised when Topsy, having been taken North by Miss Ophelia, never becomes part of the "deliberative body whom a New Englander recognizes under the term *'Our folks'*" (432). Topsy's real family remains elsewhere. She leaves "our folks" for her folks: she becomes a missionary, goes to Africa, and devotes her life to "teaching the children of her own country" (433, emphasis added). By claiming that Africa is Topsy's "own country," despite the fact that Topsy was born and raised in the United States, Stowe implicitly invokes a racial notion of nationality. Topsy is African simply because she is Black; her personal history is subsumed by her racial identity. Although Topsy grows up in the South and is educated in the North, Stowe nevertheless imagines that Topsy has more in common with Africans than Americans.

Stowe's yearning for the success of such a racialist logic explains why the novel ends not simply by revealing that so many Negroes are actually related to each other but also by miraculously reuniting these families: Cassy turns out to be Eliza's mother, Cassy's son and Eliza's brother turns out to be alive, and Madame de Thoux turns out to be George Harris's long-lost sister. That this racialist logic is fundamentally tied to a notion of the polity becomes clearest when, as soon as these families are re-united, they begin attending to questions of where their national allegiance belongs. At the novel's conclusion, George Harris reveals the extent to which Stowe's appeals for freedom are grounded in the material permanence of race. In a letter explaining why he has decided to leave the United States and settle in Liberia, George argues for the priority of race:

> But, you will tell me, our race have equal rights to mingle in the American republic as the Irishman, the German, the Swede. Granted, they have. We *ought* to be free to meet and mingle, – to rise by our individual worth, without any consideration of caste or color; and they who deny us this right are false to their own professed principles of human equality. We ought, in particular, to be allowed *here.* We have *more* than the rights of common men; – we have the claim of an injured race for reparation. But, then, *I do not want it*; I want a country, a nation, of my own. I think that the African race has peculiarities, yet to be unfolded in the light of civilization and Christianity, which, if not the same with those of the Anglo-Saxon, may prove to be morally, of even a higher type (431).

The movement of George's thought from the moral register of "ought" to personal language of "want" is matched by a shift from an explicitly liberal to an explicitly racialist logic. George begins in a traditionally liberal fashion by discussing equality and citizenship in terms of individual rights and merits and as deriving from choice. Such rights, he claims, should be color blind. But he then alters his account of rights and argues a position that some modern social theorists would label "affirmative action." He claims that the shared oppressions of his race entitle them to be granted *more* rights as compensation for past inequities. George's argument pivots on the idea that one can make discriminations on the basis of race provided that such acts correct previous wrongs committed as a result of racial prejudices. The rhetoric of equal rights gives way to a call for preferential treatment precisely because George sees social justice as best expressed not by an assertion of a universal identity but in terms of the acknowledgment of racial difference.

Indeed, it is because George comprehends equality not as sameness but as the recognition of difference that the traditional abstractions of equal rights fail him altogether. According to George, all efforts for Negroes to gain rights in the United States are empty as long as such rights are insistently characterized in purely formal terms, independent of one's racial identity and without any "consideration. . .of color" (432). George cannot imagine rights as the abstract entitlements guaranteed to raceless "persons," because George articulates a version of the "person" that is inseparable from race. For George, rights gain importance only if they are affiliated with one's communal identity, with one's family, and with one's nation: with, in short, one's race.[57] What George's speech ultimately makes clear is the distance between Stowe's racialist understanding of human rights and the formalism of contemporary liberalism.

I have been arguing that Stowe generates the "progressive" politics of *Uncle Tom's Cabin* by means of racial essentialism.[58] The lesson of *Uncle Tom's Cabin*, in other words, is that arguments that begin from the premise that racial essences are intrinsically destructive to the expression of "personhood" need to be modified. As K. Anthony Appiah has compellingly argued, not all uses of race are equally invidious:

> Racialism is not, in itself, a doctrine that must be dangerous, even if the racial essence is thought to entail moral and intellectual dispositions. Provided positive moral qualities are distributed across the races, each can be respected, can have its "separate but equal" place.[59]

Scholars, it seems, have demanded that both racial essentialism and slavery be opposed even though racial essentialism does not necessarily support slavery (Lincoln, in addition to Stowe, clearly disrupts the continuity between the two) and even though color blindness does not necessarily produce egalitarian politics. Indeed, the recent success of the New Right's equation of race consciousness with racism powerfully disrupts the continuity between emancipatory practices and anti-essentialism.[60] Neo-conservatives have deployed a color blind civil rights discourse in defense of a "neutral" social policy that in the end opposes practices (such as affirmative action) designed to redress on-going racial injustices. This invocation of a race-neutral policy, in other words, not only has a disparate impact on different racial groups, but also obscures the significant differences between the race-consciousness of the Ku Klux Klan and that of the University of California. Neutral principles simply embed a specific set of interests as if such interests have evaporated.[61]

If claims for abstract sameness do not inevitably promote social justice, the question arises why is it assumed that racial essentialism is axiomatically insidious and implicitly analogous to slavery. Racial essentialism and slavery have so been deeply linked, I would suggest, because both are imagined as parallel denials of "personhood," each violating what a "person" truly is. Indeed, the reason that so many wonder whether color-conscious public policies conform to the liberal democratic ideal is that they are working with an absolute notion of the "person," imagining that the "person" is raceless and that such an identity must be protected and recognized by liberal representation. Such an assumption places the "person" before any investigation of the consequences of a particular conception of the "person" and thus refuses historical questions about the specific effects and limits of specific conceptions of the "person."

The fact that we have comprehended the antebellum cultural practices that most persuasively "personified" slaves as little more than a series of elementary and potentially dangerous errors is a testament to how deeply we have removed the "person" from history and treated it as a pre-existing concept that either is to acknowledged or distorted, expressed or repressed. To shift from ontological claims about what a "person" is to more expressly political ones is to break from the liberal model of representation that has structured readings of Stowe's argument against slavery. Once we abandon the liberal premise that there exists a transcendental "person" that in and of itself guarantees freedom and promotes justice, we can begin to explore what kind of effect particular versions of the "person" have in particular contexts. Indeed, I would suggest that such challenges to the priority we give to a particular color blind conception of the "person" as universally progressive are especially crucial today when, as critical race scholars have powerfully charted, the trope of blindness that currently governs antidiscrimination law has served to validate the very forms of social stratification that such laws were ostensibly designed to dismantle.[62]

Or to put this another way, the question of whether Stowe is a racist (i.e. makes vicious distinctions between the races) cannot be reduced to the question of whether Stowe accepts racial essences unless one imagines that racial essences necessarily distort what a "person" is. If knowledge about the "person" is approached as fundamentally contested rather than as an absolute, then the question becomes not whether Stowe misrepresents "persons" but what her representation of "personhood" enables or disables in a particular context. To ask that we move from axiomatically repudiating to investigating the consequences of racial essentialism should not be taken to mean that one cannot critique racial essentialism. It is only to claim that the notion of the "person" cannot in itself generate such a critique because the notion of the "person" is precisely what is under debate.

In the next chapter I will focus on what has been regarded as one of the primary signs that Stowe's politics are not progressive: her investment in colonization. In particular, I am interested in the way critics have opposed Stowe's apparent endorsement of colonization (a solution based on essential difference) to the logic of the sentimental (a practice imagined as based on universal similarity).

CHAPTER 3

Eva's hair and the sentiments of race

If one reason that *Uncle Tom's Cabin* has proven particularly troubling is that the novel seems to sanction colonization as the political solution to "the problem" of free Blacks, *Dred* (1856), Stowe's second anti-slavery novel, has recently been championed for being a substantial revision of *Uncle Tom's Cabin*'s implicit endorsement of colonization. Indeed in *Dred*, Stowe not only seems to distance herself from the American Colonization Society's infatuation with Liberia by having some of the surviving Black characters migrate to interracial communities in Canada and others move to New York, but also replaces Tom's nonviolence – a nonviolence questioned by many for the way it has "stranded his [Tom's] power in the realm of sentiment" – with the militancy of a prophetic Black revolutionary.[1] Arguing that Stowe's engagement with Black abolitionists – in particular with Frederick Douglass and Martin Delany who both criticized the motives and goals of the American Colonization Society – provoked her to reject African colonization and to acknowledge Black desire for retributive justice, Robert Levine has asserted that "can be regarded as an African American-inspired revision of *Uncle Tom's Cabin*."[2]

Levine privileges *Dred* for the way it includes the African American voices that *Uncle Tom's Cabin* incompletely represented, convincingly demonstrating that Stowe modifies her political response to slavery and her representation of a Black hero because she listened to Black intellectuals for whom the Liberian solution was thoroughly discredited and for whom Tom's martyrdom seemed to discount the slave's right to violently resist slaveholders. Given Stowe's sensitivity to "black self-representations," Levine is suspicious of the way that the complexity of Stowe's racial politics has been reduced, criticizing "the current disciplinary rage" of "disciplining Stowe for her patronizing and racist attitudes towards blacks" and urging critics to "resist the paternalistic tendency of regarding blacks as always the 'victims' of racialist representations" (145, 155).

As I have argued, one reason that critics have simultaneously noted Stowe's investment in racialist categories and repudiated this investment is that an unexamined model of the "person" has structured such readings. What is most compelling about Levine's argument is how it examines the particular effects of Stowe's racial politics rather than simply assume that such racialism is axiomatically unjust because it misrepresents what a "person" is. Thus, for Levine *Dred* makes powerfully anti-racist statements, even as it continues, as many critics have lamented, to represent the African in racialist terms, noting the race's "abundant animal nature," their innate proclivity for "music, dancing, and elocution," and their child-like willingness to "yield themselves up in admiration of a superior friend."[3] Indeed, one might say (extending Levine's argument) that Stowe's sense of the limits of her perspective and the stimulus to seek out and listen to African American voices are themselves generated by her assumption that there remain fundamental, biological differences between the races, differences that cannot be overcome imaginatively but can only be recognized and appreciated.

If, *Dred*, just like *Uncle Tom's Cabin*, exemplifies how racialism can produce numerous political outcomes, generating neither inevitably regressive nor inherently progressive social practices, the abiding tendency to nonetheless condemn the "problematic racial politics" of Stowe's work suggests the extent to which we have substituted an absolute conception of the "person" for a context-bound account.[4] To condemn Stowe's racial essentialism as intrinsically racist is to invoke an absolute notion of the "person" that forecloses any exploration of the consequences and motives of Stowe's political project. It is to impute an inevitable political outcome to a particular account of personal identity rather than acknowledge the specific and multitude effects that can originate from such an account. That is, to argue that the "final configuration" of *Uncle Tom's Cabin* "plainly fails to imagine African Americans as full participant citizens in an American democracy" is to reduce the complexity of Stowe's political project just as deeply as designations of affirmative action as "reverse racism" evacuate not only history but also ethics, allowing formulaic abstractions (all forms of race-consciousness are identical) to replace any investigation of what a particular course of action accomplishes in a particular circumstance.[5]

The invocation of a decontextualized model of the "person" is perhaps most evident in the way that Stowe's reconsideration of the racial separatism that underwrites the conclusion of *Uncle Tom's Cabin* is represented as continuous with a move beyond racial difference. That is, the progressivism of *Dred* is imagined as being in direct proportion to Stowe's representation of interracial communities and these interracial communities are imagined as exorcising race as a crucial identity marker. Thus, critics have privileged the moment at the end of the novel when the white reformer Clayton visits the ex-slave Aunt Milly. Having settled in New York with her grandson as well as with the former slave Tiff and his white foster children, Milly lives "in a neat little tenement. . . surrounded by about a dozen children, among whom were blacks, whites, and foreigners," children to whom she gave "all the attention and affection of a mother" (546). Impressed by the inclusiveness of Milly's "family," Clayton notes, "I see you have black and white here." To which Milly responds:

> I don't makes no distinctions of color – I don't believe in them. White chil'en, when they 'haves themselves, is jest as good as black, I loves 'em jest as well (546).

This moment has been designated as a moment of "transracial love," a moment that resolves the two most powerful discourses in Stowe – that of colonization (i.e. racial separatism) and sentimental love (i.e. color blind unity) – in favor of love (Levine, 174).

To champion this scene as paradigmatic because it invokes love to transcend race, however, is to assume that racial difference and sentimental love are fundamentally opposed discourses. But this opposition is premised on forgetting how Stowe consistently imagines sympathetic feeling in raced (as well as gendered) terms. That is, rather than assume that the "person" to be liberated from oppression must always be liberated from racialized categories, Stowe's anti-slavery project leads one to question how imputing a fixed effect to racialism separates the "person" from any specific political practice.

In a newspaper article about the accomplishments of three Haitian students, Stowe makes clear the way in which the sentimental's success in arguing against pernicious hierarchies cannot be automatically opposed to racialism. Blacks, Stowe explains, require a supportive environment to succeed intellectually:

> The Africans as a race are exceedingly approbative. They are sensitive to kindness or unkindness. They need a warm, kindly atmosphere to grow in, as much as tropic plants. The pitiless frosts and pelting storms of scorn, ridicule, contempt, and obloquy which have fallen upon them [in the United States] could not have found a race more sensitive, more easily beaten back and withered.[6]

Stowe explains (in a logic recognizable from *Uncle Tom's Cabin*) the social conflict between the races in racialist terms: the African, warm and loving, is fundamentally different from the cold and unsympathetic Anglo-Saxon.[7] Although Stowe's explanation of social relationships and historical differences between races is framed in biological terms that certainly resemble the logic of those who seek to naturalize inequality and justify racism, her goal is clearly different. To imagine that her representation of the Negro is equally invidious is to hold onto an absolute notion of the "person." This tension between interrogating and deploying the concept of the "person" foregrounds how often the sentimental has been acknowledged as a central force in "personifying" slaves, but, at the same time, discussed as if the "person" is not produced by the sentimental but has always already been produced. That is, the sentimental has ultimately been deployed to avoid the problem of examining the act of producing more and more "persons."

In particular, this has happened because prevailing accounts of sentimental "personification" have been grounded by the claim that the sentimental generates similarity and promises to elide all difference. Sentimental literature, as one critic has explained, "subordinates" a politics that "values diversity" for "a politics of affinity, employing a method of affective representation that dissolves the boundaries between 'self' and 'other'."[8] It is this understanding of the sentimental as grounded upon similarity and as undermining of diversity that has organized recent accounts of the sentimental, both negative and positive. This chapter will explore how recent readings of Stowe have so thoroughly segregated notions of essential racial differences from the rhetoric of the sentimental because the sentimental has been understood as fundamentally continuous with modern liberalism. That is, scholars have used the sentimental as a covert way either to affirm or condemn liberal political theory, and in doing so have reified the notion of the "person," removing this conceptual category from the context in which it operates. To distinguish the "person" produced by Stowe's sentimentalism from the assumptions now ascendant, I will focus on the scene traditionally seen as exemplifying the logic of the sentimental: the death of Eva St. Claire. This scene crucially encapsulates the way in which the sentimental love that incites readers to make the Black slave into a "person" can depend upon intractable differences between the races.

SENTIMENTAL UNIVERSALISM

Realizing that she is about to die and wanting to make certain that everyone knows how much she loves them, Little Eva calls her family and all her family's slaves into her sickroom. At this meeting, Eva, part child and part Christ, gives each one of those assembled a lock of her beautiful golden hair, explaining that she wants to give them a part of herself so that "when you look at it [the curl], think that I loved you and am gone to heaven, and that I want to see you all there" (*Uncle Tom's Cabin*, 288). Not only the African slaves, "a sensitive and impressionable race," but also Eva's father and Eva's severe aunt from New England, Miss Ophelia – whose name Stowe ironically renders in slave dialect as "Miss Feely" – burst into tears upon seeing Eva's pure display of Christian love.

Although Stowe claimed that a vision of the death of Uncle Tom inspired her to write *Uncle Tom's Cabin*, readers have consistently felt that this moment, the death of Eva St. Clare, is the defining moment of the novel.[9] Testimonies about how the sainted death of this pious and innocent white child has reduced both male and female readers to tears have become legendary.[10] Modern critics, moreover, have continued to regard Eva's death as the most potent image of the novel, consistently turning to it as the paradigmatic instantiation of the sentimental logic of *Uncle Tom's Cabin*. Indeed, it often appears that those critics who champion and those who condemn the sentimental novel converge only upon one point: that Eva's deathbed scene is the "epitome of Victorian sentimentalism," "archetypical" of the sentimentality that motivates Stowe's novel as a whole (*Sensational Designs*, 127; *Feminization of American Culture*, 4).[11]

If this scene has long been regarded as the "apotheosis of sentimental narrative" because in it is writ small the mechanics of sentimental identification, I will argue that it is more appropriate to see this scene as the apotheosis of how modern misreadings of the sentimental have conflated the logic of the sentimental with the logic of liberalism (*Culture of Sentiment*, 132). Rather than a moment when the reader transcends the material differences separating the Anglo-Saxon and the African, this scene exemplifies the extent to which Stowe is not interested in establishing an identitarian correspondence between Blacks and whites, but in granting "personhood" to slaves by acknowledging the force of the essential, material differences between the races. That is, if the particular body of the Black slave has been typically imagined as an impediment in the production of liberal identity, for Stowe the particularity of the body is the source of identity. This scene is paradigmatic of how Stowe never imagines it necessary to transcend racial difference in order to love or recognize the "personhood" of African slaves precisely because such essentialist notions constitute the very means by which she thinks about "personhood."

The primary touchstone for interpretations of the sentimental power of the novel, this scene has been invoked to represent dramatically different accounts of the cultural work of sentimentality. Ann Douglas, for example, cites the scene as representative of the way in which "anti-intellectual sentimentalism" systematically worked "to gut" the "intellectual rigor and imaginative precision" of Calvinist orthodoxy (*Feminization*, 13, 8, 7). "Stowe's infantile heroine," Douglas asserts, "anticipates the exaltation of the average which is the trademark of mass culture," for Eva's "greatest act" is "dying, something we all can and must do" (4).[12] Douglas argues that Eva's death is "essentially decorative"; it powerfully stirs the emotions of readers precisely because it "is not particularly effective in any practical sense" (4). Affective rather than effective, aesthetic rather than pragmatic,

> Little Eva's beautiful death, which Stowe presents as part of a protest against slavery, in no way hinders the working of that system. The minister and the lady were appointed by their society as the champions of sensibility. They were in the position of contestants in a fixed fight; they had agreed to put on a convincing show, and to lose. The fakery involved was finally crippling for all concerned (12).[13]

Douglas' criticism of the genre is relentless: Eva's death "is there to precipitate our nostalgia and our narcissism"; her only "real demand on her readers is for self-indulgence" (*Feminization*, 4). Foreshadowing the eventual debasing or feminization of the vigor of America's elite culture, this moment privileges the "saccharine simplification" of feelings and thereby not only conflates the private and the public spheres but also encourages the substitution of idle, self-flattering tears for authentic political action (*Feminization*, 5). Sentimentality, in short, actively brings about "the commercialization of the inner life" that, Douglas claims, characterizes modern American consumer culture (*Feminization*, 254).

Critics, of course, have rescued the sentimental in general and *Uncle Tom's Cabin* in particular from condemnations such as Douglas' and have argued for the substantive political force of the sentimental novel. In doing so, they have focused a different kind of attention on this scene. In such a reading Eva's pious death is not simply ornamental melodrama, but rather central to Stowe's reformist project. For example, Philip Fisher, in his landmark reading of *Uncle Tom's Cabin*, has argued that the sentimental novel allowed middle class readers to identify with otherwise "foreign" social positions.[14] According to Fisher, Eva's death is "the most completely dramatized scene in Stowe's novel" because the death of a young child "is the only common experience that the white reader has that Stowe can use to [make white readers] comprehend slavery as separation, as the loss of a member of a family" (*Hard Facts*, 109). In contrast to Douglas, who argued "sentimentalism might be defined as the political sense obfuscated or gone rancid," Fisher asserts that sentimentality is not merely politically progressive but actually revolutionary (*Feminization*, 254). Seeking to extend "full and complete humanity to classes of figures from whom it has been socially withheld," the sentimental novel, Fisher declares, is "the primary radical methodology" of the nineteenth century (99, 92). Sentimental representations, Fisher asserts, are integral to political liberalism's production of more and more persons who deserve liberal rights, because the emotions that the sentimental elicits both appeal to and constitute a universalist notion of humanity.

For my purposes, what is most important is that, despite Douglas' and Fisher's obviously conflicting accounts of the ideological role played by the sentimental novel, both critics describe sentimentality as a genre dedicated to the erasure of difference. Although each presents opposite versions of what this fundamental sentimental principle accomplishes, both ultimately represent the sentimental novel as operating according to an identical logic, one that privileges universals rather than particulars. Douglas, as we have seen, denounces the sentimental novel for the way it dangerously effaces any distinction between self and other and thus allows private, self-involved fantasies to substitute for authentic public activity. Fisher, in contrast, celebrates the genre for erasing the distinctions of race, gender, and class invoked to justify invidious social hierarchies; or, as he puts it, the sentimental works to extend "full humanity" to those denied such "normal states of primary feeling" (94, 98). Although Douglas and Fisher disagree on how to evaluate the genre's fundamental antagonism to the category of difference, both regard the sentimental as defined by its insistent opposition to this category. What Douglas regards as "narcissism," however, Fisher calls "the liberal humanism of sentimentality" (*Feminization*, 4, *Hard Facts*, 92). Indeed, one could argue that Fisher's discussion of the sentimental implies that narcissism contains within itself an egalitarian and democratic political program. For, whereas Douglas condemns the sentimental novel for modeling the relationship between subjects and objects on a subject's relationship to him-or-herself, Fisher argues that sentimental readers, by recognizing themselves in another, come to recognize "a universal human nature," to see the "deep common feelings of the reader and the exotic but analogous situations of the characters" (*Hard Facts*, 123, 118).

The notion that the sentimental is committed to the effacing of distinctions – the assumption driving both Fisher's and Douglas' accounts – has become so accepted that debates over the ideological work performed by this genre now pivot on precisely this issue.[15] On one side of this debate are critics who share Fisher's perspective and positively characterize the sentimental as an emancipatory strategy, one that "produces or reproduces [emotional] spectacles that cross race, class, and gender boundaries," creates a "democratic readership" by "the subordination of physical difference to psychological and emotional sameness," and dissolves corporeality in order to "mediate across racial boundaries" (Samuels, 4–5, Barnes, 92, Burnham, 131[16]). Underlying this reading of the genre as a crucial strategy in the extension of basic human rights is the assumption that the genre works according to "a logic of equivalence based on affect" (Hendler, 688). Although an "intensely bodily genre," the sentimental novel, according to this line of argument, ultimately invokes a response in the reading subject that is abstracted from the bodily particularity of the object of compassion. The sentimental may jerk a physical reaction from the reader, but this reaction effectively militates against conventionally held beliefs in social or natural difference. In the words of one critic, sentimental narratives produce an "unrestricted extension of sympathy," one based on "affective" rather than "biological" bonds (Hendler, 689, 690). According to this account, *Uncle Tom's Cabin*'s exemplary sentimental logic is politically progressive to the extent that it evokes emotional responses that overcome the intractability of the physical differences commonly cited to legitimate nineteenth-century American relations of domination. Indeed, within this tradition, the sentimental so successfully overcomes notions of bodily difference that it threatens to inspire "indiscriminate identifications."[17]

In opposition to the tradition that apprehends the sentimental's foregrounding of abstraction as fundamentally progressive stands a line of argument that foregrounds the dangerous cultural work the genre performs. For example, Karen Sanchez-Eppler examines the ideologically problematic implications of the figural force of sentimentality, emphasizing the way that the genre's universalizing imperative can work to devalue and dematerialize bodily particularity and notions of difference.[18] Sanchez-Eppler accuses the sentimental novel of enforcing an "obliteration of the body," of conjuring affective alliances "between the figure of the woman and the figure of the slave" that in the end ignore the particularity of "black bodies" and thus fails to "imagine an America in which blacks could be recognized as persons" (51, 29, 50, 47–48). Even if it advertises itself as helping to expand the category of those deserving liberal rights, the sentimental, according to this critique, is guilty of a fundamental blindness to the body: it "evades" bodily differences and "masks" the "extent to which the body determines identity" (8, 48). Most insidiously, the sentimental, according to Sanchez-Eppler, acts as a rhetorical strategy by which white women ultimately divest Black slaves of their particular, materially distinct identity. Because sentimental narratives foreground the possibility of an emotional commonality that transcends the body, the genre, at least as it is deployed by white middle class women, imagines the Black (most often male) body and the white female body as if they could "appear as one," thereby turning "moments of identification" into "acts of appropriation" (31).

Since the act of sentimental identification, according to Sanchez-Eppler, depends upon the "asymmetry" between white female bodies and Black bodies, Sanchez-Eppler, like Fisher and Douglas, argues that the sentimental makes Otherness disappear, but argues, unlike Fisher, that this erasure of Otherness is not progressive but restrictive. That is, although Sanchez-Eppler's argument pointedly disputes Fisher's claims as it simultaneously distances itself from Douglas' claims, her influential criticism of the sentimental is founded on the same assumption that generates Fisher's and Douglas' work: that the sentimental is committed to the eradication of difference and the construction of a theoretical identicalness. It is only because she imagines that the sentimental is predicated upon the (she would claim ideologically problematic) overcoming of physically based social differences that she seeks to reassert the essential "corporeality" of personal identity. In other words, her critique of the genre depends upon the claim that the sentimental novel works to transcend the particularity of individual bodies for the sake of a universal emotional equivalence.[19] Or, as Dana Nelson has similarly argued, "sympathy assumes *sameness* in a way that can prevent understanding of the very real, material *differences* that structure human experience in a society based upon unequal distribution of power."[20]

Such critiques make clear how thoroughly sentimentality is represented (whether positively or negatively) in terms that render it deeply homologous with the logic of abstraction, a rhetorical structure in which materiality is elided in the service of an ideal equivalence, equivalences that Douglas condemns and Fisher praises. What these prevailing accounts make manifest, in short, is the extent to which the sentimental has come to stand as another name for the abstract universality that has been commonly equated with liberalism, or more accurately with what modern critics have understood as liberalism. Indeed, both those who defend and those who condemn the sentimental ground their arguments in a shared assumption about the sentimental: the telos of the sentimental, like the telos of liberalism, is assumed to be abstract equality. Both the sentimental and liberalism are understood to endorse and idealize a bodiless, generic "person" whose identity can be universal because it is fundamentally non-corporeal. If the sentimental is represented either as enabling the extension of liberal rights or as veiling white privilege, it does so precisely for the same reason that liberalism does: each enforces a logic of disembodiment. The sentimental, in short, has come to function as a kind of shorthand both for all that is good and all that is bad about the logic of abstract equality.[21]

This conflation of the sentimental and of liberalism in terms of a common drive towards abstract universality has been perhaps most forcefully articulated by Lauren Berlant. In several essays, Berlant discusses how the sentimental institutes a homogeneous and monolithic account of feeling that privileges the abstract, general, and universal at the expense of the concrete, the local, and particular. Berlant argues that the problem with the sentimental is not so much how it disembodies us, but how it embodies us in a way that undermines the political threat of material particularity, or, as Berlant puts it, sentimentality conjures "transpersonal linkages and intimacies [that] all too frequently serve as proleptic shields, as ethically uncontestable legitimating devices for sustaining the hegemonic field" (54). For Berlant, the fetus, the central icon of anti-abortion activists, is representative of the ideological work performed by the sentimental:

> The fetus's sanctified national identity is the opposite of any multicultural, sexual, or classed identity: the fetus is a blinding light that, triumphant as the modal citizen form, would white out the marks of hierarchy, taxonomy, and violence that seem now so central to the public struggle over who should possess the material and cultural resources of contemporary national life (56).

The sentimental, according to Berlant, ultimately works to buttress inequality and to confuse changes in feeling with substantial social change because its exemplary object of feeling is an innocent, typically a child, who is "not yet bruised by history" (55). The sentimental, in other words, does not simply subordinate the particularistic "I" to a universal "we," it, more dangerously, transforms pain from "a property of political personhood" to "a rhetoric" of "the true self," identifying subaltern pain not as "*universal*" (only some, after all, experience it) but as "universally *intelligible*" (and thus subject to the law) (72). This translation of subjective experience into the quintessentially public experience not only renders pain banal, but "congeals" one's truest identity in terms of the "present tense," in terms of a forgetting of history, a foreclosing of the habitual practices and the social structures that produced the concrete and material suffering in the first place (83).[22]

For Berlant, the problem with the sentimental is precisely what links the sentimental to liberal theory: both are in the service of the very things – the "state, the law, patriotic ideology" – that have "traditionally buttressed" the "cultural hierarchy" (53). Or as Berlant puts it in another version of this essay, she is suspicious of the way in which "national sentimentality," the "liberal rhetoric of promise historically entitled in the United States," avows that "a nation can best be built across fields of social difference through channels of affective identification and empathy," promoting a deeply felt but "stubbornly uncongealed form of personhood" as the center of politics.[23]

That the sentimental has come to be a stand-in for liberal theory (in both its positive and negative aspects) is understandable both historically and theoretically.[24] The age of humanitarian reform that began in the eighteenth century was coincident both with the ascendance of liberal theory and of an increasing revulsion against pain, which, though now regarded as inevitable, is distinctly modern.[25] Moreover, if one follows Judith Shklar and defines liberalism as an ideology that thinks, "cruelty is the worst thing," then the relationship between the proliferation of sentimentality and of liberal rights becomes almost tautological.[26] Extrapolating from Shklar, one could say that liberalism is the philosophy and sentimental discourse is the practice, the ideal rhetorical form to implement liberalism's "determination to extend humanity" and increase the scope of liberal rights.

Rather than disrupting this longstanding correlation of liberal theory to sentimentality, I am interested in foregrounding how much the affiliation of these cultural formations depends upon the assumption that both share a common will toward disembodiment: just as liberalism postulates a universal substrate of "personhood" that is beyond (either in a liberatory or a repressive way) the contingent predicates of color, sexuality, ethnicity, class, gender, so too does sentimentality posit pain as a universal category that attests to our abstract equality. But, as I have been arguing, liberal theory does not necessarily depend upon such a fixed notion of the "person," and similarly, neither does Stowe imagine feeling as a universalizable.

Indeed, as I argued in the last chapter, Stowe's argument for Negro "personhood" crucially depends upon the claim that the Negro inevitably feels more than other races do.[27] During the antebellum period, indeed, accounts of feeling were inseparable from the debate over "personhood." Thus, in contrast to Stowe, physicians such as P. Tidyman argued against the humanity of the Negro by citing evidence that the Negro's nervous system exhibited "less sensibility and irritability than is generally witnessed among whites" and therefore did not feel the pain of whipping or deprivation as deeply as the white race would.[28] Lawyers, such as Thomas Cobb, argued that rather than loving their family (as Stowe claimed), the Negro's "natural affections are not strong, and consequently he is cruel to his offspring, and suffers little by separation from them."[29] As one Southern lawyer declared, the Negro, on account of "the peculiar physical conformation of the head," is constitutionally incapable of feeling suffering, asserting that – in contrast to what the "authoress of *Uncle Tom's Cabin* has kindly informed us" – only "lust and beastly cruelty" not the "emotions of parental and kindred attachment" define the race's "instinctual feelings."[30]

If such a debate over the nature of Negro suffering suggests the deep relationship between feeling and "personhood," it simultaneously suggests that this argument was not based on an identitarian logic. Negroes feel more or less than Anglo-Saxons, it was not assumed that they feel exactly the same. If today liberals such as Richard Rorty equate feeling and "personhood" in terms of an egalitarian logic, one that – for animal rights activists – inevitably exceeds the boundaries of the human, during the antebellum period the relationship between pain and "personhood" operated according to a more differentiating logic.

To explore how feeling was racialized rather than universalized during the antebellum period, I want to turn in more detail to the paradigmatic scene of the paradigmatic sentimental novel: the death of Eva St. Claire. In particular, I am interested in the sentimental token at the heart of this scene: the locks of her hair that Eva distributes to her family and slaves. This token of love, I will argue, is simultaneously a token of race. These tokens overlap precisely because Negroes were "personified" according to a sentimental logic that inscribes rather than transcends racial difference. In this scene, sentimental love is driven by an impulse to recognize difference rather than impose, as modern critics have asserted, an abstract equality. In this sense, Stowe's project follows the antebellum conception of equality as a term that needed to take into account essential difference. Equal rights were not necessarily identical rights precisely because there remained essential differences between the sexes and the races. Thus, when discussing the right of women to enter the public arena Wendell Phillips, one of the period's most forceful proponents of equality, stated in a speech on gender and racial equality:

> Woman now takes the stand to give us her views of God's works and her own creation; and exactly in proportion as *woman, though equal, is eternally different from man,* just in that proportion will the literature of the next century be doubly rich (emphasis added).[31]

Rather than being contradictory, the coincidence of equality and eternal difference indicates the distance between antebellum and modern notions of "personhood" and of rights.

Modern discussions of how the sentimental diminishes notions of difference and particularity suggest how deeply accounts of the sentimental have presumed an abstract account of the "person." During the antebellum period, however, the sentimental crucially extended liberal rights not because it generated abstract identities but because it cherished difference. The problem with attributing a universalizing imperative to either liberalism or the sentimental is that such an account removes the object of sentimentality and the subject of liberal thought from the very debate in which both are inevitably embedded: the debate over who counts as a "person."

EVA'S DEATH

When describing Eva's distribution of her locks of hair to her family's slaves, Stowe dwells on the slaves' grief:

> It is impossible to describe the scene, as, with tears and sobs, they gathered around the little creature, and took from her hands what seemed to them a last mark of her love. They fell on their knees; they sobbed, and prayed, and kissed the hem of her garment; and the elder ones poured forth words of endearment, mingled in prayers and blessings, after the manner of their susceptible race (288).

Clearly, Stowe's staging of Little Eva's death, her representation of loved ones crowding around a dying child and yearning for a precious memento, participates with a vengeance in the antebellum United States' fascination with mourning.[32] Historians of the period have detailed the "sentimental cult of mourning" that developed around tokens of the deceased. As one manual on mourning recounts:

In every home there is an enshrined memory, a sacred relic, a ring, a lock of shining hair, a broken plaything, a book, a picture, something sacredly kept and guarded, which speaks of death, which tells as plainly as words, of some one long since gone.[33]

But the scene does more than simply exploit the nineteenth-century's cult of death.[34] It is also designed to demonstrate Eva's Christ-like, evangelical love. Stowe deliberately emphasizes Eva's giving away a part of herself in order to foreground the way in which Eva "is an impersonation in childish form of the love of Christ" (*The Key to Uncle Tom's Cabin*, 51).[35] Eva's dispersal of her body operates according to the Christian logic of communion, on the one hand recalling the communal breaking and sharing of Christ's body in the sacrament of the Eucharist and on the other anticipating the redemptive moment of eschatological commingling when the saved shall be reconciled with God.[36]

But the significance of the part of herself that Eva gives away is exhausted neither by antebellum conventions of mourning nor by the Christian notion of the relic, both of which discourses the scene certainly rehearses. The lock of hair at the center of this iconic scene has a notorious history in popular and scientific debates over racial difference. That is, by fetishizing Eva's hair, Stowe is not simply representing a moment when Eva's love, incarnated in the locks she distributes, overcomes bodily difference, but also enters into an on-going argument over hair as an indelible and ineffaceable racial marker. To read this scene as a moment when love transcends all racial difference thus erases the extent to which hair was a highly charged signifier of racial difference during the antebellum period. Since hair raises crucial questions about the eternal force of race, this scene needs to be explored as confronting the problem of racial knowledge and as foregrounding the possibility that Stowe mobilizes a politics of affect by recognizing rather than overcoming race. This scene, indeed, suggests that race has been read out of the sentimental for the same reason that it has been read out of liberal "personhood."

THE RACE OF A HAIR

During the antebellum period, all hair, much like all men, was not created equal. Hair functioned in both scientific and public discourse as a parallel to skin color: it was typically cited as a means by which human groups could be empirically sorted, as a natural part of the surface of the body, like skin, that must possess inherent significance. Since antebellum scientific and popular discourse was obsessed with how the body signified, this identification of hair and race makes sense.[37] It was not unusual, in fact, for some to claim that hair served as a better indicator of racial identity than skin color.

Peter A. Browne, for example, the period's foremost expert on trichology (the study of hair) argued in a paper presented to the American Association for the Advancement of Science in March 1850 (about one year before Stowe began to serialize *Uncle Tom's Cabin* in the *National Era*) that the relationship between hair and race is more stable than the relation between color and race. Building on his earlier work on how the Negro's head was covered with wool rather than hair, Browne set out to prove this superiority by comparing the hair from two "Black" and two "white" albinos. Using this group, one in which skin color was an inadequate signifier of difference, Browne examined the length of the hair, its shape, color, luster, direction of growth, as well as its ductility, elasticity, and tenacity at a given temperature, barometric pressure, and dew point; he investigated the manner in which it fractured; the characteristics of button, sheath, follicle, cortex, intermediate fibers, apex, and cross-sections. Browne discovered that the hair of the albinos matched hairs from others in their respective races and therefore he concluded that albinos were not a separate species but merely a variety of either the Black or white races.[38] For Browne, this fact meant that the whitening produced by albinism (and implicitly by racial amalgamation) did not make the Negro a member of the white "species."[39] Though his skin may be white, the distinct differences of the hair of the Negro albino proved him a Negro.[40]

If albinism is representative of the gap that is beginning to open up between color and racial identity, Browne claims that one can turn to hair to definitively close this gap. At a moment when questions of the color line threatened to be unsatisfactorily answered by appeals to the skin, Browne seeks to publicize an objective and stable identity marker. According to Browne, hair will always render racial difference visible (albeit microscopically so). According to Browne, since wool is "*permanently native*" to the Negro, it is more than "sufficient ground for a *specific* division of a genus" ("*Classification*," 19).[41] Because "the white man has hair upon his head, and the negro has wool, we have no hesitancy in pronouncing that they *belong to two distinct species*" (20). Browne, in essence, is not examining race as much as he is refining its operation, establishing a more sophisticated methodology for proving the objectivity of racial difference.

Browne's focus on hair as an object of analysis participates in a well-established scientific tradition of founding an effort to determine the diversity of mankind on the assumption that there are manifest physical differences between the races that can be measured and classified.[42] Subscribing to the conclusion reached by the American School of Ethnology that the races were separate species produced by separate creations (polygenesis), Browne opposed his scientific work to the work of the British ethnologist James Cowles Prichard (1786–1848), the foremost champion of monogenesis, the theory that there was one origin for all human kinds and that racial differences developed over time. Throughout his writings, Prichard defended the concept of one human species, arguing that though there may be permanent varieties these differences were analogous to the diversity among species of dogs.[43] Recognizing that "the short crisp hair of the Negro" seems "the greatest anomaly" in efforts to claim the unity of mankind, Prichard set out to prove that the Negro has hair, which, although dramatically and obviously different from the hair of Europeans, is not, as is "generally considered," wool (Prichard, 80–81). According to Prichard, the Negro is covered not with wool, but with hair that differs from the European's only in the "degree of crispation."[44]

Browne argued that Prichard's examination of hair lacked scientific rigor. In his paper "The Classification of mankind, by the hair and wool of their heads," which he read before the American Ethnological Society, and then more extensively in his books, particularly *The Classification of Mankind by the Hair and Wool of their Heads* (1852), which he published with the "Patronage of the Commonwealth of Pennsylvania," and *Trichologia Mammalium* (1853),[45] Browne argued that one could scientifically distinguish three species of mankind by examining "pile," the term he coined to describe both hair and wool whether on men or animals. Using a variation of the microscope that he invented specifically for measuring the various properties of pile, called the "trichometer," Browne claims that his careful study of pile revealed that there exist three shapes of pile: oval, cylindrical, and eccentrically elliptical. These three shapes are in turn "inseparably connected" to what he called three different "directions" of pile: cylindrical pile "must necessarily be straight and lank," oval pile "must necessarily flow from or curl upon" the head, and eccentrically elliptical pile is always "crisped, frizzled, or spirally curled" (*Classification,* 4–6). The third "exceedingly important" quality of pile is its "inclination" (*Classification,* 6–7). According to Browne, both oval and cylindrical pile grows out of the epidermis at an acute angle, while eccentrically elliptical pile emerges at a right angle. Taken together, these prominent, specific, and ineradicable differences in pile, Browne argues, correspond to the three races of mankind. Since "there are three portions of men who now exist, and who from time immemorial have existed, the covering of whose heads respectively, do, and have, uniformly corresponded with these three species of pile. . . there will be no difficulty in pronouncing that (judging from the pile of their heads) they belong to three distinct species of men" (*Trichologia*, 59). The white race always has oval, flowing or curled, hair; the Indian race always has cylindrical hair that hangs straight and lank. Both of these types of hair have "an oblique angle of inclination." Negro pile, on the other hand, is always eccentrically elliptical, crisped or frizzled, and pierces the epidermis perpendicularly.

Animating Browne's argument is the claim that if one knows how to use a trichometer, an objective tool, miscegenation will no longer threaten the purity of the races. For example, Browne found that the hair of the European was pierced by a canal through which flowed the coloring matter while the hair of the Negro had "no central canal"; if Negro pile had any color at all, (which Browne argued it rarely did) the coloring agent was "disseminated through the cortex."[46] In addition to the shape and color of Negro pile, Browne found "scales" upon the cortex of Negro pile that cause Negro pile to mat together like wool, while the hair of the Caucasian had no such scales. He, therefore, noted that "the hair of the white man will not felt, but the wool of the negro will felt" (*Classification*, 8).

The fact the Negro has wool rather than hair becomes of particular interest to Browne because it allows him to continue his account of the relationship between hair and the purity of the races in a more thoroughly controlled experimental setting. Taking very seriously his discovery that the only significant difference between the wool of the Negro and the covering of sheep is the "degree of felting power," Browne extended his investigations of human species to the study of sheep-breeding (*Classification*, 20). Many, he argues, make the same mistake with sheep that is made with the Caucasian and the African: they identify as a single species what should be defined as separate species. Some sheep, Browne claims, have hair, while others have wool. Sheep, in other words, recapitulate the species difference between the white and Black man. Browne considers the two species of sheep crucial knowledge for the sheepbreeder who wants to produce a particular kind of sheep. He develops the following scientific rule: "THE SHEEP-BREEDER SHOULD NEVER CROSS THE TWO SPECIES OF SHEEP, VIZ: THE HAIRY SHEEP AND THE WOOLLY SHEEP – This is the most important direction we have to give – it is the *golden rule* – the primatus principatus" (*Trichologia*, 158). Browne, it seems, cannot overemphasize the importance of this rule against the mixing of separate species. It appears, in short, that sheep offer the standard by which to understand the relationship between the distinct species of Man.

The vehemence with which Browne protests any effort to mix these species barely camouflages the fact that he *racializes* sheep breeding, imagining it as reproducing the situation of whites and Blacks. Thus, he stresses the "natural abhorrence" and "natural disgust planted in the minds of all animals to the mixture of species," claiming that if such an order is violated "the whole animal commonwealth would be converted into a disgusting assemblage of unsightly monster!" (161, 162, 165, 167). "Let us suppose," Browne writes, "that nature were to resign the reigns of creation to man, what a picture would soon be presented":

> Cows rioting in blood, while Lions and Tigers were grazing and chewing the cud; Fishes clambering up trees, or building and inhabiting three-story brick houses; Turkies in uniform, strutting at the head of regiments of Geese and fowls; Hogs dressed in brocades and adorned with pearls and diamonds, while woman, lovely woman, is grunting Italian airs, as she lies wallowing in the mire! (170).

Browne has no doubt that interbreeding would turn the world upside down. Indeed, by culminating his apocalyptic vision with the image of a degraded and darkened (white) woman, Browne makes clear the extent to which his entire discussion of sheep barely conceals an obsession with the danger of miscegenation.

Browne's ferocious condemnation of man's potential ability to "mar and destroy" nature with "artificial varieties" is compensated for by his faith in the power of hair. Browne claims that although the appearance of the hybrid will seem to combine its essentially different parent species, its hair will remain separate. Although people may commingle, hair will never do so. The mixing of two species will only produce creatures that possess the pile characteristics of each of their parent species. In the same way that the hair of a mulatto born of a "pure" Negro and a "pure" white race will have some hair (i.e. whiteness) and some Negro wool, Browne argues that the mixing of the two species of sheep will produce a similar tangle of pile. According to Browne, hair is a pure sign of race, so intractable that no mixture can dilute its expressive force or damage its integrity. For Browne, one might say, the significance of hair was more than skin deep.

THE SEMIOTICS OF HAIR

Although Browne's classificatory schema may seem too obvious in intent to be taken seriously, Browne cannot be dismissed as a crackpot.[47] Browne's work on hair did not exist on the margins of antebellum society. Josiah Nott, the premier ethnologist in the United States, along with Samuel Cartwright, for example, were enthusiastic supporters of Browne's work. And Browne's *Classification of Mankind, by the Hair and Wool of their Heads* was reprinted in John Campbell's influential pro-slavery collection *Negromania.*[48] Browne's appeal, moreover, was not limited to apologists for slavery. Favorable reviews of Browne's work were common in the periodical press, and his methodology was referred to by the US Army's Provost Marshal-General's Bureau's massive anthropometric investigations of Union recruits, an examination that was central to setting the anthropological statistics for the second half of the nineteenth century.[49] Indeed, later in the century, when craniometry began to lose prestige, distinguished anthropologists such as Broca, Muller, Huxley, Haeckel, and Keane all examined human hair, claiming that it served as a more constant and reliable basis for the classification of racial differences than skull measurements.[50]

Hair, in fact, was not represented as a crucial identity marker only by apologists for slavery or for racial inequality. For example, William Wells Brown in *Clotel* repeatedly discusses how Black slaves comb and oil their woolly hair "to death" in order to appear more white (194) and how few would suspect that one character was Black since his hair "was straight, soft, fine, and light" (262). Brown also quotes from a newspaper story in which an Ohio court attempts to determine whether one Thomas West could vote since there were "*constitutional doubts* as to whether his color was orthodox, and whether his hair was of official crisp" (original emphasis, 221). In another instance, Henry Box Brown, in his very popular narrative about how he escaped from slavery by enclosing himself in a box and mailing himself to the North, describes the way in which his sister, anxious to be saved, "shaved the hair from her head, as many of the slaves thought they could not be converted without doing this".[51] Brown's sister, having internalized the racist teachings of some religious leaders, does not think it possible to be saved as long as her "frizzy" and "woolly" hair distinguished her as fundamentally Black.

Indeed, hair served as such a powerful index of African identity that one ethnologist of the period tells the story of a Negro pastor. The preacher, seeking to quiet the fears of members of his congregation who had just heard scientific proof that they were a different species, assures them that they were under special protection of God. As evidence of this fact, he explains that the Negro is literally the lamb of the world, a race to whom God has given wool instead of hair.[52] One did not need to follow Browne and believe that the Negro hair was scientifically classifiable as wool in order to invoke Black hair as a manifest and significant sign of Negro identity.[53] Thus, Frederick Douglass in considering the "ethnological unfairness towards the Negro" remarks how leading ethnologists have developed elaborate arguments to prove the Egyptian was distinct from the Negro even though they were as dark as the Negro and "their hair was far from being of that graceful lankness which adorns the Anglo-Saxon head."[54]

Certainly, the relationship between hair and racial identity developed during the nineteenth century has not wholly disappeared. African American hair continues to possess a powerful ideological force. One thinks, for example, of how Malcolm X, looking back on his efforts to straighten his hair, recognizes his desire to have "white" hair as symptomatic:

> I had joined that multitude of Negro men and women in America who are brainwashed into believing that black people are "inferior" – and white people "superior" – that they will even violate and mutilate their God-created bodies to try to look "pretty" by white standards.[55]

The Negro's desire for processed hair makes Malcolm wonder "if the Negro has completely lost his sense of identity, lost touch with himself" (*Autobiography*, 55). Also one thinks of the big dance number from Spike Lee's *School Daze* which takes place in Madam Re-Re's beauty parlor. There the Black co-eds sing "Straight and Nappy," a debate between the "Wannabees" and the "Jigaboos" over the relationship between one's hair and one's interiority:

JIGABOOS: I don't mind being BLACK
go on with your mixed-up head
I ain't gonna never be 'fraid
WANNABEES: Well you got nappy hair
JIGABOOS: Nappy is alright with me
WANNABEES: My hair is straight you see
JIGABOOS: But your soul's crooked as can be. . . . .[56]

Hair has not stopped signifying racial identity. It may signify differently and have been thoroughly resignified, but hair nonetheless remains a crucial identity marker. Rather than having been emptied of social significance, it has become central to a liberatory politics, raising critical issues about standards of beauty and Black self-definition.[57] As Kobena Mercer has stated, "our hair, like our skin, is a highly sensitive surface on which competing definitions of the 'beautiful' are played out in struggle."[58]

Thus, Browne's work, rather than being anomalous, is emblematic of a widespread and continuing belief in hair's expressive force in matters of racial identity. Browne, in some sense, merely puts the conventional antebellum wisdom that hair is a crucial marker of absolute racial difference into the enlightened register of science. And, he was not alone in pursuing such work; the contemporaneous anatomists Dr. Seidy and Dr. Robert W. Gibbes also did extensive work on hair and racial difference, examining how the pure African, like many animals, shed his hair once a year and how Negro hair attracted a particular kind of lice.[59] Such work was regarded as so reputable that antebellum judges commonly turned to hair to guide their rulings about racial identity. Thus, in a case of a girl who was "supposed to be a negro" and was purchased to be a slave but who claimed to have "been stolen from a roving band of Cherokees," Gibbes offered testimony about the difference between Negro, Caucasian, and Indian hair. Gibbes testified that under "microscopial observation" it is clear that "in the mulatto cross the hair of one or the other parent was present," and sometimes hairs of both, but never a mongrel hair. . .no amalgamated hair existed. The reason is that although the Indian and Caucasian have "true hair," the Negro has "not hair, but wool, capable of being felted."

The Virginia Supreme Court of Appeals, for example, relied on hair in *Hudgins v. Wright* (1806) when presented with the problem of deciding what constituted proof of one's race. In this case, three generations of women sued for their freedom, arguing that they were Indians rather than Negroes and thus could not be enslaved. The ancestry of these women was in dispute because their birth records and public testimony about their birth were inconclusive. The court decided the case by arguing that the physical appearance of the women stood as sufficient proof of their identity and that no other evidence was necessary to decide whether or not they were slaves. Reaffirming the logic of visibility grounding the earlier ruling of George Wythe, the Chancellor of the Richmond District Court of Chancery, Judge St. George Tucker declared that:

> Nature has stampt upon the African and his descendants two characteristic marks, besides the difference of complexion, which often remain visible long after the characteristic distinction of colour either disappears or become doubtful; a flat

nose and woolly head of hair. The latter of these characteristics disappears last of all: and so strong an ingredient in the African constitution is this latter character, that it predominates uniformly where the party is in equal degree descended from parents of different complexions, whether white or Indian; giving the jet black lank hair of the Indian a degree of flexure, which never fails to betray the party distinguished by it, cannot trace his lineage purely from the race of native Americans. Its operation is still more powerful where the mixture happens between persons descended equally from European and African parents. . . . So pointed is this distinction between the natives of Africa and the aborigines of America, that a man might as easily mistake the glossy, jetty clothing of an American Bear for the wool of a black sheep, as the hair of an American Indian for that of an African, or the descendant of an African. Upon these distinctions as connected with our laws, the burthen of proof depends (11 Va. at 134).

The freedom of these women, in fact, ultimately depended upon their hair not their skin (the court noted that the youngest woman "was perfectly white"). The court decided that the appellees are "absolutely free" because "The witnesses concur in assigning to the hair of Hannah [the mother]. . .the long, straight, black hair of the native aborigines of this country" (11 Va. at 140).[60]

Another court case suggests how powerfully hair was appealed to as an immutable and foolproof test of racial identity, one more reliable than skin color. In 1857 a slave known as Jane was sold in the slave market of New Orleans; she ran away and filed suit against her owner, claiming that she was white and thus wrongly enslaved. Her whiteness was ostensibly manifest; she had blond hair and blue eyes, and "white features."[61] But in New Orleans, in particular, appearance was often deceiving. And since her personal and sale history was unclear and her appearance and behavior inclusive, Jane's lawyers cited as decisive evidence the fact that strands of Jane's hair when cut transversely, revealed themselves to be the "moderate" ovals of a white person rather than the longer ovals of the black race. Such evidence was considered compelling, and Jane was declared white and eventually freed.

The widespread understanding of the relationship between hair and race does not, of course, prove that Stowe was directly aware of Browne's work or that she was responding to cases like the ones mentioned above. There exists little conclusive biographical evidence concerning Stowe's engagement with Browne's work on hair as a signifier of absolute racial difference. Thus, rather than ask whether Stowe was directly influenced by work such as Browne's, I am interested in how Stowe's representation of Eva's hair reveals her investment in an analogous understanding of hair as intrinsically racialized.

If traditionally Eva's distribution of her hair has been interpreted as exemplary of how sentimental love overcomes bodily particularity, such an interpretation assumes that Eva's hair holds a merely contingent relationship to her identity. It is to assume that Eva's hair is an arbitrary and self-consuming artifact, a merely vehicular, rather than essential and organic, signifier. In contrast, I focus on the way that Stowe represents Eva's lock as the primary fetish object of the novel. That is, Stowe bestows upon this token of love an intrinsic force that suggests how deeply she imagines hair as essential to identity, a marker inseparable from the quiddity of racial difference. Rather than being an innocent token, hair serves as the central symbol of sentimental love precisely because it carries a racial trace.

Readers have foreclosed the ways that hair operated as a crucial signifier of race because they have cut it from the particularizing and racialist discourse of antebellum liberalism and located it within the universalizing discourse of modern sentimental liberalism. The sheer weight of Eva's lock of hair, in short, has been forgotten because critics have been working with the premises of modern liberalism and have mistakenly assumed Stowe to be working within these same premises. For Stowe, however, hair carries in and of itself a substantive racial meaning, one that supplements rather than conflicts with the power of the sentimental to "personify" slaves.

EVA'S HAIR

Although Eva dies midway through the novel, her hair lives on. Indeed, it returns in a wholly different style at a crucial moment in the novel. Long after Eva's death and in a totally different context, Simon Legree discovers the lock of hair that Eva gave Tom at the notorious deathbed scene. Legree's slave Sambo brings Legree the piece of paper which holds the lock of Eva's hair, a lock that Sambo believes is a "witch thing," a fetish object given to slaves by witches to keep the slaves "from feeling when they's flogged" (369). Legree unwraps the paper, and there drops "a long shining curl of fair hair – hair which, *like a living thing*, twined itself round Legree's fingers" (369, emphasis added). Legree is horrified:

> Damnation!" he screamed, in sudden passion, stamping on the floor, and pulling furiously at the hair, as if it burned him. "Where did this come from? Take it off! – burn it up! burn it up!" he screamed, tearing it off, and throwing it into the charcoal. "What did you bring it to me for? (369).

Like the scarlet letter, Eva's hair burns; it possesses an intrinsic and mysterious power. "What was there in a simple curl of fair hair," Stowe asks, that could "appall that brutal man, familiar with every form of cruelty?" (369).

The answer Stowe offers is that Legree believes this lock of hair to be the lock of hair sent to him by his mother when she was dying. Legree's mother, the reader is told, intended the lock to be an emblem of her love and of her prayers for his salvation. When he received that lock it also "twined about his fingers" (370). For Stowe, in other words, hair is not a dead symbol, but a living emblem, one that scares Legree because it seems to mysteriously "rise from the dead," from the fire into which he threw his mother's token. And as Stowe explains:

> Ah, Legree! that golden tress was charmed; each hair had in it a spell of terror and remorse for thee, and was used by a mightier power to bind thy cruel hands from inflicting uttermost evil on the helpless! (372)

Legree's terror at Eva's lock of hair suggests that the curl itself contains an intrinsic charge long after its owner's death. Although Legree misreads the origins of this lock of hair, his understanding of the lock as incarnating Christian love is correct. Legree is right to see the hair of his mother and of Eva as fundamentally equivalent signs since both locks embody the power of Christian love.

But, of course, this lock circulates not only in narratives of Christian love, but also in narratives about African voodoo and pagan superstition.[62] And it is this tremendous signifying force that suggests the extent to which the hair is powerful in and of itself. That is, just as scientific, legal, and popular narratives about hair begin from the premise that hair possesses an inherent meaning, Stowe deploys hair as a signifier with immanent meaning, a meaning that cannot be repressed and that continues to signify no matter what the context. Thus, while Stowe certainly represents Legree's reaction to this hair as fundamentally superstitious (and thus as unChristian), his understanding of hair as possessing a mysterious and essential power is never undermined.

Indeed, most significantly this piece of hair initiates a process of racial identification and particularizing that suggests how hair is always already a raced object. Legree, it is crucial to note, never imagines that this lock of hair has anything to do with Tom himself. In fact, the lock affects Legree only because he recognizes it as fundamentally alien to Tom, as a physical token obviously belonging to a white woman. Underlying this moment, in other words, lies a recognition of the abiding difference between white and Black hair. Recapitulating the power of racial difference that informs *Uncle Tom's Cabin* as a whole, this scene emblematizes the extent to which the effect of hair is predicated upon the fact that it is the hair of a white "person," not on the fact that it could be mistaken for anybody's or everybody's hair. Underwriting this scene is the assumption – one so embedded in the fabric of the text that it does not need comment – that hair is a raced artifact, one whose symbolic force is intimately tied to its racial origin.

Stowe's representation of this lock of hair as independently significant and obviously "white" suggests how deeply this emblem of love depends upon and reproduces the logic of racial essences. In hair, the metaphysics of love and of race converge. At this moment it becomes clear how deeply Stowe's sentimental project is ultimately premised upon essentialism. Sentimental love, like race, transcends contingency. The influence of both remains independent of context and eternal to environment and culture. Indeed, it is precisely because hair has already been so powerfully branded as an objective marker of identity that Stowe chooses this symbol to incarnate love.

It is this essential power of hair that suggests that the traditional alignment of sentimental love with an anti-essentialist and disembodied logic needs to be reevaluated. Hair in the novel is represented as a motivated sign, a symbol whose material form is deeply connected to its spiritual content. The incarnational logic of this lock suggests that the materiality of the hair cannot be forgotten. And it is this materiality that explains why Stowe installs a primary token of race as a token of love: Stowe depends upon the objective force of racial difference to confirm the power of love. The power of hair, in fact, stands as an ideal expression of how the sentimental works. Just as the sentimental requires that it is possible for an image, object, or text to create particular feelings in a subject, racial identity operates according to an analogous confidence in the reproducibility of identity.

Stowe's resurrection of Eva's hair reinforces the inevitability of sentimental love. The racialist claim that physical and mental traits of an ancestor will reveal themselves in future generations and Stowe's representation of the haunting influence of love intersect in this lock of hair. Rather than excise the logic of the sentimental from the logic of race, Eva's hair conjoins racial essences to the sentimental. Indeed, if, during the antebellum period, the mechanism by which biological traits are transmitted from one generation was commonly represented as fundamentally mysterious, the influence of Christian love was considered no less inexplicable. As Charles Loring Brace explained in his *Races of the Old World*:

> The mysterious and far-reaching property of blood – of Race, is becoming more and more recognized in modern science. The power, whereby the most distant ancestor shall influence his remotest descendent, and – still more wonderful – that accumulated effect of a line of ancestors in the final progeny, so that a clear stream of inherited physical and mental peculiarities can flow unmingled through human history in every variety of external circumstances and internal influences – is something not to be lightly weighed in the philosophy of man or in history of his actions.[63]

Brace's description of the magical and inexorable force of race looks a great deal like the way in which the power of sentimental love was commonly imagined to be able to influence others no matter what the distance and no matter what the circumstance. The power of the novel to engender sentimental relationships between its readers and its characters is, in short, most powerfully confirmed by the power of racial markers to signify no matter what the context.

If the process by which racial distinctions perpetuate themselves seems supernatural, at least to the antebellum observer, this process is no less supernatural than the power of sentimental sympathy. Indeed, claims for the ineluctable power of the sentiment depend upon an essentialist logic; particular scenes are counted upon to inevitably produce certain reactions. The fact that Stowe represents the lock of Eva's hair as possessing an inherent significatory power uncovers the deep homology between the logic of race and of the sentimental. It is a natural sign and thus enforces a necessary belief in the possibility of a spontaneous link between a sign and the content of that sign, between a representation and a reaction. In this sense, essentialism enables the emancipatory logic of the sentimental.

The scene long regarded as the ultimate expression of Stowe's universalism, in other words, is predicated upon and reinscribes essentialist premises. Rather than solidifying the possibility of a perfect community universal in scope because it is based on the transcendence of the body and on the delegitimation of the material differences between Black and white, Eva's hair plays a central role in the emancipatory project of the novel because hair is clearly an intractable identity marker, one that highlights rather than refuses the inevitability of difference. Stowe's sentimental sympathy always remembers race precisely because race is what makes us what we are.

Thus, the "personifying" impulse that critics have identified at the heart of the sentimental needs to be reread in terms of the historical contingency of the notion of the "person" that the sentimental seeks to make representable. That we tend to erase race from our reading of the sentimental and assume that the sentimental enforces an abstract similarity points to how deeply our account of this formation is predicated upon an unexamined notion of the "person." Rather than explore how the sentimental works to expand the category of those who deserve rights differently at different times or how it marks that the concept of the "person" operates differently in different historical contexts, we have smuggled a decontextualized notion of the "person" into our reading of this genre and projected this static notion onto antebellum culture. In doing so, we have misidentified how the sentimental produces more and more "persons." *Uncle Tom's Cabin* suggests the extent to which the novel's success in producing "persons" is inseparable from its sentimental essentialism.

If Stowe is committed to representing slaves as "persons," the next chapters focus on the work of Nathaniel Hawthorne, a figure who remained committed to a more conservative account of "personhood." Where Stowe worked to produce more and more "persons," Hawthorne opposed such efforts. In order to foreground how interpretations of Hawthorne have neglected Hawthorne's participation in antebellum debates over "personhood" I want to focus on what is perhaps the most powerful and influential reading of Hawthorne's most canonical novel: Sacvan Bercovitch's *The Office of The Scarlet Letter.*[64] Bercovitch's interpretation of the text that has come closest to standing as the national novel not only offers a brilliant synthesis of the prevailing modes of reading US literary and political history but also makes clear the extent to which a particular notion of the "person" has served as the unacknowledged and unexamined center of the most influential interpretations of US liberal culture. That is, I will approach Bercovitch's reading of *The Scarlet Letter* as a kind of shorthand for the kind of readings of US liberal culture that I am challenging.

CHAPTER 4

A is for Anything: US liberalism and the making of The Scarlet Letter

It is a truth now universally known that the scarlet letter on Hester Prynne's chest designates much more than her adultery.[1] In fact, one might argue that every post-World War II reading of the novel has, albeit in strikingly different ways, been dedicated to consolidating the notion that the A signifies anything and everything but Adultery: Able, Artist, Angel, Antinomian, Admirable, Apathy, Ambiguity, Author, Allegory, and America are just a few of the possible meanings that critics have offered.[2] This anti-literalist style of reading the letter has developed into the current critical consensus that the A is an indefinite article, an impossibly overdetermined figure that ultimately represents nothing but the dynamics of representation itself. According to this account, Hawthorne's letter, rather than specifying anything in particular, connotes the "inconclusive luxuriance of meaning," the "constitutive uncertainty" of language.[3] Indeed, it has been precisely by claiming that the A is indeterminately polysemic that critics have successfully redescribed Hawthorne as an ironist rather than a moral absolutist, as a proto-modernist rather than a superannuated Puritan, as a complex symbolist rather than a dogmatic allegorist.[4] *The Scarlet Letter*'s congeniality to modern criticism, in short, has been directly proportional to the degree to which the scarlet letter has lost its official meaning and gained an ambiguous, symbolic one – or, to put this another way, this congeniality increases in direct proportion to the ways the scarlet letter has come to constellate the modern assumption that "personhood" is a fundamentally abstract identity category, one in which both embodiment and the material markers of identity are rendered inessential and contingent.[5] By grounding interpretation in something beyond the literal meaning of the scarlet letter, the most influential modern readings of Hawthorne's classically American novel, in particular, and of US literary culture, in general, reveal themselves to be organized in terms of a decontextualized account of the "person" and thus to reproduce the foundational fantasy of liberal thought.

The publication of Sacvan Bercovitch's *The Office of The Scarlet Letter* offers an ideal occasion to re-examine this anti-literalist style of reading.[6] Bercovitch can be said to have extended this style of interpreting the scarlet letter into a far-ranging and powerfully influential reading of US liberal culture. If *The Scarlet Letter*'s status as a representative American classic has, in the words of Frank Kermode, been an effect of "its failure to give a definitive account of itself," then *The Office of The Scarlet Letter* extends claims for such indefiniteness perhaps as far as they can go, translating such anti-literalism into a grand unified theory of American liberal culture.[7]

According to Bercovitch, the A makes visible "the strategies of what we have come to term 'the American ideology'," incarnating "the system of symbolic meanings that encompasses text and context" and expressing "all the tenets of modern liberal society [that] find their apotheosis in the symbol of America" (xvii, xxi). For Bercovitch, the A is an ideological relay point, an object that registers the deep correspondence between the interpretation of the scarlet letter and the "premises of American liberalism" (xx). The office of the scarlet letter, Bercovitch argues, is synonymous with the office of American liberalism precisely because the political symbol America is simply the A writ large.[8] As Bercovitch puts it, "the process by which the United States [as a nation-state] usurped America [as an ideological construct] for itself" is symbolic (xxi).

Whereas earlier chapters traced how some of the most influential readings of US slavery have been energized by placing the "person" beyond history, this chapter approaches Bercovitch's brilliant reading of this nation's "first instant classic" as representative of how the dominant style of reading US literature has worked according to an analogous premise. Readings of *The Scarlet Letter* exemplify how the logic of liberal representation has been reproduced in a text that does not take race-based slavery as its explicit topic.[9] The United States, in short, has been made into a liberal nation not only by the way race-based slavery has been discussed but also by the way US literary culture has been read.

Bercovitch's account of America (as an ideological symbol) turns on a reading of the scarlet A as an identity marker with no essential content, as something whose meanings, like clothing, can be put on or taken off. This understanding of the A assumes, I will argue, a particular relationship between surface characteristic and identity that itself is symptomatic of the liberal imperative to place the "person" out of history. That is, although

Bercovitch's explicit purpose is to critique US liberalism, I examine *The Office of The Scarlet Letter* as the most sophisticated and comprehensive example of how the imperatives of liberal representation have reproduced themselves even in the work of those who set out to critique the premises of liberal representation. By deploying rather than examining the assumption that surface markers (such as the A) bear only an arbitrary rather than determining relation to one's true identity, Bercovitch reproduces a style of reading that erases any historical disputes over the nature of the "person," disputes that often hinged on the question of the relationship between identity markers (such as race) and one's eligibility for "personhood." By extending the prevailing modern reading of the A as a purely contingent signifier into a reading of American liberal symbology, Bercovitch's text itself performs a significant liberal office: it fulfills the liberal imperative to mystify the origins of a historically particular account of the "person." If Bercovitch reads Hawthorne's symbolic and indeterminate A as the source of American liberal ideology, I, in contrast, examine such an understanding of the A as the primary effect of US liberal thought.

THE OFFICE OF LIBERAL EXEGESIS

Before one can claim that Bercovitch's argument about liberal representation itself exemplifies the logic of liberal representation, it is necessary to rehearse the elegant way in which Bercovitch uses Hawthorne's novel to link the two principal strains of US political and literary culture: the claim that this nation's literary imagination is symbolic and that its politics are liberal. According to Bercovitch, "the process by which the United States usurped America for itself, symbolically, is also the process by which liberalism established its political and economic dominance" (*Office*, xxi). Bercovitch, in essence, sees the scarlet letter as yoking the dominant literary style of America (symbolism) with what has traditionally been nominated as the dominant style of American politics (liberalism).[10] For Bercovitch, *The Scarlet Letter* is "the liberal example par excellence of art as ideological mimesis" because the letter's semantic elasticity is paradigmatic of the insatiable ideological capaciousness of America (*Office*, xxi).

To explain how the A instates the mechanics of liberal thought, Bercovitch begins by focusing on a textual incident that has long perplexed critics, "the dramatic moment when Hester decides to come home to America," and reattaches the A to her body (*Office*, xxii). This moment is crucial to any account of the novel's liberalism since liberal theory traditionally stands or falls on the notion of consent. In this final gesture, Hester seems to abandon the values which had energized her heroic rebellion; she not only reclaims the symbol that had been her torment, but also, apparently, repudiates her previous dream of tearing down the "whole system of society" and suddenly dedicates herself to consoling the socially disaffected, promising them that "some brighter period" will eventually come (*Scarlet Letter*, 112). Unlike most recent critics, who regard this transformation of an individualistic rebel into a social worker as unnaturally and violently grafted onto Hester's "real" story, Bercovitch argues that this incident manifests the liberal imperatives underwriting not only the novel but American culture as a whole. Rather than disrupting the tenor of *The Scarlet Letter*, Hester's "dramatic change of purpose and belief" possesses the "force of necessity"; indeed, "the entire novel has been our preparation" for this moment of Hester's *voluntary* reconciliation with the A (*Office* 2, 3, 93). According to Bercovitch, the scarlet letter's office is only fulfilled when Hester learns to interpret the scarlet letter in such a way that she no longer feels the need to reject it. In the end, the scarlet letter reveals itself to be so spectacularly inclusive that its meaning can comprehend even Hester's rebelliousness.

Bercovitch finds it particularly significant that the basis for Hester's acceptance of the letter remains "entirely unexplained" (*Office*, 2). Lacking a certain answer, readers are implicitly asked to explain why Hester reattaches the scarlet letter. Their answer, according to Bercovitch, "depends on our interpretation–or more precisely, on our capacities to respond to Hawthorne's directives for interpretation," what Bercovitch calls the "principles of liberal exegesis" (*Office*, 4, 22). Bercovitch, of course, is following a long line of critics by approaching the scarlet letter as an object whose primary claims on the reader are hermeneutic.[11] But unlike previous critics, Bercovitch focuses on the act of interpretation as an exemplary enactment of the American liberal ideology. As Bercovitch explains, the symbol has a "certain office" in

> the double sense of "certain," as certainty and as something still to be ascertained. The office of the letter is to identify one with the other–to make certainty a form of process, and the prospect of certain meanings a form of closure and control (*Office*, xii).

According to Bercovitch, Hawthorne's symbol identifies the commitment to the process of interpretation as superior to any particular interpretation and represents the lack of any definite meaning as the truest expression of meaning and as the best form of closure.

It is this characterization of the undecidability of symbol that Bercovitch distinguishes as the "model" of the "dominant patterns of cultural expression" of America (*Office*, xvii). America and the A signify without a determinate meaning (*Office*, xviii).[12] To believe in America, according to Bercovitch, is not to believe in nothing, but to believe, above all else, in the metaphysics of the symbol. It is to accept that the only way to specify America's meaning is to reduce what America means.

Bercovitch understands American liberalism, in other words, not simply as a political, social, scientific, or philosophic discourse, but as a synonym for the background, the social imaginary, against which and by which all forms of meaning are produced and interpreted within American culture. The word "liberal," he explains, is the "catchall term to convey the continuing relation between social process and cultural symbology" in America (*Office*, xvi). What Bercovitch distinguishes as exceptional about the American ideology is the particular "interpretative framework" that America has established. It is America's ability to mean without the limitations of a specific content that has made American liberalism "the single most cohesive ideology of the modern world" (*Office*, 112).

AMBIGUITY, IRONY, AND PARADOX

To unpack these interpretative practices, Bercovitch redescribes traditional techniques of reading *The Scarlet Letter* as instances of "ideological mimesis." For example, in his first chapter, "The A-Politics of Ambiguity," Bercovitch argues that ambiguity, the rhetorical mode that is perhaps most consistently associated with interpretations of *The Scarlet Letter*, is "directly based" upon a particularly liberal "concept of truth" (*Office*, 13). Instating a "politics of both/and," Hawthorne's relentless and absolute ambiguity "requires" readers to deny the potentially radical "politics of either/or" (*Office*, 9). Hawthorne's fundamentally open-ended text teaches readers that no interpretation can ever be either "entirely wrong" or "in itself satisfactory" (*Office*, 19). Ambiguity, according to Bercovitch, is a "strategy of pluralism" (*Office*, 19). By representing the choice of a single interpretation as fundamentally limited, ambiguity directs readers "*not to choose*" one meaning (*Office*, 22).

Hawthorne's directive "not to know the truth but to embrace many possible truths," Bercovitch argues, not only reflects the paradigmatic pluralist "premises of liberal society," but also functions as a strategy to enforce liberal consensus:

> To make choices involves alternatives; it requires us to reject or exclude on the ground that certain meanings are wrong or incompatible or mutually contradictory. To have choice (in Hawthorne's fiction) is to keep open the prospects for interpretation on the grounds that reality never means one thing or another but, rather, is Meaning fragmented by plural points of view. . . And by these principles, to opt for meaning in all its multifariousness. . .is to obviate not only the conflicts embodied in opposing views but also the contradictions implicit in the very act of personal interpretation between the fact of multiple meaning and the imperative of self-assertion (*Office*, 13, 21–22).

Ambiguity's aesthetic pluralism, in other words, is fundamentally ideological. Since ambiguity configures truth as an aggregation of points of view rather than as any particular perspective, it undermines the foundation that generates political conflict: ambiguity thwarts one's confidence in the rightness of one's opinion.

This revisionary account of ambiguity as a liberal strategy for disabling "self assertion" is amplified by Bercovitch's discussion of irony in his next chapter, "The Ironies of A-History." In this chapter, Bercovitch turns his attention to irony – a trope that has been nearly as endemic to modern Hawthorne criticism as ambiguity – redescribing it as "the complementary" pole of "Hawthorne's aesthetics of liberalism" (*Office*, 39). If ambiguity encourages a mode of interpretation that foregrounds competing versions of synchronic meaning, irony, Bercovitch argues, extends this complication of singular meaning onto a diachronic register. Irony introduces a historical pluralism into the process of interpretation. By situating the act of interpretation within a historical continuum, irony demonstrates the limitations of any temporally situated interpretation. Irony installs a temporal predicament at the center of the act of interpretation. Establishing an inevitable rupture between the historical specificity of an intention and its long-range consequences, irony demonstrates the necessity of a more comprehensive temporal framework than any time-bound individual can hope to attain.

Irony's function in liberal thought, according to Bercovitch, is to represent History as operating according to

> a devious, unpredictable, often 'tortuous,' but eventually benevolent pattern, and [irony] invites us to recognize that our best recourse is to let it be (*Office*, 41).

That is, irony asserts the presence of a higher order of historical coherence only to inscribe the illegibility of the present. Irony provides History with a "providential unconscious"; it educates one to privilege "normal," "oblique," "gradualistic," and "cumulative" change because it classifies particular calls for revolutionary change as at best hopelessly ineffective and at worst profoundly dangerous (*Office*, 65, 39). Irony renders liberal society the historical society par excellence, but this drive to contextualize meaning ultimately serves to delegitimate radical action. Irony reassures one that such action is unnecessary: "Man's accidents," as Hawthorne was fond of saying, "are God's purposes" (*Office*, 39).

Bercovitch presents these literary tropes as the primary techniques for enforcing a liberal consensus because these tropes direct the force of the particular, the concrete, and the local towards the abstract and universal. Ambiguity enforces multiple meanings by representing any concrete meaning as a reduction of the many semantic possibilities contained within a sign; and irony deracinates the notion of historical change, shifting the source of progress from the historically particular to a perspective that transcends such embeddedness. And as becomes graphically evident in *The Office of The Scarlet Letter*'s next chapter, "The Red Badge of Compromise," Bercovitch assumes that particularism poses the greatest threat to the symbolic unity of America. Examining the failure of compromise during the antebellum period, Bercovitch explains this failing as a sign of the nation's collective unwillingness to subsume individual and substantive differences within the notion of America. Such a failure of the symbolic, Bercovitch argues, is what ultimately leads to the Civil War.

As Bercovitch explains, in 1850 the concept of "consensus through concession" (i.e. compromise) did not "carry the primarily pejorative meaning it does today" (*Office*, 100). Imagined as a heroic expression of an American tradition, the act of compromise still possessed the authority of the Constitution and meant, "above all," "'to bind by mutual agreement,' where the principles binding had the doubled force of contract and covenant" (*Office*, 100). However, according to Bercovitch, between 1848 and 1852, the years Bercovitch sets as the context of *The Scarlet Letter*, the notion of compromise "was undergoing decisive change," taking on the increasingly negative sense of a shameful concession (*Office*, 100). During these years, as the North and the South, abolitionists and slaveholders, Whigs and Democrats were growing more and more committed to the absolute truth of their opposing, partisan beliefs and thus less and less willing to negotiate the particularity of their positions, the positive connotations of "compromise" were replaced by the notion of compromise as a disreputable and dangerous surrender of principles.[13] According to this narrative, as meaning grew more and more material, literal, and definite, America's aesthetic strategies for consensus and cohesion collapsed. The particularity of different substantial meanings overwhelmed liberal ideology's ability to unsettle the threat of substantive meaning – the symbolic apparatus of American liberalism was failing.

In the last chapter, "The Paradoxes of Dissent," Bercovitch makes clear the implicit homology between America's representation of materiality and definite meaning and its idealization of individualism. In this chapter he returns to the question of Hester's rebellion, focusing on how the American ideology reproduces itself on the level of the individual. According to Bercovitch, the antagonism between the individual self and the oppressive restraints of society (the fundamental opposition that structures liberal political thought) ultimately reflects the representative American strategy for social cohesion and control, recapitulating America's relentless effort to subsume particularity. Because radical individuality has always already been translated into an abstract and formal language of individualism, America actually promotes "tolerance, accommodation, pluralism, acquiescence, inaction" by championing individual rebellion (*Office*, 8). As he puts it, in America "socialization is a matter not of repressing radical energies but of redirecting them, in all their radical force, into a continuing opposition between self and society" (*Office*, 120). By dissolving the political specificity of any radical action into the an amorphous category of *the rebel*, America renders the liberal "conviction that society is the enemy of the self" the foundation "upon which consensus paradoxically depends" (*Office*, 147). In America, difference ends up signaling nothing but our commonality, in the same way that interpretative difference ultimately abolishes itself.

As this summary of Bercovitch's argument suggests, Bercovitch is troubled by the way that the symbol of America rewrites radical difference (whether of meaning, act, or identity) in terms of a higher-level, abstract sameness. Thus, for Bercovitch, the scarlet letter fulfills its office when it finally subordinates the urgency of Hester's particular situation: by reattaching the letter, Hester is not submitting to any specific interpretation of the meaning of the *A*, but rather learning to "deflect, defuse, or at least defer" definite meaning, to transmute the "inherently explosive conflict" generated by particular interpretations of the letter (the "politics of either/or") into "a faith" in the harmonious "politics of both/and" (*Office*, 12, 9).

Although such a critique of liberalism for its impulse toward abstraction resonates with the suspicion of universalism currently ascendant in discourse on US literature, it departs from a tendency in recent political discourse to critique American liberalism for abandoning communal coherence. For Bercovitch, the triumph of American liberalism is not the triumph of the private self over the intrusive state, of the *oikos* over the *polis*, but the transformation of individuality into the basis of a hegemonic collective identity. The problem with liberal individualism in America, according to Bercovitch, is that it has never really been individual enough.[14]

LIBERAL FORMALISM

As is probably clear, the terms (ambiguity, irony, symbol, and paradox) structuring Bercovitch's description of the ideological power of America bear an uncanny resemblance to the terms that the New Critics privileged in their accounts of poetic meaning. Although Bercovitch never explicitly makes the connection between his account of liberal hermeneutics and the New Critical model of literary interpretation, the filiation is not difficult to uncover. Not only are the tropes which Bercovitch designates as guiding liberal exegesis the primary analytical tools of the New Critics, but also these tropes of apparent conflict and uncertainty, according to both Bercovitch and the New Critics, actually produce continuity, coherence, and unity rather than difference and discord. Indeed, after reading *The Office of The Scarlet Letter* one is left with the impression that "the principles of liberal exegesis" are essentially the principles of New Critical hermeneutics and that a century later the New Critics simply paraphrased the "enormous imaginative resources of mid-nineteenth-century American liberalism" in order to develop their literary theory (*Office*, 22, 155).

By linking the aesthetic idiom of New Critical formalism with the political register of liberal pluralism, *The Office of The Scarlet Letter* can be viewed as an ideological revision of Charles Feidelson's *Symbolism and American Literature*, perhaps the most influential New Critical reading of "the American Renaissance." According to Feidelson, the "American Renaissance" is the period in which the symbol grew dominant (the scarlet letter, the white whale, Walden Pond). Although Feidelson declares that his is a purely aesthetic argument, the vision of the literary symbol that he presents suggestively prefigures Bercovitch's ideological account of America.[15] Focusing on the formal properties rather than the particular content of this nation's "great" literature, Feidelson celebrates the symbol's focus on "mean*ing* rather than the meant" as the ideal aesthetic device for transcending the "patent dualisms" that threaten to divide perception (*Symbolism*, 53, 214). Arguing that the symbol abjures any attempt to "absolute knowledge," Feidelson explains that symbolism presents meaning as "essentially fluid" and "indeterminate" (*Symbolism*, 72,73). Symbolism "embraces the infinity of poetic meaning," and in doing so redefines meaning neither as the security of determinate meaning, nor as the nihilism of the "meaninglessness of meaning" but as the "drama" of "the meaningfulness of meaning," (*Symbolism*, 74).[16] Bercovitch suggests that Feidelson's aesthetic appreciation of the literary symbol's semantic overload is simply liberalism by other means. It appears that Bercovitch is arguing that the office of *The Scarlet Letter* is to teach its readers the principles of the New Criticism, as if the closer one comes to being a proleptic New Critic, the more one becomes ideologically liberal.

The tropes of New Criticism offer Bercovitch an ideal vocabulary with which to describe logic of the American ideology because Bercovitch, as if a latter-day Whitman, imagines America as the world's greatest poem. If the New Critics argued that the kind of knowledge that the poem presented was hermetic, unavailable in and superior to any other linguistic formulation, precisely because the poem exceeded the protocols of normal reference, Bercovitch, similarly, foregrounds how the symbol America exceeds all substantive meaning.[17] America simply means itself. For Bercovitch, the crucial ideological fact about America is aesthetic: America, like the poem, has eluded the categories of a specific reference and of an intelligible content.[18] What the New Critics called the "heresy of paraphrase" (any effort to derive an explicit meaning from a poem), Bercovitch translates as a form of unAmericanness. Thus, whereas the New Critics legitimated their claim for the unique cultural significance of poetry by declaring that whatever the poem "communicated is mauled and distorted if we attempt to convey it by any vehicle less subtle than that of the poem itself," Bercovitch argues that America proves itself impossible to oppose according to the same logic.[19] And since the "meaning" of America is that it does not "mean" in any definite referential manner, America remains fundamentally beyond the referential language of politics.

That is, although Bercovitch seeks to examine an object that the New Critics would consider inappropriate and violates the New Critical conviction that literary texts are essentially autonomous, he perhaps must be seen not as overturning but as extending the principles of the New Critics to spheres under-illuminated by the New Criticism. The very strategies that the New Critics deployed to explain the irreducibility of a poem, Bercovitch re-identifies as the means by which America has mystified itself as a transcendent space emptied of any specificity or literality. Although one may imagine that such a lack of meaning would either produce anarchy or inspire a search for more definite meaning, Bercovitch, like the New Critics, argues that it is specifically this abjuring of an *a priori* meaning that has allowed America to triumph, to evade the dangerous fall into particularity that has inevitably disabled traditional ideologies (it is such a substantial foundation that permits an ideology to be disputed and subjected to determinate critiques). It is because America has been so thoroughly figuralized that it has managed to remain an invulnerable ideological icon, one that can absorb all forms of difference and dissent, categorizing such difference and dissent as merely partial expressions of a more comprehensive vision of America.[20]

By foregrounding the deep linkages between liberal politics and a particular style of interpretation, Bercovitch suggests an ideological explanation for why allegory has been so definitively exiled from classic accounts of American literary history. If to have no essence is the essence of American liberal culture, then it is to be expected that dominant accounts of US literary history have denounced allegory, the figure that has traditionally (at least since the Romantics) been cast as enforcing a particular, dogmatic interpretation. To the degree that allegory has been imagined as infected by a bias for content, it violates the principles of American liberal exegesis. Similarly, to the degree that the symbol has been imagined as infinitely plural and as exceeding both materiality and any literal content, it incarnates the American Way.[21]

The continuity between Bercovitch's New Americanist description of the directives of American liberal hermeneutics and Feidelson's exemplary New Critical principles, of course, signifies neither that Bercovitch desires to resurrect the New Criticism, nor that he is an unwitting disciple of the New Critics. Rather, the similarity foregrounds the extent to which Bercovitch identifies American liberalism itself as a kind of formalism, as a structure which subordinates particular questions about the substance or content of a poem to abstract questions about its form. Bercovitch appropriates the terminology of New Criticism because its interpretative procedures offer a powerful means to isolate the ideological formalism that he claims sustains the coherence of America. The institutionalization of such formalism suggests that this nation sanctions and encourages dissent (as a category) only because it simultaneously homogenizes, renders insubstantial, and disempowers any particular act of dissent. By uncovering the latent ideological force of the symbol, Bercovitch, one might say, fulfills with a vengeance Feidelson's claim that symbolism is the "*governing* principle" of US literature (*Symbolism*, 43, emphasis added).

DEONTOLOGICAL LIBERALISM

I have rehearsed Bercovitch's argument in depth because it makes clear how profoundly interpretations of the A as an overdetermined symbol, a sign that signifies no definable content, have everything to do with the imperatives of liberal representation. For Bercovitch, the crucial feature of the American ideology is its ability to instaurate a hermeneutics that empties the signifier of a specific content, conjures the loss of such specificity as an advance in meaning, and creates America as figural space that embodies this process. But whereas, traditionally, America's capacity to absorb difference has been championed as progressive, Bercovitch reveals the darker aspects of this capacity, arguing that this displacement of specificity renders any call for radical change incoherent and thus enforces an inevitable acceptance of America. That is, to the extent that Bercovitch identifies literary formalism with liberalism, *The Office of The Scarlet Letter* allows us to appreciate not only Feidelson's *Symbolism in American Literature* as an implicitly political document but also John Rawls' *A Theory of Justice*, probably most significant post-World War II text on liberal political theory, as an implicitly aesthetic text.[22] Bercovitch's description of liberalism as fundamentally formalist suggestively echoes with Rawls' procedural and deontological account of liberalism. Bercovitch's representation of American liberalism as a structure that seeks to evacuate the force of particularity can, in short, be read as so capacious that it even incorporates Rawls' effort to establish a liberalism that avoids comprehensive and teleological premises within the symbolic logic of the scarlet letter.

A Theory of Justice attempts to develop a system of rights that does not anchor itself in any particular teleological theory of the Good. A teleological theory, i.e. one that defines a right action in terms of maximizing some ultimate sense of the Good (in the case of utilitarianism, for example, "the greatest good for the greatest number"), assumes an objective view of the individual and, Rawls argues, ultimately does not acknowledge the plural conceptions of the Good that individuals may hold. To the extent that a political theory depends upon an ontology of the Good, it fails, according to Rawls, to take seriously these competing versions of the Good and thereby conflates all people and diminishes the inevitable and substantive plurality of human desires and interests. In order to eschew a substantive conception of the Good, Rawls' deontological liberalism aspires toward a morally neutral proceduralism, one that privileges the individual by establishing a framework that avoids "claims to universal truth, or claims about the essential nature and identity of persons."[23] Such a version of liberalism is, in essence, a philosophy that is dedicated to bracketing definitive content. Rawls advocates a liberal theory whose primary commitment to individualism resides in its neutrality, its refusal to affirm any preferred substantive purpose, value, or end.

What Rawls calls deontological liberalism and a "thin theory of the good" corresponds quite strikingly with what Bercovitch calls the symbolic logic of American liberalism. Bercovitch's account of the American symbology shares with deontological liberalism the claim that liberalism offers only a set of formal principles rather than a particular or predetermined interpretation. According to each, one might say, liberalism offers a set of interpretative procedures – for Bercovitch the symbol, for Rawls the Original Position – that share a common logic: accepting the pluralistic equivalence of concrete cultural, personal, and political contents by diminishing any reference to the particularity of such contents. For both, liberalism is a structure, which, in contrast to substantive theories of social organization, brands any specific meaning or identity as arbitrary and contingent and thus attempts to transcend such particularism. Even though Bercovitch, unlike Rawls, sees the jettisoning of all unique or distinguishing characteristics not as a utopian promise (allowing an individual to choose ends) but as a dynamic of control (devaluing any individual choice), both hold onto an analogous account of liberalism. For both, liberalism privileges abstract form over the specificity of content. The question of how this version of liberalism (liberalism as abstraction) has achieved its ascendancy is what a rereading of the scarlet letter most powerfully allows. That is, what needs to be examined is not whether such abstraction is in itself progressive or regressive but how liberalism came to be linked so indissolubly with the logic of abstraction.

'THE SCARLET LETTER' AS IDENTITY MARKER

If Bercovitch's argument brilliantly explores how American liberalism (as both a political and a literary formation) has been characterized by a constitutive prejudice against specificity, I want to suggest a counter-narrative, to explore the assumptions on which such an account of the US liberal tradition depends. For my purposes, what is significant about Bercovitch's account of liberalism as an apparatus that relentlessly conspires to efface concrete content or exact meaning in multiple spheres of American culture is how this account depends upon a particular set of assumptions about the identity of the "person."

The notion of the "person" informing Bercovitch's reading of America becomes explicit when Bercovitch explains the relationship between Hester's "sainted individualism" and Emerson's transcendental metaphysics. According to Bercovitch,

> Emersonian self-reliance identifies dissent as the quintessentially American gesture and then universalizes it as the radical imperative to subjectivity. From either perspective, the gap-to-be-bridged elicits our opposition by providing a barrier to the *wrong kind of process – the kind, for example, that would "reduce" dissent to the "merely social" terms of race, class, or gender.* Or in positive terms, it directs our opposition toward American dissent by *translating such categories as race, class, and gender as social "limitations," to be transcended en route to representative individualism,* a sainted subjectivity of one's own, like Hester's prophecy of the ideal woman actualized in her own penitence *to be* (*Office*, 146, emphasis added).

In this account, "race, class, or gender" do not mark the representative American because such identity categories have been fashioned as too particular, too full of content. Race, class, and gender are merely "social limitations," accidents "to be transcended en route to representative individualism," inessential or secondary features to be included within the abstract American self. These identity categories, Bercovitch suggests, signify in the same way that the scarlet letter signifies: their substantive meaning is subsumed into a larger liberal narrative.

At this moment it becomes clear that reading the A as an indeterminate and inessential sign is itself affiliated with a set of assumptions about the "person" and about race, gender, and class. *The Scarlet Letter*, Bercovitch suggests, undermines the ascription of any crucial content to the A in the same way that American liberalism renders race, gender, and class merely contingent signs. Bercovitch's analogizing the A to race, class, and gender reveals the extent to which readings of the A have everything to do with a particular understanding of the significance of markers of personal identity. The linking of the A and race, for example, signals how ascriptive markers (like the A and like race) have been emptied of any specific content, have, in short, been imagined as no more defining of identity than a wig, an article of clothing, or jewelry. Readings of race, gender and class, in other words, have come to look a lot like readings of the A: each is seen as merely an incidental signifier.

Contained within the affiliation between interpretation and ideology that Bercovitch establishes, in other words, is a second story: a story about how the style of interpretation incited by Hawthorne's text simultaneously enforces a way to understand the nation and to understand the "person." American liberal hermeneutics, Bercovitch suggests, constructs a style of interpretation that works simultaneously on the national and the personal level, neutralizing empirical differences in understandings not only of America but of Americans. And it is the A that incarnates this ideological process of emptying the content of everything American.

Bercovitch, of course, is quite aware that this nation has, at various moments in its history, declared women, African-Americans, Native Americans, immigrants, Catholics, and the poor essentially ineligible to claim the protections of liberal rights precisely because they were understood as irreducibly and materially different – indeed, it is because he is acutely aware of such practices that when discussing race, gender, and class, he puts the words "merely social" and "limitations" in scare quotes. Nonetheless, Bercovitch focuses on how liberalism defers and departicularizes substantive differences rather than on how liberalism has historically sanctioned and depended upon certain substantive notions of the "person" to construct both national and personal identity. Imagining the exclusion of such groups as less defining of American liberalism than their eventual inclusion, Bercovitch implies that such groups incorporated themselves within America by redescribing their intractable material differences as fundamentally contingent, as inessential qualities that do not encumber the abstract equality of the American Self.

Bercovitch, in short, makes clear that the way one reads the scarlet letter carries with it a set of assumptions about the "person." I want to suggest that Bercovitch's reading of the scarlet letter as a contentless sign is itself incited by the liberal imperative to remove the "person" from history. Bercovitch's linking of readings of the A and readings of race, gender, and class (I will focus predominantly on race) reveals how deeply modern readers have read the A as a polyvalent symbol because modern readers begin with the premise that the meaning of one's identity cannot be reduced to surface markers, whether they be the A or race. That is, rather than argue that *The Scarlet Letter* is the "liberal example par excellence of art as ideological mimesis," I want to approach *The Office of "The Scarlet Letter"* as a liberal example of criticism as ideological mimesis. If Bercovitch suggests that Hawthorne's text enforces a particular style of interpreting, I want to reverse Bercovitch's claim in order to explore how the style of interpretation that Bercovitch identifies as governing the logic of *The Scarlet Letter* is itself a symptom of liberalism.

The style of interpretation (New Critical, anti-literal) that Bercovitch builds upon, I want to suggest, emanates from a historically particular moment, a moment when a formal rather than a substantive account of the "person" appears nearly self-evident. It has become easy to read the scarlet letter as a contingent marker, I am suggesting, precisely because we now regularly read identity markers (like race) as contingent markers, as identity categories to be transcended for one's true "personhood" to be expressed. It is precisely such contingency, however, that needs to be the subject of historical inquiry rather than taken as the ground of an interpretation.

The anti-essentialist and disembodied model of the "person" that orients Bercovitch's account of America's genius at absorbing difference, in other words, is neither as obvious nor as historically continuous as Bercovitch's reading of American liberalism assumes it to be. In this sense, Bercovitch puts the cart before the horse, deploying rather than interrogating the notion of the "person." Although Bercovitch homologizes American liberalism and the A because he assumes that liberalism, at least in theory, is always driven by such a contentless account of the "person," it is precisely this account that was in question during the antebellum period. Thus, to render both America and the A in terms of the liberal imperative to represent all identity markers as merely interesting accidents is far from an innocent interpretation. It proceeds as if the relationship between "personhood" and identity markers (such as skin color, hair, the size of the skull, or the A) is always already self-evident. This issue is beyond debate today, but during the antebellum period it was the subject of intense national debate. During the 1850s, the question of whether identity markers possessed a merely contingent relationship to "personhood" was far from obvious. Bercovitch's reading of the ideological office of *The Scarlet Letter*, in other words, never confronts the question of how the novel and his reading of the novel might be entering into on-going debates about "personhood" very differently.

The facility with which Bercovitch builds a model for reading America from a reading of the A marks the extent to which we have foreclosed readings of the scarlet letter as anything but an indeterminate signifier because we have always already been working with a particular account of the "person," one in which race, gender, class etc are arbitrary signifiers, signs that bear merely a contingent relation to true identity. In the following section, I want to focus on what prevailing interpretations have regularly precluded: the possibility that the A possesses a fixed content. I will not be offering a new reading of the scarlet letter as much as suggesting that readings of *The Scarlet Letter* have persistently suspended the possibility of the A as a determined sign, and by doing so, have linked the A to a modern anti-essentialist conception of the "person" and dislinked the meaning of the letter from antebellum debates over the notion of the "person." Prevailing anti-literalist readings of *The Scarlet Letter* have implicitly precluded significant historical questions about the "person," assuming that the A is obviously an open sign rather than asking what assumptions are involved in interpreting the scarlet letter as an essential or a contingent sign, as literal or figural. That is, I am not disputing Bercovitch's point that the A functions like a racial marker, but questioning whether during the antebellum period racial markers so clearly work in the way that Bercovitch represents them.

BERCOVITCH AND TOCQUEVILLE

Bercovitch makes America into a deontological construct, I have suggested, because he is following a long tradition that conflates liberalism with a thoroughly abstract and disembodied "person." In order to foreground the extent to which the "person" motivating Bercovitch's account of the relationship between surface markers and identity is itself a thoroughly contested one, I will turn to an antebellum observer of US liberal culture, one often seen as a precursor of Bercovitch, who understands identity as originating in, rather than transcending, particular aspects of the body and who appeals to rather than denies the fact that the visible surface of bodies determined the substantive content of "personhood."[24]

When Alexis de Tocqueville looked at the antebellum United States, he predicted that the liberal equality he discovered there would inexorably expand to encompass the entire world. Tocqueville explains that he wrote *Democracy in America* in order to prepare his readers for the time when equality would be as total in the rest of world as it had become in the United States. The work exhorts readers to try to control equality's seemingly ineluctable momentum: although the movement is "too strong to be halted," it is "not yet," Tocqueville avers, "so swift that we must despair of directing it."[25] Since Tocqueville believes that equality threatens to abolish all distinctions and to foster a despotic uniformity, *Democracy in America* is full of warnings about democracy's leveling impulse, the tyranny of majority opinion, and the atomization produced by the equality of social conditions.[26]

In fact, the grand theme of *Democracy in America* is the tension between the equivalences initiated by democracy or equality – Tocqueville uses these terms interchangeably – and the differentiation that individual liberty demands. "I know of no country," Tocqueville asserts, "in which, speaking generally, there is less independence of mind and true freedom of discussion than in America" (254–255). More than a system of government, democracy, as Tocqueville describes it, is a cultural force, which effaces particularity in every aspect of modern life. The American love for equality explains why the "passions" of Americans have "a sort of family likeness," one, which Tocqueville complains, "soon renders the survey of them exceedingly wearisome" (240). Democracies install such abstract sameness not only within a citizen's heart, but also within a citizen's head: "Democracies," Tocqueville explains, "have a taste, and often a passion, for general ideas . . . generic terms and abstract words," because it is believed that such generality "widens the scope of thought," allowing a word or idea to function more democratically, to circulate in many different contexts and among various speakers (482–483). The democratic citizen loses any appreciation of difference and develops an "ardent and often blind passion" to discover "common rules for everything, to include a great number of objects under the same formula" (439).

In *Democracy in America*, Tocqueville, however, does more than just conjoin the traditional opposition between equality and individual liberty with a discursive antagonism between generality and particularity. Not only is the erasure of particularity in the political sphere coincident with the loss of particularity in the realm of language, but, Tocqueville predicts, democracy will extend its sway beyond the structure of politics and of language and eventually reach a society's literal expression: in "our day," Tocqueville laments, "everything threatens to become so much alike that the particular features of each individual may soon be entirely lost in the common physiognomy" (701). In Tocqueville's view, equality, as if possessed by an overpowering urge to eliminate distinctions of all kinds, manifests a dangerous rage at all forms of non-identity. The imperialist force of equivalence, Tocqueville fears, will totalize equality and thereby eradicate all aspects of differentiation, even those of a physical order.

So far, it appears that Tocqueville's account of America closely parallels Bercovitch's. Tocqueville's description of democracy's elimination of difference resembles the formalizing that Bercovitch will later identify as the sustaining principle of liberal America. The loss of individualizing content that Tocqueville dreads has, according to Bercovitch, been fulfilled. But, even as Tocqueville voices his fears concerning the ominous force of democratic abstraction, he, nevertheless, confirms that in the United States there are still material limits to the seemingly all-inclusive reach of equality. He acknowledges that even though the democratic citizen may see "nothing but people more or less like himself" and cannot "think about one branch of mankind without widening his view until it includes the whole," the "Negro and the Indian," the two other "races" which inhabit the United States, stand beyond the logic of equivalence that dominates America (439).

Indeed, Tocqueville is especially disturbed by America's intolerance of racial difference. Thus, Tocqueville recounts the way the United States has been able systematically to enforce the gradual disappearance of the Indian with "wonderful ease, quietly, legally, and philanthropically, without spilling blood and without violating a single one of the great principles of morality." "It is," he sarcastically concludes, "impossible to destroy men with more respect to the laws of humanity" (339).[27] Although Tocqueville never explicitly states why the "red man" is killed rather than absorbed into America, he suggests that such systematic genocide occurs because America cannot accept the Indian's essential racial difference from the white man. In other words, the leveling force of American equality cannot overcome the hard fact of the "red man's" material difference and therefore America claims that the "red man" is outside the category of the "person" and can be legitimately exterminated. Tocqueville finds such thinking barbaric. But he condemns this practice not because he imagines the Indian as fundamentally the same as the American (he clearly does not). Rather what he condemns is America's inability to recognize such essential difference as justifiable. The "Indian race," Tocqueville concludes, "is doomed to perish" not because democracy fails, but because democracy succeeds too well: democracy's universalizing imperative cannot acknowledge the inexorable reality of racial difference (326).[28]

When Tocqueville turns to a discussion of the position of the "Negro" in the United States, he offers a similar assessment of the limits of America's drive toward abstraction. Tocqueville recognizes the inevitable movement of democratic formalism, but he simultaneously recognizes that such a formalist drive cannot figuralize racial essences. Tocqueville acknowledges that the law may abolish slavery and institute equal rights, but the Negro, Tocqueville claims, will always be a "stranger" to the American since "only God can obliterate [slavery's] traces" in the material appearance of the Negro (341). The problem that modern slavery uniquely produces, according to Tocqueville, is that in it, unlike in the case of ancient slavery, "the insubstantial and ephemeral fact of servitude is most fatally combined with the physical and permanent fact of difference in race"; the Negro, Tocqueville explains, always "transmits to his descendants at birth the external mark of his ignominy" (341). All who hope that the European will one day mingle with the Negro are therefore "harboring under a delusion." Slavery may be a historically contingent institution and produce historically particular inequalities, but having been linked to the eternal fact of race, slavery becomes more than an alterable status; its effects become natural. Thus, what separates the two races, according to Tocqueville, are not merely "artificial barriers" but an inequality "founded on visible and indelible signs" (342). Since the material difference of the Negro "is immovable," the social differences of the Negro will always remain (344).[29]

Thus, even though Tocqueville shares Bercovitch's suspicion of abstraction, he does not share Bercovitch's understanding of identity markers (such as race) as contingent. For Tocqueville, some somatic characteristics are signs of natural differences. Tocqueville's classically liberal discussion of the inevitable threat of equality is founded upon the fear that material differences are not sufficiently solid and therefore can be threatened by democracy's drive for abstract or formal equivalencies, but this fear is not synonymous with the claim that all material differences are equally formalizable.[30] According to Tocqueville, some differences are objective facts – existing as physical markers to be acknowledged, markers that reflect an essential content to be discovered not erased. Like Bercovitch, Tocqueville argues that the mechanics of America works to obliterate the specific content of individual bodies, but, unlike Bercovitch, Tocqueville never imagines that such figuralism can overcome the marks of nature. For both, the erasure of particularity is threatening, but Tocqueville never imagines America's leveling impulse as erasing the differences of race.

It is clear to us why Tocqueville comprehended race in such essentialist terms: he was embedded in a century when race was seen as crucially structuring identity, as determining social practice rather than reflecting it. And it is equally clear why Bercovitch does not see race in such ways: he is embedded in a moment when race is seen primarily in constructionist terms, the very category itself having been rendered a dubious biological certainty by scholars in innumerable disciplines. Thus Bercovitch, like most contemporary thinkers, regards identity categories such as race as contingent, while Tocqueville, like most during the nineteenth century, imagines Blackness as inscribed by Nature. Whereas Bercovitch sees race as a mark imposed by convention and practice (he calls it a "merely social" term), Tocqueville shares an antebellum account of race as an essential sign, one that precedes practice rather than one produced by practice. The dissolution of the body as a certain marker of personal identity can perhaps be regarded as inaugurating modern liberal thought, but during the antebellum period corporeality was not yet an empty sign.

Bercovitch, in other words, is not simply wrong in claiming that the values of liberalism are fundamentally equivalent to the values embodied in the New Critical symbol and in assuming that liberal political theory repudiates the literal and the material. The liberalism of Rawls and New Critical hermeneutics are such kinds of formalisms. But to claim that the cultural symbology of antebellum America initiated a similar formalism assumes that the relationship between racial markers and "personhood" structuring modern liberal representation also structured antebellum liberal representation. Bercovitch, one might say, is right about the wrong version of liberalism.[31]

Bercovitch is giving an account of the cultural work that identity markers, like the A, now perform for us, offering a reading of the A that foregrounds the relationship between the A and "personhood" but ultimately obscures antebellum arguments over the "person." Indeed, since Bercovitch interrogates liberal representation without interrogating the historicity of the figure that grounds liberal representation, his reading exemplifies rather than critiques the logic of liberal representation. Bercovitch is not misreading the particular liberal office of the scarlet letter but he is reading it in a way that reflects contemporary assumptions about the "person." Bercovitch reading of the cultural symbology of America, in other words, itself participates in the institutionalizing of the historically contested claim that markers of identity (such as the A) do not determine "personhood." Thus, if on one hand, Bercovitch makes visible the reciprocity between interpretations of the indeterminacy of American literature and liberal pluralism, he simultaneously demonstrates how such readings of US literary and political history have reproduced the liberal impulse to deploy rather than examine the notion of the "person." What is missing from Bercovitch's argument, in short, is an account of how reading the scarlet letter in formal rather than substantive terms itself participates in a debate about "personhood."

THE SCARLET LETTER

I am arguing that the tradition of championing the unlimited multiplicity of the A testifies to how readings of *The Scarlet Letter*, the nation's "first instant classic," have carried with them a specific set of assumptions about the significance of identity markers (*Office*, xix). By pre-empting literal readings of the A, an unexamined anti-essentialist notion of the "person" has, for all intents and purposes, been installed at the center of readings of US literary history. Just as the physical markers of racial identity are now assumed to be signs without content rather than crucial markers of the "person," the A is almost axiomatically regarded as much more than its literal meaning. Thus, unlike Sophia Hawthorne who understood her husband's novel as representing how "the Law cannot be broken," modern critics have been excited by *The Scarlet Letter* because the A is polysemic, a signifier that exceeds any effort to specify its significance.[32] In the distance between Sophia Hawthorne's understanding of the A as possessing a fixed content (adultery) and contemporary readings of the A as without any specific content is writ small the movement from antebellum to contemporary culture, the transition from debating to denying any self-evident correlation between surface markers and "personhood."

To say that modern readers have interpreted the A in the same way that the material phenomenon of race has been interpreted is not to say that Hester is covertly Black, but to call attention to how critics have implicitly established an analogy between the A and identity markers like race and then interpreted such an analogy within a wholly modern framework. That is, I am not arguing that Hawthorne is representing the A as a racial marker – even though the novel suggestively represents Hester's A as the mark of the Black Man – but claiming that modern critics have set up such a correspondence and having done so, proceed to read this racialized mark in anachronistic terms.[33]

To the extent that the signifier of race has now been securely branded a false signifier – a distortion of what a "person" is – critics have located the complexity and interest of the letter in its contingency and have separated the historical problem of racism from the signifying logic of the scarlet letter. And to the extent that the letter is regularly read as rehearsing "the difficulty of understanding the inner state from the outward signs," modern readings of the A recapitulate the contemporary (but not contemporaneous) assumption that ascriptive markers of identity are fundamentally mistaken.[34] Thus, moments, such as the one in the forest when Pearl compels her mother to reattach the A, that seem to foreground the problem of deciding whether the A is a permanent or provisional identity marker have been approached as if the question were always already answered. This moment, however, could be read as offering two legitimately conflicting accounts of the A: whereas Hester treats the letter as if it were an article of clothing that can be fastened or removed, Pearl understands the letter not as a contingent token but as a sign that expresses Hester's essential identity. To the extent that the A is always already interpreted as wholly social, a particular understanding of the relationship between surface markers and identity has been incorporated into a reading of the A.

By the conclusion of the novel, however, Hester has abandoned the reading of the A she held in the forest and has come to believe that she will never be able to resignify the meaning of the A:

> Earlier in life, Hester had vainly imagined that she herself might be the destined prophetess, but had long since recognized the impossibility that any mission of divine and mysterious truth should be confided to a woman stained with sin, bowed down with shame, or even burdened with a life-long sorrow. The angel and apostle of the coming revelation must be a woman, indeed, but lofty, pure, and beautiful; and wise, moreover, not through the dusky grief, but the ethereal medium of joy (263).

Indeed, in the end it is the townspeople, rather than Hester, who interpret the A as a crucially fluid token, as a mark whose meaning is plastic, now filled "with awe" and "reverence too" (262). In accepting the unalterable force of the letter, Hester once again stands apart from the people of Boston.

Given this trajectory of Hester's understanding of the A, one could say that modern readers tend to comprehend the A in the very way that Hester learns to reject: modern readers foreground how the A can be embroidered and elaborated upon, assuming its meaning to be open and revisable rather than natural and fixed. The fact that the A's meaning as a polyvalent sign has become consistently privileged – despite the changing cast of characters in the novel who maintain this line of argument – suggests the extent to which modern readings are committed to a particular mode of interpretation in and of itself, going so far as to separate this style of reading from the context of the text. What is being championed is the assumption that surface markers of identity are contingent. What is being passed over is that such an assumption may be self-evident today but is a question in the text and was in question during the antebellum period. The degree to which the A is imagined as fundamentally removable, in other words, has come to be directly proportional to the degree that race has been imagined as fundamentally inessential.

Indeed, the axiomatic linking of the A to a contingent understanding of the relationship between identity markers and "personhood" has incited critics to distinguish the A from antebellum conceptualizations of race. That is, if the A is idealized as a fundamentally contingent sign (how race is now read), antebellum culture is typically represented as operating according to a mistaken and obsolete signifying logic of racism. Thus, Brook Thomas, in a recent discussion of Hester as an exemplar of how a civil society develops, observes how Hawthorne's description of the A as "a mark, a brand, a badge of shame, and a stigma" uncannily anticipates Chief Justice Taney's use of similar metaphors to explain in the Dred Scott case why Blacks – whether free or slave – could never become citizens of the United States.[35] As Thomas notes, Taney argued that

> 'the deep and enduring marks of inferiority and degradation' implanted on blacks had so 'stigmatized' them that they were excluded from the sovereign body constituting the nation.

Contrasting the way that a "badge can be removed" from the way a stigma is immovable, "implanted for a lifetime," Thomas dislinks the rhetoric of stigma (Blackness) and the rhetoric of the badge (the A).[36] According to Thomas, African Americans were denied citizenship through their individual efforts because "their race meant that, as group, they inherited a badge of slavery, whose stigma persisted," in contrast Hester's A is "her 'badge of shame'," a marker that she can choose to wear (202). Thomas privileges the logic of the A and is anxious about the way that "race. . .marks an important limit" to the novel's emphasis on civic choice (201).

Thomas' argument is significant because it notes the possible continuity between readings of the letter and antebellum readings of race and then interrupts it. And it is a modern certainty about the contingency of race (as opposed to the essentialism of racism) that produces this interruption. This certainty exemplifies the extent to which readings of the A and modern readings of the "person" have converged, foregrounding the extent to which readings of the A's semantic undecidability are tied to an idealized and decontextualized understanding of the "person," one that inevitably rejects any racialized conception of identity. We read the A in the same way we read race and never imagine that race could ever be legitimately comprehended as an essential identity marker. Such a position is itself a symptom of the distance between antebellum and modern culture. Readings of the letter as obviously elastic and of the liberal imagination as fundamentally driven by abstraction, in short, are a function of twentieth-century historiography.

In this chapter rather than arguing that Hawthorne intends *The Scarlet Letter* to be, either explicitly or implicitly, an allegory about race or slavery – indeed, it is unclear if such a claim could be substantiated except suggestively through metaphoric resonances – I have focused on the way that modern criticism has constructed readings of the novel's central identity marker that are informed by a particular set of assumptions about race and identity. Since I am not arguing that the A be read as a racial marker, no specific reading is inevitable from this argument about the way that readings of the scarlet letter have been grounded on a decontextualized notion of race. I am only claiming that such an analogy between the A and race has structured modern criticism and that this analogy has not been historicized. I am suggesting that this analogy has not been historicized because the antebellum debate over the relationship between race and "personhood" has been erased.

The following chapter will focus on Hawthorne's last completed romance *The Marble Faun* to suggest how Hawthorne explicitly participated in antebellum debates over how to represent "personhood." That is, if this chapter has foregrounded how modern readings of Hawthorne's hypercanonical novel have depended upon the mystification of the "person," the following chapter will turn to *The Marble Faun* to foreground what Hawthorne imagines the "person" to be.[37]

CHAPTER 5

The art of discrimination: The Marble Faun, *"Chiefly About War Matters," and the aesthetics of anti-black racism*

In the Postscript he claims to have added "reluctantly" to the second edition of *The Marble Faun* (1860), Nathaniel Hawthorne addresses his readers' numerous demands "for further elucidation respecting the mysteries of the story."[1] Although presumably intended to resolve the story's mysteries, this Postscript is, for the most part, Hawthorne's lament over the fact that so many of the book's literal-minded readers want to know whether Donatello really is a Faun. Standing precariously "between the Real and the Fantastic," this anomalous creature, Hawthorne states, should have "excited [the reader] to a certain pleasurable degree, without impelling him to ask how Cuvier would have classified poor Donatello, or insist on being told, in so many words, whether he had furry ears or no" (463–464). Hawthorne's point is clear. If readers translate Donatello into the realist register of comparative anatomy, all they will discover is that they do not know "how to read a Romance." Hawthorne urges his readers to let Donatello simply be; let him, that is, remain a purely aesthetic creature, one who incarnates the epistemological instability of the Romance.

Given Hawthorne's insistence that the figure of the man/faun is subject only to the rules of the Romance, it is striking that shortly after writing *The Marble Faun*, Hawthorne himself resurrects this creature in his only piece of journalism on the Civil War. In "Chiefly About War Matters" (1862), his ostensibly realistic account of his trip to Washington DC to gather first-hand information about the war, Hawthorne comes across a group of fugitive slaves heading North:

> They were unlike the specimens of their race whom we are accustomed to see at the North, and, in my judgment, were far more agreeable. So rudely were they attired, – as if their garb had grown upon them spontaneously, – so picturesquely natural in manners, and wearing such a crust of primeval simplicity (which is quite polished away from the northern black man) they seem a kind of creature by themselves, not altogether human, but perhaps quite as good, and *akin to the fauns and rustic deities of olden times.*[2]

Apparently, the faun has escaped the realm of the Romance and entered the literal premises of Hawthorne's non-fiction. Indeed, even though Hawthorne claims that the seriousness of the Civil War has "compelled him" to "suspend the contemplation" of the "fantasies" he customarily writes, going so far as to assert that it would be "a kind of treason" to think such "idle thoughts in the dread time of civil war," it appears that when he looks closely at slavery – the social and moral problem at the center of the Civil War – he cannot help but apprehend it in Romance terms (299–300).

Although this hyper-aesthetic flourish may seem incongruous given the self-professed aims of Hawthorne's essay, it accords, as I have discussed in the Introduction, with a critical consensus concerning Hawthorne's notorious insensitivity to the historical problem of US slavery. Scholars have long been disturbed by Hawthorne's apparent refusal to take race-based slavery seriously, a refusal marked by his unwillingness to discuss slavery in anything but purely aesthetic terms, as a metaphor for psychological bondage. Typically, such aestheticizing has been approached in one of two ways: either as an unfortunate consequence of Hawthorne's chronic inability to engage the "real world" – temperamentally detached from his time, Hawthorne is more interested in Puritans than in Abolitionists, more devoted to slavery as an allegorical rather than a contemporaneous practice – or, as a deliberate and alarmingly conservative political strategy – Hawthorne intentionally constructed texts to encourage despair about concrete political action.[3] If one line of argument sees Hawthorne's interest in aesthetics as blinding him to politics, the other argues that Hawthorne invokes the aesthetic to blind others to political realities. This latter view is the one currently in vogue; Hawthorne is regularly indicted for a "derealizing style," a mode of representation that incites a relentless "indeterminacy" about the substance of politics and thus mystifies the possibility of concrete action.[4] Where once Hawthorne had no politics, now it seems that all he has are bad politics. Where once Hawthorne simply wanted to avoid the real world, now he is viewed in more insidious terms, regarded as actively misrepresenting the real world.

As scholars have increasingly emphasized Hawthorne's unpardonable politics, this *fauning* of Black slaves has come to stand as merely the most egregious instantiation of the primary ideological failing of Hawthorne's writing and thought: his use of the aesthetic to excuse, contain, or conceal the political problem of race-based slavery. Thus, Eric Cheyfitz has argued that Hawthorne's aestheticizing of Black slaves provides "an alibi" for the status quo, i.e. the continuing "dehumanization of these people," while Nancy Bentley contends that such aestheticizing allows Hawthorne to simultaneously acknowledge and "safely enclose" an "emblem of the real political crisis," and Evan Carton traces how the complex aesthetics of *The Marble Faun* attempts to repress the "actualities" of race and slavery (Cheyfitz, 556; Bentley, 59, 24; Carton, 109).[5] It is imagined, in short, that Hawthorne exploits the aesthetic to confound the hard facts of slavery.[6]

To discuss Hawthorne's representation of slaves as fauns in terms of a strategy of disavowal or distortion is to understand Hawthorne's aesthetic as in competition with the reality of slavery. Such an understanding dismisses the possibility that Hawthorne deploys the aesthetic to produce rather than deny real knowledge about slavery. Taking for granted that the truth of slavery is stable, self-evident, and always already produced, this account simply posits that US slavery obviously misidentifies "persons" as things. What is lost by such an approach is an appreciation of how it was precisely the question of whether the Negro is a "person" – a being who naturally deserved inalienable rights – that was being fiercely disputed during the antebellum period.

Although no longer a question for us, during the antebellum period, as I have discussed, questions about the "personhood" of the slave were being debated not only in the political and legal arenas, but also in scientific, religious, and aesthetic discourse. And, as I have argued, these debates hinged on the question of whether the Black slave was a "person." This nation's most influential scientists were debating the question of whether the Negro constituted a separate species and Biblical scholars were heatedly debating the question of whether there were multiple Creations. Once one appreciates how deeply antebellum arguments over the legitimacy of race-based slavery turned on the issue of whether the Negro was a "person" and how centrally the issue of "personification" (the question of whether Donatello or the fugitive slaves can become "persons") preoccupies both *The Marble Faun* and "Chiefly About War Matters," then these apparently escapist texts start to resonate quite eloquently within contemporary political discourse.

Most significantly, it is precisely the deeply political question of whether one can become a "person" that the purely aesthetic figure of the faun crystallizes in both texts. In *The Marble Faun*, Hawthorne invokes the man/faun Donatello in order to explicitly raise the question of whether such a creature can acquire a moral sense and becomes fully human, and in "Chiefly About War Matters," Hawthorne represents slaves as fauns at the very moment when he explicitly raises the question of whether a Negro slave, now in the liminal space between freedom and slavery, can enter the North and be suddenly transformed (both legally and morally) into a "person." It is the self-consciously aestheticized figure of the faun, in other words, that serves as the relay point in these two stories of "personification" and that foregrounds the question fundamental to antebellum debates over slavery.

In this context, it becomes particularly significant that in April 1862, as Hawthorne was writing "Chiefly About War Matters," slavery was being declared illegal in the District of Columbia and Lincoln was contemplating issuing a more expansive Emancipation Proclamation (something he would do about a month after Hawthorne's essay was published). That is, the central ethical dilemma of *The Marble Faun* is literally being re-enacted at the moment that Hawthorne sees these contraband slaves entering the District, moving from slave to potential citizen.[7] It is neither surprising nor coincidental that Hawthorne returns to the figure of the faun at the very moment that he wonders about such a transformation (the title under which the Romance was published in England).[8] It is in terms of this figure that he has already most thoroughly interrogated the problem of what it means to become a "person." Foregrounding questions about the moral development of Donatello, *The Marble Faun* can be seen as Hawthorne's preliminary mediation on the question of "personification."

Having worked out the problem of this transformation within the imaginary realm of the Romance, Hawthorne then uses what he has learned to understand the problem at the heart of the Civil War. Indeed, if *The Marble Faun* can be seen as an experiment in bestowing personhood upon the man/faun Donatello, then "Chiefly About War Matters" can be seen as Hawthorne's redaction of this literary experiment as an explicitly political one.[9] By aestheticizing slaves, Hawthorne expresses and constitutes rather than represses and avoids knowledge about slavery, race, and personhood. Hawthorne's representation of an essential correspondence between fauns and slaves, in other words, is inseparable from antebellum disputes over what the indisputable reality of the slave is. He participates in this debate by claiming that the political problem of race-based slavery can best be understood as a fundamentally aesthetic problem. Or to put this another way, "Chiefly About War Matters" does not testify to how Hawthorne "finally did respond imaginatively to the centrality of race and slavery in America" but how powerfully he had already responded to these issues.[10]

Since Hawthorne's account of the truth of the Black slave has been thoroughly superseded – become a debate beyond debate –, it has become too easy to condemn Hawthorne's aestheticizing as a fundamentally inadequate response to the reality of slavery. However, to presume that Hawthorne is making an obvious mistake about what slaves essentially are (displacing or mystifying the truth) not only erases how intensely the facts of slavery were being contested during the antebellum period but also treats the conceptual category of the "person" as if it were an identity beyond contingency and history. It is, in short, not to take seriously how Hawthorne enters (albeit in a way that we would certainly dispute) into contemporaneous arguments about the essential nature of slaves. If conventionally critics have set the real (slavery) against the aesthetic (fauns) and have been unsettled to the extent that in Hawthorne the aesthetic overwhelms the real, this chapter explores how in *The Marble Faun* and "Chiefly About War Matters" the aesthetic identifies rather than stands external to the reality of slavery. It explains why the Negro, even though he (like the faun) may seem "really so human," simply is not a "person."[11]

THE SLAVE AND THE FAUN

The Marble Faun is very clearly a text obsessed by aesthetic issues: it takes place in the galleries of Rome, all its characters are artists or artworks or both, and most of its pages are devoted to the making, discussing, and examination of art.[12] If this text is explicitly about art, it is less obviously but no less about race.[13] Race circulates suggestively throughout the Romance.[14] The Romance's romantic pairs, for example, are simultaneously divided along racial and national lines: the good American couple, Hilda and Kenyon (who are explicitly associated with whiteness), and the genealogically dark European couple, the man/faun Donatello and the Jewish Miriam, about whom it is rumored that there is "one burning drop of African blood in her veins" (23). In particular, the metaphoric echoes between the faun of *The Marble Faun*, Donatello, and antebellum accounts of the Negro are quite striking. Donatello is repeatedly described as a primitive being: affectionate, imitative, childish, overly emotional, and quick-tempered. He is represented as lacking a developed moral sense. All these qualities were commonly attributed to the Negro race during the period.[15] And all are brought into play in the act that sets the novel's plot in motion: Donatello's impulsive murder of Miriam's mysterious nemesis, known only as the Model, apparently in submission to a vindictive look from Miriam.

Perhaps the most tantalizing rhetorical correspondence between the African and Donatello is that Hawthorne presents Donatello as biologically distinct from the other characters of the Romance. When Kenyon says that Donatello seems "not precisely man, nor yet child, but in a high and beautiful sense an animal" he rehearses, albeit in more mannered terms, an opinion that members of the American School of Ethnology had declared to be a scientific truth about the Negro: "betwixt man and animal," "[n]either man nor animal," the African is a distinct and inferior species (*Marble Faun*, 10). This observation resonates powerfully with the work of antebellum ethnologists, who persistently argued that they had scientifically proven that the African was essentially different from the Anglo-Saxon, a distinct species, produced in a separate act of divine creation. Donatello, one might say, looks a lot like a statue and feels a lot like a Negro.

This convergence of racial and aesthetic discourse, of course, is not surprising. During the antebellum period, questions about race were never far from questions about beauty.[16] Racial classifications were regularly translated into the hierarchical language of beauty and ugliness, and such standards of beauty were, in turn, considered as offering crucial information about the way in which the political and social sphere should be organized. As might be expected, Blacks were represented as the antithesis of the beauty of the Anglo-Saxon.[17] Not only was the Negro consistently represented as ugly, but the race's intrinsic ugliness was commonly regarded as Nature's determinative proof of Negro inferiority.

However, neither Donatello nor the fugitive slaves are represented as ugly. Donatello, in fact, is conspicuous for his beauty. Both figures disrupt the traditional alignment of racial superiority to beauty. Indeed, Hawthorne is fascinated by the faun, as he makes clear when he discusses in his notebooks several faun statues in the Capitoline Sculpture Gallery (among them Praxiteles' sculpture of *The Faun*), precisely because they cannot be comprehended by conventional narratives about beauty and race:

I like these strange, sweet, playful, rustic creatures, *almost entirely human as they are, yet linked so prettily, without monstrosity, to the lower tribes*. . . .In my mind, they connect themselves with that ugly, bearded woman, who was lately exhibited in England, and by some supposed to have been *engendered bewixt a human mother and an orang-outang*; but she was a wretched monster – the faun, natural and delightful link betwixt human and brute life, and with something of a divine character intermingled.[18]

Hawthorne's reference to "the lower tribes" and to "the orang-outang" (a creature that, as Poe's "Murders in the Rue Morgue" vividly clarifies, was a conventional metaphor for the Negro) makes clear how deeply the figure of the faun constellates questions about race, humanity, and aesthetics.[19] This connection is not unusual; the faun was often seen as a missing link comparable to the Negro. As John Blair Dabney explained in his overview of scholarship on the monkey, satyrs "were not altogether fabulous, but were, doubtless, monkeys in the transition, or chrysalis state."[20] For Hawthorne, however, what is significant about the faun is that this liminal creature does not incite the corporeal horror of an analogously raced and hyper-symbolic emblem of miscegenation (the "ugly, bearded woman"). Standing between the human and the nonhuman, the faun, like the human/orang-outang hybrid, collapses categories that should remain distinct, but the faun, unlike most other hybrids, does so without evoking disgust.

ANTEBELLUM RACIST AESTHETICS

Although Hawthorne clearly affiliates aesthetics, race, and personhood in *The Marble Faun*, this linkage, as I have suggested, cannot be understood as simply reiterating the well-rehearsed conflation of beauty and racial superiority. Indeed, one can only appreciate Hawthorne's racial aesthetics if it is distinguished from contemporaneous accounts of the relation between race and aesthetics, accounts that tended to focus on the physical characteristics of the African – the thick lips, broad nose, dark skin, and "woolly" hair – as visible material signs of the race's inner and essential "ugliness."

Traditionally, the Negro's morphology was classified as negatively aesthetic, while the Anglo-Saxon's physical nature was regarded as the natural standard of beauty. The obvious *ugliness* of the Negro provided certain knowledge about the order of things. The aesthetic, in short, was never an autotelic category; it always revealed significant proof of the superiority of the Anglo-Saxon in the "real world." The process of taxonomizing particular physical signs as representing Blackness, of identifying these signs as absolutely ugly, and of drawing social conclusions from these obvious empirical facts dates back in US political discourse at least to Thomas Jefferson's *Notes on the State of Virginia* (1785/1787).

In the *Notes*, Jefferson, citing among other things the Negro's monotonous skin color, woolly hair, and inelegant form, summoned aesthetic categories to support his claim that it was impossible to "incorporate the blacks" into the United States.[21] According to Jefferson, the Negro race itself emits physical proof of its aesthetic inferiority: "Negroes secrete less by the kidnies, and more by the glands of the skin, which gives them a very strong and disagreeable ordour" (*Notes*, 138). Jefferson justifies his call for racial nationalism in terms of the aesthetic nature of each race. Jefferson's confidence in the social relevance of ugliness reveals not only that notions of beauty and ugliness were thought to be "natural" facts but also that the visible differences between the races were regarded as transparent signs of eternal differences, immovable markers of racial essences impervious to alteration by human intention, political action, or history. To abandon the obvious "inferiority of form and features" of the Negro race would be to concede, as William Harper, Chancellor of the University of South Carolina later declares, that there is "no universal standard of truth and grace and beauty."[22] Since beauty speaks the language of the absolute truth, to deny the proof of beauty is to deny truth.

During the antebellum period, as the moral and political attacks upon slavery increased and as the threat of a free Negro population was emerging as a possibility, the notion of the Negro's self-evident and self-incriminating physical ugliness surfaced as a particularly effective strategy for legitimating the non-personhood of the Negro. In *Negromania* (1851),[23] for example, John Campbell explains that

> the grand secret of separation or rather of the separate existence of races is to be found in the love of the beautiful. Man, even savage man will stop to gaze at a beautiful statue or picture, and the fair-haired white caucasian woman has been always sought as a wife by every race; while on the other hand the white race of men have drawn back in disgust from anything like general intermingling with the female of an inferior species (547).

According to Campbell, who is less interested in legitimating the institution of slavery than in refuting claims for Negro equality, the universal truth of aesthetic categories – embodied, as one might expect, in the figure of the woman – makes clear the inevitability of existing racial divisions.[24] The Beautiful and the Ugly, Campbell explains, are matters of universal assent, clear even to the African himself. In Campbell's account, this self-evident physical ugliness of the African proves the unnaturalness of any claim that the Negro may have to social equality. Man not only should not but also cannot interfere with the immutable and transcendent principles of aesthetics. He must simply assent to these unalterable and undeniable facts.

Campbell's representation of the transparent ugliness of Black women makes clear the ideological force of aesthetic arguments: Campbell, intent on asserting the inferiority of the Negro, asserts that no white master would rape a Negro slave precisely because the Negro is an intrinsically repulsive and alien species.[25] Claims for the ugliness of the Negro, however, were conspicuous not only in blatantly racist pro-slavery discourse but also in the objective rhetoric of the scientific community. Indeed, few ethnological treatises of the period lacked a chapter on beauty.[26] It was considered an empirical fact that beauty is a question of "primary importance in the natural history of several species," determining "not only the permanent separation of the species, but the actual advance, retardation, or retrogression of any, and every species in moral and intellectual power."[27]

In the assumption that beauty was truth, scientific and personal discourse converged. Thus, Louis Agassiz, the Swiss naturalist who settled in the US in 1846 and gave the American School of Ethnology international respectability, describes in a now notorious letter to his mother how profoundly the Negro's physical appearance repelled him. Upon first seeing the Negro waiters who served him at a Philadelphia hotel, Agassiz could not contain his aesthetic horror:

> In seeing their black faces with their thick lips, and grimacing teeth, the wool on their head, their bent knees, their elongated hands, their large curved nails, and especially the livid color of the palm of their hands, I could not take my eyes off their face in order to tell them to stay far away. And when they advanced that hideous hand towards my plate in order to serve me, I wished I were able to depart in order to eat a piece of bread elsewhere, rather than dine with such service (1846).[28]

Simultaneously disgusted and fascinated by the Negro's anatomical features, Agassiz suggests that only the conventions of polite dining restrained him from fleeing the room. Agassiz draws a profound conclusion from this experience of visceral disgust: "What unhappiness for the white race – to have tied their existence so closely with that of negroes in certain countries! God preserve us from such contact!" (45).

To the extent that the "ugliness" of the Negro is seen as inevitable, it is represented as preceding and causing social relationships. Such a racist aesthetics claims that the aesthetic is external to politics and thus provides a secure foundation for social and political judgments. Since an individual's disgust with the Negro is natural, any attempt to legislate this response out of existence can only be understood as unnatural. As Calvin Colton succinctly stated 25 years earlier in *The Americans* [1833], race prejudice is "doubtless as wrong as it is natural."[29] Or as William Graham Sumner will write about 25 years later, state ways cannot overcome folkways. Indeed it is precisely this logic that *Plessy v. Ferguson* (1896) will eventually codify: racial prejudice reflects the order of things, a natural response antecedent to and independent of the scope of the law.

This form of racist aesthetics imagines itself as "objective" not only because it considers racial hierarchies a universal truth beyond dispute, but also because it is predicated on the stability of object, on the belief that the material specifics of Blackness are irreducible attributes, characteristics that resist history and abide with an ontological stability through the generations. As pro-slavery thinkers were fond of stating, "the Ethiopian cannot change his skin, nor the leopard his spots."[30] The reason that antebellum ethnologists expended such energy on the study of hair, skin color, facial structure, and skull size was that they believed that these morphological features were permanent and specific to particular races, a self-evident expression of race that could always be relied on to categorize racial difference.[31] Antebellum ethnologists assumed that such somatic and physiological features reflected the transcendent taxonomy of Nature. Antebellum ethnologists subscribed to a fundamentally physicalist logic, one predicated on the claim that these material and exterior markers manifested the interior essence of racial difference. Aversive racial feeling is simply an inevitable reaction to these markers.

Racial aesthetes, in other words, depend on the fact that inferiority is permanently written on the surface of the Negro. And although such an account of racial difference can certainly function as an effective guarantee of the social and political hierarchies, it is accompanied by a danger: it requires that the material signs of race justify such certainty. In order for these visible signs of "ugliness" to signify properly, they must remain clear and unchanging, independent of the observer and of contingency. These somatic structures function as legitimate markers only to the extent that they continue to reflect the object's identity in defiance of the vagaries of climate, social condition, or cultural perspective. Since the antebellum aesthetics of race regarded these racial differences as empirical indices that could be scientifically measured and classified, this discourse fundamentally depended upon the visible, external materiality of racial difference.

CHIEFLY ABOUT WAR MATTERS

If conventional accounts of racial aesthetics assumed that the material markers of race were stable, it is precisely such stability that Hawthorne seems most anxious about in "Chiefly About War Matters" when he represents these fugitive slaves as fauns. Indeed, the essay seems to mock the reliability of the materialist logic that underwrites aesthetic racialism, foregrounding the assumptions that underwrite the dominant aesthetic ideology of race only to weaken any racist account of aesthetics that relies on objective, visible markers.

Hawthorne explains that he "felt most kindly" toward the fugitive slaves he came across because they were still "wearing such a crust of primeval simplicity," such visible inferiority allowing Hawthorne's extension of sympathy. But he continues less affectionately, lamenting that such a natural "crust" has been "quite polished away from the northern black man" (318). Since these creatures have made no attempt to "polish away" the natural surface markers of their race, they enchant Hawthorne. Northern Negroes, in contrast, are less appealing precisely because they have attempted, somewhat nefariously it appears, to obscure the exterior signs that identify them as Black. Given that aesthetic judgments about the Negro crucially depended on the stability of the race's visible morphology, one can understand the cultural significance of such efforts to "polish away" the markers of Blackness: Northern Negroes are dangerous because they threaten the foundation of any racial aesthetics.

To the extent that Northern Negroes undermine the possibility of a racial aesthetics, these fugitive slaves satisfy the fantasy of natural markers of race. Hawthorne's description of their exterior appearance (their clothes, their manners, and their "crust" of simplicity) seems to fulfill with a vengeance the demand that the Negro be categorizable according to stable surface markers. Hawthorne analogizes the clothes and the skin of these slaves: "so rudely were they attired, – *as if* their garb had grown upon them spontaneously" (emphasis added). Hawthorne is representing these clothes as if they were natural garments. Although clothes may appear to be a contingent and removable rather than an essential or permanent sign of identity, Hawthorne, nonetheless, describes these clothes as a second skin, not exactly replacing skin with clothing but imagining that, at least ideally, the clothing of these slaves should function as a supplemental and natural marker of race, expressing rather than concealing their nature.

If on one level, Hawthorne is mirroring the widespread assumption that free Blacks take too much pride in their appearance – a pride supposedly excited by their natural love of pretty colors, a pride that excited caricatures in the North depicting apelike creatures absurdly decked out in garish tuxedos and preposterously elegant gewgaws – he is also expressing the deeper anxiety that informed such obsessive concern about Black appearance.[32] His excessively rhetorical conjuring of clothing as epidermal augmentation registers an anxiety about the possibility that there are no immovable signs of Blackness. Hawthorne's privileging of the naturally generated clothes of the unpolished Blacks suggests not a confidence in material signs but an apprehension that the surface signs of Blackness not only can, but more crucially, are being erased.[33] His fantasy that the man-made coverings of these fugitives are Nature's garments foregrounds the extent to which he fears that the empirical markers of Blackness are becoming increasingly unreliable. External evidence of racial difference, these Northern Blacks make all too clear, is not beyond alteration.

One could say that Hawthorne is representing the transitional space between South and North where he comes across these fugitive slaves as a sort of metaphysical changing room: these fugitives are about to change from slave to freeman as they simultaneously change from one garb to another.[34] By linking the potential transformation of slaves into citizens to a departure from a realm in which exterior and interior states correspond, Hawthorne suggests that the impending transformation of the slave is superficial, a metamorphosis that should not be mistaken for evolution or true progress, but only as a masking of the slave's nature.

Hawthorne, thus, has not mistaken a social sign (clothes) for a natural one (skin), rather, by conflating clothes and skin, he has drawn attention to the precariousness of ostensibly natural signs. Indeed, at a moment when many slaves did "look" white, such anxiety over the mutable materiality of racial signifiers would be understandable. However, Hawthorne, as will become clear, is not critiquing racist hierarchies; he is critiquing the materialist logic on which such hierarchies have been conventionally predicated. Hawthorne is not abandoning racial hierarchies just because he is questioning a particular (materialist) version of racial aesthetics. For Hawthorne, unlike for many of his contemporaries, the crucial question is not whether the Negro is physically beautiful or ugly precisely because he is suspicious of the aesthetic itself. Hawthorne can align the Negro with the beautiful precisely because he is not interested in critiquing standards of beauty, but in revealing how the Negro must be understood as a fundamentally aesthetic problem. Hawthorne's understanding of racial aesthetics, in other words, needs to be distinguished from arguments that turned to the self-evidently ugly surface of the Negro as objective proof of Negro inferiority as well as from those that sought to challenge prevailing claims about Negro inferiority by foregrounding the beauty of the Negro.

Hawthorne establishes a critique of conventional racist aesthetics that looks nothing like the effort of Black intellectuals to invert hierarchies of racial beauty or to discredit claims about the universality of the aesthetic. Given that notions of beauty were politically charged, it is not surprising that anti-racist thinkers sought to contest conventional linkages between the universality of beauty and the naturalness of racial hierarchies. Some Black intellectuals, such as William Wells Brown, sought to undermine the logic of racist aesthetics by asserting that slaves often were "as white as their masters, and a great deal better looking."[35] This strategy challenged any claims of Black inferiority based on the material difference of the Negro, arguing that such material markers were disappearing. If some foregrounded the instability of racial markers, others, such as Dr. John S. Rock, the noted Boston physician and first Black attorney admitted to the bar of the US Supreme Court, sought to redefine the notion of beauty itself. Rewriting beauty according to a Black standard, Rock asserted that the "fine tough muscular system, the beautiful, rich color, the full broad features, and the gracefully frizzled hair of the Negro" must be contrasted "with the delicate physical organization, wan color, sharp features and lank hair of the Caucasian." Such patent aesthetic deficiencies, Rock concluded, suggested that "when the white man was created, nature was pretty well exhausted – but determined to keep up appearances, she pinched up his features, and did the best she could under the circumstances."[36] Although far from identical, both lines of argument ground their challenge to prevailing arguments about the inferiority of the Negro on the claim that beauty instated meaningful knowledge about the order of things.

The strategy to resignify Black as beautiful, indeed, was crucial to many arguments about Negro personhood. As William Wilson explained in *Frederick Douglass' Paper*:

> At present, what we find around us, either in art or literature, is made so to press upon us, that we depreciate, we despise, we almost hate ourselves, and all that favors us. Well may we scoff at black skins and woolly heads, since every model set before us for admiration, has pallid face and flaxen head, or emanations thereof."[37]

Having internalized a standard of beauty that is implicitly white, Negroes, Wilson laments, too often regularly identify their own race as essentially ugly and thus participate in their own degradation.

Some extrapolated from the way that statements of beauty concealed a racial politics that beauty itself ultimately had nothing to do with universal truths and everything to do with social power. That is, rather than maintain that Black beauty is the true universal, some maintained that the concept of beauty was itself nothing more than a particular perspective that had become politically dominant and mistakenly inflated into a universal and objective one. As Frederick Douglass explains, he would be handsome "if public opinion was changed."[38] Pretending to espouse radically universal principles, the aesthetic, according to this account, embeds a specific set of interests at its origin but is invoked as if such embedded interests have evaporated.

In contrast to claims that the aesthetic only reveals the contours of existing relations of power, Hawthorne's critique of racial aesthetics neither questions aesthetic standards nor declares aesthetic claims of universality to be counterfeit. As will become clear in *The Marble Faun*, Hawthorne relentlessly complicates and repudiates the materialist logic of antebellum racist aesthetics without ever doubting the legitimacy of racial hierarchies or the universality of beauty. He accepts that the aesthetic is a transcendental category. Motivated neither by the claim that aesthetic judgments are actually political judgments nor by the belief that Black could ever become beautiful, Hawthorne's rejection of the materialism that informs prevailing accounts of racial aesthetics is motivated by a suspicion of the aesthetic itself. Indeed, rather than undermining the authority of racial hierarchies, *The Marble Faun* sets out to place racial difference upon a more secure foundation than a materialist logic allows: it explains why the aesthetic and the Negro must be renounced simultaneously. Hawthorne, in essence, rejects the aesthetic in order to preserve racism.

THE AESTHETICS OF 'THE MARBLE FAUN'

Although many critics have considered it a proto-post-modern text, *The Marble Faun* elaborates a very conservative view of art.[39] Hawthorne relentlessly sets up an antagonism between the transcendence of the aesthetic and the materiality of the object. As the opening scene of the Romance immediately makes clear, Hawthorne imagines that the aesthetic exists in tension with the imperfect forms (paint, marble, or marble) that express it. The Romance's four main characters, standing in the Capitoline Gallery, are gazing at "the famous productions of antique sculpture" that are still shining in the undiminished majesty and beauty of their ideal life, although the marble, that embodies them, is yellow with time, and perhaps corroded by the damp earth in which they lay buried for centuries (5).

Though the physical appearance of these artworks has been seriously compromised, Hawthorne imagines that their aesthetic worth nonetheless remains "undiminished."

In order for this version of the aesthetic experience to be possible, the literal surface must never become the object of the viewer's attention; it must be clearly segregated from and wholly subordinated to the unchanging "ideal life" of the aesthetic. The aesthetic tenor of the art object, Hawthorne suggests, only emerges if the viewers are engaged in this process of hierarchization. According to this essentially allegorical model of the aesthetic, the only relation that temporal objects must have with the aesthetic is purely vehicular: they carry the viewer to the ideal sphere of the aesthetic that is eternally protected from the vagaries of history and from the inevitable damage and change that defines the temporal world. The miracle of art is that even though the vehicles of the aesthetic decay, the aesthetic endures.

Hawthorne's account of the aesthetic experience allows for no mediation between the materiality of the object and the transcendence of the aesthetic: the chasm is unbridgeable because the material is represented as inexorably corrupting the aesthetic. Given this absolute opposition, it is perhaps not surprising that the model Hawthorne sets up is consistently confounded. Characters in the Romance cannot stop themselves from being fixed by the materiality of the object itself. For example, even Hilda, whom the Romance holds up as the ideal observer of art, acknowledges the difficulty of placing the physical aspects of an object out of the picture. After scrutinizing the Faun of Praxiteles for a while, she realizes that she has become so conscious of the statue itself that the aesthetic experience has vanished: "I have been looking at him too long," she laments, "I see only a corroded and discoloured stone. This change is very apt to occur in statues." Kenyon, her fellow countryman and a sculptor, immediately adds, perhaps feeling his medium is being singled out, "And a similar one in pictures, surely!" (17).

If the aesthetic requires that the material surface of the art object be strictly governed, Hawthorne repeatedly shows the difficulty of establishing this governance in Rome where every art object is besmirched by the dirt and marked by decay. Art objects, in essence, become the occasion for the transcendent and material to uncomfortably collide. What the aesthetic ultimately requires, according to Hawthorne, is not only the subordination of the material to the transcendent, but more significantly, the subordination of the viewer. The Romance, in other words, represents the aesthetic as besieged both by the transience of its materials and the inconstancy of its viewers.

Hawthorne repeatedly foregrounds the reader's power to disrupt the aesthetic experience.[40] As the American sculptor Kenyon declares, "It is the spectator's mood that transfigures the Transfiguration itself. I defy any painter to move and elevate me without my own consent and assistance" (17). Hawthorne, in fact, repeatedly acknowledges the extent to which the aesthetic depends upon the viewer:

> A picture, however admirable the painter's art, and wonderful his power, requires of the spectator a surrender of himself, in due proportion with the miracle which has been wrought. Let the canvas glow as it may, you must look with the eye of faith, or its highest excellence escapes you. There is always the necessity of helping out the painter's art with your own resources of sensibility and imagination (335).

Although Hawthorne shows the aesthetic to be threatened simultaneously by the materiality of its object and the particularity of the viewer, it would be a mistake to see *The Marble Faun* as anxious about the fragility of the aesthetic. Rather, the aesthetic is itself the problem. It becomes a problem precisely because the subordination of materiality (required by the aesthetic) is inseparable from the subordination of the viewer. Indeed, since Hawthorne establishes the transcendent universality of the aesthetic as a fundamental threat to the individual subject, he is ultimately more concerned with the fragility of the individual than that of the aesthetic experience.

Hawthorne's representation of Hilda, the Romance's ideal artist and viewer, most clearly foregrounds the degree to which the Romance imagines the assertion of the aesthetic and the assertion of the individual as ontologically opposed. Hilda, Hawthorne explains, becomes "incomparably the best copyist in Rome" by "sacrificing herself to the devout recognition of the highest excellence in art" (59). Although one might expect that Hilda's skill as a copyist would express itself as a perfect mimesis, she is, in the most literal sense, a very poor copyist. What she paints is not visible in the original: "she had been enabled to execute what the great Master had conceived in his imagination but had not so perfectly succeeded in putting upon canvas" (59). Her copies, in short, look nothing like the original. What Hilda imagines as copying, therefore, looks a great deal like creation. Paradoxically, Hilda's "generous self-surrender" to "the Old Masters" allows her to paint what they never could (60).

Hawthorne's seemingly confused description of Hilda's "copying" as creation, however, is precisely the point. For Hawthorne, copying and creation are identical acts, indistinguishable because both are predicated on the subordination of the individual to the universal. Hawthorne replaces a romantic aesthetic that aligns self-expression with creativity with the classical notion that the aesthetic demands self-abnegation. The price of both producing and reproducing great art, Hilda demonstrates, is the loss of a personality. Indeed, the distinction between creation and imitation, originality and reproduction is predicated upon the very assumption that the Romance is dedicated to repudiating: that the aesthetic can ever be connected to the expression of individuality.

Hawthorne thus repeatedly emphasizes how completely Hilda's devotion to the aesthetic blocks her from becoming an individual. Although such a "sensitive faculty of appreciation" and "generous self-surrender" may seem to mark Hilda as an ideal of the feminine – devoted, humble, and pure – her aesthetic bondage to the "Old Masters" actually exiles her from the true concerns of women. As long as she is "the handmaid to the Old Masters," Hilda will never marry, never tend to her family's rather than the Virgin Mary's hearth, and never be, according to Hawthorne's conventional Victorian imagination of the feminine, a complete woman (334). "Hilda," as Kenyon sadly reflects, "does not dwell in our mortal atmosphere." And as long as Hilda continues to sacrifice herself to the universality of the aesthetic, she will neither recognize Kenyon's love for her nor exist herself as more than an imaginary figure.

Hilda, however, is redeemed. For, after witnessing the murder of Miriam's mysterious tormentor, known only as the Model, Hilda loses her sublime negative capability. The murder compels her to think about temporal matters and to contemplate her particular situation. And it is only when she begins to think about her particularity that she can escape her bondage to the Old Masters. Her depression and self-absorption may ruin her skill – she is no longer able to "yield herself up to the painter so unreservedly as in times past" – but she gains a self-consciousness that preserves her individuality from the tyranny of the aesthetic. "Her character," the narrator explains, now "developed a sturdier quality, which made her less pliable to the influence of other minds" (375).

In Hilda's experience, Hawthorne clearly aligns the restoration of individuality with the reassertion of the materiality of art objects. It is precisely at the moment that she begins to think about herself that Hilda suddenly sees the paintings that she had previously worshiped as "empty" and apprehends the painters whom she had previously "venerated" as seduced by "venal beauty":

> Heretofore, her sympathy went deeply into a picture, yet seemed to leave a depth, which it was inadequate to sound; now, on the contrary, her perceptive faculty penetrated the canvas like a steel probe, and found but a crust of paint over an emptiness. Not that she gave up all Art as worthless; only, it lost its consecration (341).

Hilda's redemption requires that the art objects become material and coarse. That Hilda's fall from the aesthetic is fortunate becomes obvious when, on the "very afternoon" after experiencing "the emptiness of Picture-Galleries," Kenyon "felt Hilda's hand pulling at the silken cord that was connected with his heart-strings" (343). Finally, Hilda can recognize her love for Kenyon and begin to think proper thoughts about home and marriage.

Although the gender-inflected character of Hilda's devotional stance towards the aesthetic cannot be dismissed, it is important to note that Kenyon, Hilda's fellow expatriate, recapitulates this conflict between individuality and the aesthetic. Near the end of the Romance, Kenyon, hoping to find Hilda, who has mysteriously disappeared, follows the instructions of an anonymous communication. Instead of Hilda, Kenyon discovers the fragments of a statue. Collecting the fragments, Kenyon reassembles the figure, a lost model for the celebrated *Venus de Medici*. Reattaching the head, he appreciates his find:

> the effect was magical. . . . The beautiful idea at once asserted its immortality, and converted that heap of forlorn fragments into a whole, as perfect to the mind, if not to the eye, as when the new marble gleamed with snowy lustre . . . The world was richer than yesterday, by something far more precious than gold. Forgotten beauty had come back, as beautiful as ever; a goddess had risen from her slumber, and was a goddess still . . . an Emperour would woo this tender marble, and win her as proudly as an imperial bride! (423–424).

For this moment the aesthetic overwhelms the gross materiality of the marble – "nor was the impression marred by the earth that still hung upon the exquisitely graceful limbs, and even filled the lovely crevice of the lips" (424).

For a moment this decayed marble bride seems to satisfy Kenyon, for a moment he (as Miriam and Donatello had hoped) forgets Hilda. But, as the narrator explains, Kenyon "could hardly, we fear, be reckoned a consummate artist, because there was something dearer to him than his art," and, "by the greater strength of a human affection, the divine statue seemed to fall asunder again, and became only a heap of worthless fragments" (424).[41] Kenyon, in other words, simultaneously proves himself a deficient artist and a worthy man. When Kenyon's individuality returns, the ethical rather than the aesthetic is expressed.

In *The Marble Faun*, to state the case most boldly, Hawthorne imagines both aesthetic creation and aesthetic appreciation as anti-self-expressive acts. Hawthorne affiliates subjectivity and materiality because of their common role in thwarting aesthetic expression. Both need to be subordinated for the aesthetic to be realized. If, in *The Marble Faun*, this subordination never completely occurs, and thus great paintings are repeatedly reduced to flecks of paint and classic sculptures transformed into chunks of stone, this failure of the aesthetic is ultimately a good thing. Rather than troubling to Hawthorne, the recalcitrance of material forms is the key to saving the individual.[42] Having set up a choice between the aesthetic and individuality, Hawthorne repudiates the aesthetic in order to choose individuality.

Hawthorne, it is important to note, is not arguing, as those who sought to undermine the connection between racial and aesthetic knowledge, that the aesthetic's claim to universality is false; he is not arguing that this experience be understood in anti-formalist, subjective, or sociological terms. He accepts the aesthetic as a purely transcendent category, one that must subordinate the particularity of the viewer. Hawthorne does not claim (as an anti-formalist would or anti-racist might) that the aesthetic is a purely contingent or illusory or political category. He acknowledges the force of aesthetic transcendence. But he identifies such transcendence as inevitably and axiomatically threatening. And it is this dynamic of subordination that he isolates in order to represent the aesthetic as fundamentally threatening.

In *The Marble Faun*, Hawthorne never seeks to mediate between the aesthetic and the subjective. In contrast to Kant, for example, Hawthorne does not make the category of the aesthetic a model for subjectivity. Hawthorne establishes the aesthetic as the antithesis of subjectivity. Moreover, unlike Coleridge, he does not attempt to fuse the particular and the universal in the concrete universal, an incarnational logic expressed most fully in the Romantic account of the symbol. The Romance is not an effort to derive the aesthetic object's determinacy and structure from the subject, nor an effort to reconcile the transcendent realm of the aesthetic with the contingent force of the material.

Defining the aesthetic as essentially antagonistic to the subject, *The Marble Faun* needs to be seen as an effort to preserve and protect the subject from the hazards of the aesthetic. And in this sense, *The Marble Faun* does not follow the common trajectory of nineteenth-century aesthetic history. Hawthorne's discussion of art does not become less objective and more subjective, less oriented toward the characteristics of things and more focused on individual psychology. In fact, he deliberately foregrounds aesthetic transcendence not as an ideal instantiation of "personhood" but as the absolute abomination of "personhood." Rather than formulate an aesthetic theory that can reconcile the subjective and objective elements of the aesthetic, Hawthorne writes *The Marble Faun* in order to elaborate the irreconcilability of the universal and the particular that aesthetic objects foreground.[43] Rather than aligning the aesthetic with the constitution of the individual subject, he positions the aesthetic as the primary antagonist of the subject and turns to the materiality of the art object to save the subject from the aesthetic. In this sense, it is almost to be expected that *The Marble Faun* is Hawthorne's last completed Romance. In it he carefully lays out the process of aesthetic expression and then wholeheartedly and thoroughly establishes the moral grounds for rejecting this process.

ROME AND THE RULE OF THE AESTHETIC

Given this opposition between individuality and aesthetics, it is not surprising that Hawthorne's Preface to *The Marble Faun* works to isolate art in the foreign world of Rome. Hawthorne firmly localizes the Romance in Rome, taking particular care to exile the twilight of Romance from the "common-place prosperity" and "broad and simple daylight" of "our stalwart Republic." Italy, he claims, rather than the United States, provides the perfect place for a Romance: it is "a sort of poetic or fairy precinct, where actualities would not be so terribly insisted upon, as they are, and must needs be, in America" (3). Despite the modern critical tradition that claims (almost reflexively) an essential relation between the Romance and US culture, Hawthorne in his last completed Romance has set the United States against the Romance.[44]

I want to take Hawthorne's claim that the United States is no place for Romance seriously. Hawthorne, after having not written a Romance for six years, repudiates the genre of the Romance for the same reason that he rejects the aesthetic: both imperil individuality. It is because Hawthorne is so intent on disconnecting the Romance from the United

States that he makes the seemingly outrageous statement that in his "dear native land" there "is no shadow, no antiquity, no mystery, no picturesque and gloomy wrong" (3). In particular, Hawthorne locates Rome as the ideal setting for a Romance because, unlike the United States, Rome is devoted to the erasure of the empirical and of particularity. As Hawthorne explains, the "state of feeling" experienced most often in Rome is:

> a perception of such weight and density in a by-gone life, of which this spot was the centre, that the present moment is pressed down or crowded out, and our individual affairs and interests are but half real, here, as elsewhere. Viewed through this medium, our narrative – into which are woven some airy and unsubstantial threads, intermixed with others, twisted out of the commonest stuff of human existence – may seem not widely different from the texture of all our lives (6).

Rome offers itself as "a place where actualities are not so terribly insisted upon" because in Rome "actuality," having already been processed by the aesthetic, simply disappears. Rome is not a place "somewhere between the Real and the Imaginary," but a space where everything becomes imaginary.[45]

Rome, in essence, universalizes everything, collapsing all differentiations into a fully aestheticized form of life. Embedded in history so thoroughly that the force of the past overwhelms the present and attenuates the seriousness of subjective experience, "individual affairs and interests are but half real here." Here the aesthetic holds sway, and the particularity of everything and everyone is transformed. That is, not only is Rome a land of ruins, it is also the land that ruins individuality. The exuberantly figurative atmosphere of Rome is, as one would expect, incomparably productive of art and destructive of particularity. Rome initiates the possibility of universal analogies: the chance that everything can seem to be something else. Hilda, the pure and innocent "daughter of the Puritans," and Miriam, the dark and fallen European, both look remarkably similar to Guido's portrait of Beatrice Cenci; Miriam's tormentor, who works (at least part-time) as an artist's model, looks eerily similar to Guido's Demon; this mobile relationality, of course, climaxes in Donatello's resemblance to the *Faun* of Praxiteles. In both Rome and the Romance the restraining force of the particular and the individual is so thoroughly erased that nothing limits the resemblances one notices or the metaphors one can make.

THE FALL

Because everything and everyone loses its individual identity in Rome, the city may be a healthy place for art, but certainly not for morality.[46]

Indeed, *The Marble Faun* culminates by foregrounding the serious moral problems raised by the aesthetic environment of Rome. Miriam, near the Romance's conclusion, offers Kenyon an explanation, one that most critics have seconded, of what *The Marble Faun* is ultimately about: "The story of the fall of man! Is it not repeated in our romance of Monte Beni?" [the subtitle of *The Marble Faun*]. In making this claim, she makes clear how deeply the problem of becoming a "person" lies at the heart of the narrative. And having noticed that Donatello has developed a moral sense after having sinned, Miriam then extrapolates from her observation of a resemblance between Donatello and Adam: "And may we follow the analogy yet further? Was that very sin,–into which Adam precipitated himself and all his race,–was it the destined means by which, over a long pathway of toil and sorrow, we are to attain a higher, brighter, and more profound happiness, than our lost birthright gave?" In short, Miriam asks whether Donatello's murder of the Model was a blessing in disguise, "a means of education, bringing a simple and imperfect nature to a point of feeling and intelligence which it could have reached under no other discipline?" Donatello, according to Miriam merely performs an archetypal transgression. Re-enacting the Fall of Man, Donatello's murder cannot be simply condemned and perhaps can even be justified as necessary for his moral development.

Miriam, it seems, is simply asking a rather traditional theological question: if sin is not educational, why else would God permit it to continue? But within the context of *The Marble Faun*, her hypothesizing is represented as profoundly scandalous. Kenyon replies that he finds her line of speculation "too dangerous." Inferring that Miriam may be suggesting that we ought to imitate Adam – or worse Donatello – and sin deliberately in order to learn, Kenyon declares that he will not follow her into such an "unfathomable abyss." Despite this refusal, Kenyon remains intrigued by Miriam's theory and adopts her argument when he and Hilda are contemplating the significance of Donatello's sudden development of a deep moral sense:

> "Here comes my perplexity," continued Kenyon. "Sin has educated Donatello, and elevated him. Is sin then, – which we deem such a dreadful blackness in the universe, – is it, like sorrow, merely an element of human education, through which we struggle to a higher and purer state than we could otherwise have attained? Did Adam fall, that we might ultimately rise to a far loftier paradise than his?" (460).

Hilda adamantly repudiates this version of the story, demonstrating "the white shining purity" – the militant orthodoxy that has so consistently vexed modern critics.[47] She responds to the sculptor's question with horror. "Oh hush!" she cries and:

> shrinking from him with an expression of horrour which wounded the poor, speculative sculptor to the soul. 'This is terrible; and I could weep for you, if you indeed believe it. Do not you perceive what a mockery your creed makes, not only of all religious sentiment, but of moral law, and how it annuls and obliterates whatever *precepts of Heaven are written deepest within us*? You have shocked me beyond words!' (460; emphasis added).

Hilda's disgust galvanizes Kenyon. He quickly retracts his statement, says he was just joking, and asks Hilda to marry him and guide him home to the United States "with that white wisdom which clothes you."

One wonders why Hilda is so shocked by what seems not only platitudinous, but so clearly the manifest theme of the Romance. As Richard Brodhead has asked, "What are we to make of a novel that so prominently hushes the speech it seems designed to express."[48] It is a mistake, however, to regard Hilda's rejection of Kenyon's version of the story as motivated by her aversion to the doctrine of the Fortunate Fall itself. For when Kenyon asks Hilda whether "The story of the fall of man. . .not repeated in our romance of Monte Beni?", he is not merely asking a theological question, he is reminding her of what she literally witnessed: she watched Donatello *throw* the Model from the summit of the Tarpeian Rocks.

The issue of the Fall lies at the center of the Romance in two very different senses. The abstract problem of the Fall of Man is set against the literal fall of one man – the Model's fall from the Tarpeian Rocks. To Hilda, the story of *The Marble Faun* is the story of the "fall of a man" not of the Fall of Man. Hilda is disgusted by the possibility that Kenyon could aestheticize a murder, allegorize an event that she has literally witnessed. Hilda is unwilling to forget Donatello's literal act.

The Romance thus sets up a competition between the literal and the figural account of the Fall. Hilda's unqualified repudiation of a Romance reading of the Fall suggests how dangerous any confusion of the literal and the figural can be. Hilda reacts so strongly not to the doctrine of the Fortunate Fall, but to the notion that Donatello's murder could be transformed from the literal act of murder into an abstract theological question. Hilda, in short, is disgusted by Kenyon's aestheticizing, more than by his theosophizing. This climactic scene reveals the extent to which the aesthetic in general and the Romance in particular are dangerous precisely because each depends on the effacing of the literal and the erasing of the individual (in this case the Model). In this text, aestheticizing looks a lot like murder.

FAUNING SLAVES

Given this account of aesthetic abstraction, it is clearly a victory for morality when, at the conclusion of *The Marble Faun*, Hilda and Kenyon abandon the "shadow" and "gloomy wrong" of Rome and return to "the broad and simple daylight" of the United States. Or to put this another way, Hilda and Kenyon leave the old world of the Romance for the literal new world. But there they will discover, as Hawthorne does two years later, that the figure of the faun is no longer indigenous to Rome or to the Romance. The United States may be a place "where actualities" are "terribly insisted upon," but nevertheless, it is not without its fauns. Thus, if we return to the question that began this chapter (why does Hawthorne faun these Negro slaves?), it becomes clear that to link slaves to the faun not to animalize them but to render them as fundamentally aesthetic creatures. This hyper-figural gesture signifies the extent to which Hawthorne deploys the aesthetic not to avoid political issues, but to make a thoroughly political statement about race. To link the Negro slave to the aesthetic is to explain (not evade) why the race cannot become "persons" even if they are emancipated. Hawthorne, in other words, is less interested in how the slaves are like animals than in how the decisive mark of Negro identity is the race's aesthetic nature.

As I have argued, Hawthorne's account of aesthetics undermines the materialist logic of antebellum racist aesthetics, but this critique does not lead Hawthorne to abandon the aesthetic as a source of knowledge. According to Hawthorne, the aesthetic remains profoundly enlightening. What it reveals, however, is not the truth of beauty but the danger of the aesthetic itself. Indeed, since Hawthorne opposes the category of the aesthetic to individuality, it is ultimately immaterial whether the Negro is beautiful or ugly. All that matters is that the Negro is a fundamentally aesthetic creature. By aestheticizing the Negro, in short, Hawthorne crystallizes his understanding of the Negro problem: the Negro is ineligible for personhood not because of how the Negro looks, but because the Negro incarnates the aesthetic experience itself.

The Negro simultaneously becomes a social and moral problem in Hawthorne's account precisely because the race reproduces the aesthetic experience. In contrast to conventional racist rhetoric, Hawthorne does not declare the Negro a "mud-sill" class, too material and too obdurately embodied to be beautiful; rather, he represents the Negro as inferior because the Negro lacks individuality, does not possess an essential material fixity.[49] According to Hawthorne, the Negro lacks a place in America precisely because the Negro, like an aesthetic object, inaugurates a tension between the literal and the figurative, between the material and the transcendent, between the interior and the exterior. By linking the Negro race to the aesthetic, Hawthorne isolates the danger of the Negro as fundamentally analogous to the danger posed by the aesthetic.

Indeed, by rendering Black slaves as analogous to aesthetic objects, Hawthorne recuperates contemporary debates about a free Negro population as an effect of the Negro's inevitably confusing being:

> I felt most kindly towards these poor fugitives, but knew not precisely what to wish on their behalf, nor in the least how to help them. For the sake of the manhood which is latent in them, I would not have turned them back; but I should have felt almost as reluctant, *on their own account*, to hasten them forward to the stranger's land ("Chiefly," 319 emphasis added)

This passage establishes Hawthorne's sympathy with these fugitive slaves but at the same time it establishes a homology between one's reaction to the Negro and to an aesthetic object: both initiate a conflict between the instability of surface markers and a more stable core, between what is visible and particular and what remains invisible and transcendent. That is, Hawthorne's confusion about how to engage the sympathy he feels for the Negro ultimately reveals more about the ontological status of the object than it does about the sympathizing subject. The moment crystallizes how Hawthorne understands his divided sympathy to be the clearest sign of the Negro Problem.

This moment, in essence, aligns the Negro with the threat of the aesthetic experience: the Negro, like the aesthetic object, confuses an individual's relationship both to oneself and to the material world. The only way to recognize and sympathize with the "manhood" which is "latent" in the Negro, according to Hawthorne, is if one suppresses one's knowledge about the Negro's present condition. By representing Negro "manhood" as fundamentally distinct from the Negro's present material situation, Hawthorne encapsulates the moral danger that the Negro presents. To think beyond the Negro's obvious lack of education, civilization, and preparation for life in the North is to forget the literal, existing world and to enter the ethically perilous and essentially foreign realm of the Romance. By opposing the Negro's visible, current condition to an appreciation of the Negro's imaginary essence, Hawthorne represents the

Negro Problem as fundamentally analogous to the problem incited by the aesthetic. Or to put this in terms of the lesson of *The Marble Faun*, the personhood of the Negro can only be expressed if Hawthorne subordinates himself to the Negro, if he denies his individuality for the sake of the Negro's. In the end, Hawthorne's point is not that these slaves look like fauns (they clearly do not), but that they reproduce the threat of the aesthetic.

That is, Hawthorne understands Negro slaves not simply as non-citizens and non-persons, but as figures that threaten the very premises of citizenship and personhood. The Negro's fundamentally unstable nature designates the Negro as the antithesis of the individual but even more importantly it reveals how the Negro provokes an aesthetic response. Thus, the removal of these inherently aesthetic creatures becomes necessary to preserve this nation's moral character. It is not by accident, therefore, that the liminal space in which Hawthorne situates these fugitive slaves is simultaneously the evanescent space of the Romance, the transitional political space between slave and potential citizen, and the geographic space between South and North. The Negro is excluded from citizenship for the same reason that the Negro is included in the realm of the Romance: the Negro is essentially a figural creature. It is not the aesthetic inadequacy of the Negro but the race's aesthetic excess that prevents them from finding a home in the United States. Locating the Negro on the side of the aesthetic rather than the particular and the individual, Hawthorne designates the Negro as outside the literalist and materialist premises of this nation. Because the Negro's essential character is to lack a materially stable character, the Negro can never be transformed into a citizen of the United States. The Negro, in essence, poses a clear and present danger to individuality and America.

Although such a complex account of Negro aesthetics is certainly not explicit in Hawthorne's texts, what I have been adumbrating are the assumptions (both conscious and unconscious) that frame Hawthorne's knowledge of what the Negro is. Hawthorne in these texts demonstrates a sustained engagement with the problem of the Negro becoming a "person," an engagement that has not been appreciated precisely because we assume that knowledge about the personhood of the Negro is inevitable. Hawthorne marks the possibility that things might be other than they are.

Most suggestively, by linking the aesthetic to an ineligibility for citizenship and "personhood," Hawthorne disrupts the association between aesthetic universalism and "personhood" that currently characterizes not only readings of Hawthorne's politics but of liberal citizenship itself. In contrast to modern claims that rights are distributed in terms of a "rhetoric of the bodiless political citizen, the generic 'person' whose political identity is *a priori* precisely because it is, in theory, non-corporeal," Hawthorne obsessively desubstantializes the Negro in order to classify them as non-citizens and as morally disruptive. He understands the indeterminate materiality of the Negro as the primary signifier of the race's ineligibility for personhood. Hawthorne, in short, comprehends the conceptual category of the "person" in terms we do not, or more precisely, no longer recognize.

That is, if we currently consider appearance as having a purely extraneous relation to personhood, imagining liberal personhood in purely disembodied terms, Hawthorne's representation of the Negro registers the historical specificity of this account. Rather than identify "persons" with the privilege of disembodiment, he represents the impulse to move beyond literality (an impulse incarnated by the Negro) as the problem incited by the Negro. Lacking a stable appearance, the Negro becomes ineligible for the right to citizenship. To the degree that the Negro can embody disembodiment, the Negro is not a "person." This account marks a significant discontinuity between the mechanics of antebellum and modern liberal thought. The abstract "person" at the heart of modern liberalism is, for Hawthorne, symptomatic of all that must be disavowed. According to the logic Hawthorne develops, the universality of the aesthetic is not the model of subjectivity, but its antithesis.

Thus, although we regularly assume that Negroes were denied personhood because they were represented as possessing a surplus corporeality (as unable to submerge their bodies), *The Marble Faun* requires us to historicize the model of personhood that underwrites liberal representation. Instead of posing a stumbling block to attaining the privileges of (white) personhood, the body of the Negro slave poses a problem precisely to the extent that the Negro lacks a fixed body and thus ominously motivates others to look beyond the body and beyond the literal. What Hawthorne's affiliation of aesthetics and race eventually suggests is that he is operating with a substantially different model of the "person" than the one we assume. Rather than enabling the extension of rights, the pull of abstraction identifies the limits of Negro identity. Rather than being the primary sign of American citizenship, abstraction endangers the ethical character of the nation. For Hawthorne, the Black body is too obligingly vehicular, offering itself too readily as a means to proliferate abstract meanings rather than as an obstacle to the producing of such meaning.

The Marble Faun, in other words, represents the aesthetic as inseparable from the question of emancipation. And in this respect, Hawthorne is not unique. Indeed, Thomas R. Dew, in his classic account of the Virginia legislature's debates over emancipation following the Nat Turner rebellion (1831), a text that collected and inaugurated many of the arguments over slavery that would come to dominate antebellum culture, also found the aesthetic the most effective means to express the problem of Negro emancipation. Dew, quoting Senator Canning, explained the difficulty of liberating the Negro by turning to literature:

> To turn him [the Negro slave] loose in the manhood of his physical passions, but in the infancy of his uninstructed reason, would be to raise up a creature resembling the splendid fiction of recent romance; the hero of which constructs a human form with all the physical capabilities of man, and with the thews and sinews of a giant, but being unable to impart to the work of his hands a perception of right and wrong, he finds too late that he has only created a more than mortal power of doing mischief, and himself recoils from the monster which he has made.[50]

Although I am not arguing that Hawthorne, like Dew, is explicitly rewriting Mary Shelley's *Frankenstein* in the service of a pro-slavery argument, I am suggesting that Hawthorne imagines the Civil War as threatening to give birth to an analogous kind of monster (albeit not as ugly a one). Both texts, I would suggest, are responding to the fear that scientists and politicians are both entertaining the possibility of making "persons." And both texts refuse to sanction such acts precisely by making clear that "persons" cannot be made.

CHAPTER 6

Freedom, ethics, and the necessity of persons: Frederick Douglass and the scene of resistance

This project has explored how an unexamined and anachronistic certainty about the "person" organizes the most influential modern readings of antebellum literary and political representation. It argues that the structure of liberal representation incites us to decontextualize the privileged referent of liberal discourse and to comprehend this conceptual category as a brute fact to be reflected rather than as the principal term that liberals construct and battle to define.[1] One of the goals of this project, therefore, has been to challenge the prevailing assumption that invoking the transparent fact of the "person" is sufficient to oppose slavery. In particular, the "person" is insufficient to oppose slavery because what seems like a transparent fact to us (that slaves are "persons") was not only far from transparent during the antebellum period, but also was precisely what was in dispute. Antebellum debates over slavery, in fact, most powerfully illustrate how the conceptual category of the "person" registers rather than resolves controversies, demonstrating how little claims about the self-evidence of the "person" ultimately accomplish when what is at stake is the question of "personhood." Such an argument may strike some as ethically perilous and politically regressive.

The problem, however, remains that at different historical moments the conceptual category of the "person" has been invoked to legitimate acts of heinous violence as well as to justify crucial emancipatory movements, to authorize segregation as well to compel integration, to sanction as well as to proscribe hierarchies that we now consider invidious. And, to the extent that we now see understandings of the "person" as having thwarted just as much as they have sustained social justice, the question to be asked is not whether projects for social justice will still be possible if the notion of the "person" is approached as political effect, but why do we, despite the preponderance of evidence to the contrary, still hold onto the "person" as a foundation of social justice rather than entertain the possibility that the "person" could both be constructed and function differently in different contexts.

Invocations of the "person" as an absolute, in other words, create two difficulties. Firstly, such invocations are inadequate historically. During moments of conflict appeals to the "person" reproduce precisely what generates the conflict in the first place. And secondly, such appeals incite a complacency about the "person" in contemporary thought. We now know that slaves obviously are "persons." But such certainty, instead of proving how compellingly the concept of the "person" definitively resolves disputes over the ethics of US slavery, marks the end of any dispute over slavery, revealing how the "person" effectively enforces a specific truth about the legitimacy of slavery only after the issue of slavery is no longer in dispute. It is only retroactively that the "person" becomes available as a means to resolve this political debate, and it is only retroactively that it becomes compelling to assert that ignorance, self-interest, or irrationality allowed the "personhood" of the slave to be misunderstood. The modern claim that slavery obviously dehumanizes, immorally distorts, and illegitimately represses "persons," in other words, is a consequence of a political change that has been rewritten as the cause of that political change.

Modern certainty about antebellum debates, indeed, depends upon the assumption that when we invoke the "person" as intrinsically ethical we are invoking a particular account of the "person" (for example, as color blind and gender neutral) that we assume is a transparent representation of what a "person" is in and of itself. A specific definition of the "person" can be universalized because it is imagined that this definition originates in the "person" itself rather than from a particular historical or political perspective. Our conviction that – despite the widespread misperceptions of antebellum culture – slaves simply are "persons" has been purchased at the price of forgetting the contested history of this identity category and extracting it from any particular context. In order to disrupt such complacency about the self-evidence of the "person," this project focuses on a moment before such inevitability was obvious and reapproaches the "person" as an identity that a liberal society makes and believes it has found. In this conclusion I want to address the ethics of such an argument. It asks what happens if one undermines the solidity of the identity conventionally summoned as the unequivocal foundation for ethics and the indispensable root of resistance.[2]

There appear, nonetheless, to be some very good reasons why the "person," in spite of everything, continues to be invoked as the irreducible foundation of social justice. It is thought that without the guarantee of the self-evident "person," one loses the essential fulcrum for denaturalizing and condemning acts such as slavery, racism, and torture. According to this account, unless the "person" remains objective, an identity beyond politics, the category drowns in history and human rights are reduced to an empty concept.[3] It is assumed, in other words, that unless the "personhood" of the slave stands outside of and above politics nothing can ground the claim that slavery is wrong and nothing can unequivocally be opposed to self-deception, existing state policy, group preferences, and the limitations of one's context. In contrast to such assumptions, this project challenges the liberal assumption that the absolute "person" is necessary to generate ethics, foregrounding how claims on behalf of such a "person" have not succeeded in doing what they are summoned to do: they have neither resolved controversies over ethical behavior nor guaranteed a progressive politics that can apply in any and all circumstances.

If one, despite the historical evidence to the contrary, nonetheless continues to believe that the conceptual category of the "person" and thus ethics itself are endangered by politics, the argument of this project might seem precariously relativistic, not only forsaking the primary foundation for social justice, but also auguring a future of doing little but accepting (and perhaps even defending) all kinds of horrific violations upon "persons" as legitimate within a particular cultural, political, or historical context. Some may thus see this project not only as incompatible with emancipatory politics but also as ultimately reproducing the logic of oppression by undermining the hard-won "personhood" of certain beings. It is precisely this deeply-held belief that the "person" is required in order to ground emancipatory thought that this chapter will explore. Although I am questioning the claim that the "person" in itself can secure social justice and am interested in reconfiguring the kind of argument we use to establish progressive thought, I am not arguing that by changing the argument or that by appreciating the ways in which we are implicated in constructing the "person," true social progress will inevitably result. I am not claiming that such a change is inherently progressive because it finally represents what a "person" truly is. Rather than preserve the representationalist logic underwriting liberal thought, I am simply claiming that an appeal to the absolute "person" is no longer useful. What I am suggesting is that changing the way in which we invoke the notion of the "person" will allow more productive and politically engaged arguments to be developed, inciting questions about how to achieve particular goals at particular moments. The epistemological and metaphysical problem of determining who is a "person" would be replaced by the political and ultimately pragmatic question of what we want a "person" to be.

In order to address the abiding conviction that the "person," no matter what its problematic history, must nonetheless remain above politics if progressive thought and emancipatory politics are not to dissolve, I turn to Frederick Douglass's *Narrative of the Life of Frederick Douglass, An American Slave, Written by Himself* (1845), the text that has come to be regarded as the classic slave narrative.[4] Because one would expect slave narratives to most forcefully express the irreplaceable power of an absolute conception of the "person," I turn to this genre to explore the assumption that the conceptual category of the "person" must rest on more than the shifting sands of historical contingency. Without the "person" as an authentic, *a priori* fact that exists before the touch of slavery, it is often assumed that these narratives would be unable to prove the categorical injustice of slavery or to secure the slave's natural right to freedom and equality. In particular, Douglass's careful representation of his becoming a Man offers an ideal occasion to examine the necessity of locating a transcendental and transcontextual "person" at the root of any compelling argument about the fundamental injustice of slavery.[5]

Or to put this another way, I am interested in how the slave narrative, in general, and Douglass's, in particular, have incited scholars simultaneously to cite the "person" as a self-evident identity even as they have discussed how these autobiographies are "the attempts of blacks to *write themselves into being*."[6] And it is in this sense that the slave narrative stands as the exemplary liberal genre. *The Narrative of Frederick Douglass* is grounded on the claim that slavery unpardonably represses the always already existing "personhood" of the slave, and therefore the *Narrative* looks a lot like a traditional liberal argument. But there is a counter-narrative contained in this hyper-canonical slave narrative. In this second story, "personhood" is produced rather than reflected, an identity that must be enacted rather than a brute fact to be cited. Douglass's narrative, despite its overt and archetypally liberal logic, contains a competing logic, one that exposes the constitutive blind spot of liberal representation, revealing how liberalism depends upon a ritualistic disavowal of the possibility that "persons" are the effect – rather than the source – of history.

Douglass's narrative, in short, ultimately exceeds the explicitly liberal argument that governs it. Challenging the claim that the "person" is the indisputable origin of a slave's right to be free, the *Narrative* is at war with its own liberal logic. Its manifest argument is shadowed by a rival account of emancipatory politics, one in which those excluded from "personhood" gain social and political authority not because their "personhood" is inherent and finally recognized, but because subaltern figures themselves finally participate in the act of representation and recognize themselves as "persons" – that is, confer this status upon themselves. This chapter will read *through* the liberal narrative that Douglass explicitly tells (one in which "personhood" is an eternal possession) to uncover the narrative that the text submerges and seeks to disown. This alternative narrative replaces questions about who always already is a "person" with questions about who controls the representation of "personhood" and what effect a particular definition produces in a particular context. This second story – a story about how "persons" are made rather than found – is the one that must be disavowed if the *Narrative* is to be apotheosized as the paradigmatic liberal text.

In particular, I will focus on the moment that has become perhaps the most discussed in Douglass's narrative: Douglass's fight with the slave-breaker Edward Covey – an event that he calls "the turning point in my career as a slave" (113). In introducing this defining moment, Douglass says that "you have seen how a man was made a slave; you shall see how a slave was made a man." The elegant balance of Douglass's formulation elides the extent to which the story Douglass tells is not symmetrical; it is not simply a story of return but of rupture.[7] This sentence, placed as Henry Louis Gates has said, "at the structural center" of the autobiography (*Figures*, 94),[8] represents the central tension not only of Douglass's story, but also of liberal thought: the tension between being "a man" and becoming one. In Douglass's archetypal story of the slave's journey from slavery to freedom, the central problems haunting discussions of slavery converge: on one hand, slave narratives are imagined as representing the inalienable "personhood" of the slave (i.e. slavery misidentifies "persons" as things), yet these narratives are simultaneously imagined as *writing* the Black "person" into existence. That is, these narratives base their anti-slavery argument on the claim that slaves are "persons" despite their "brutification" ("you have seen how a man was made a slave"), even as they represent "how a slave was made a man" – as Houston Baker has put it, the goal of these narratives "was primarily one of *creating* a human and liberated self."[9] The genre, one might say, is divided between the project of representing and making "persons."

What makes the battle with Covey especially significant is that it foregrounds precisely this division, explicitly unsettling the foundation that conventionally authorizes assertions of the immorality of slavery. The key event of Douglass's life puts the quintessentially liberal understanding of "personhood" as a pre-political truth under severe pressure, placing the claim that the slave is always already a "person" in tension with the competing claim that "personhood" is a historical effect, a consequence of praxis. By attending to an event – the act of becoming a "person" – that liberal thought imagines as having always already occurred, Douglass's text, despite Douglass's apparent intention, both highlights and forecloses questions about what grounds the claim that slavery is wrong. The reading that follows goes against the grain of Douglass's narrative, examining how the climactic moment of the text clarifies the limits of liberal representation, revealing liberal narratives about the liberation of the "person" to be written retroactively, their explicit foundation (the "person") neither as necessary nor as secure as is commonly imagined.

THE FIGHT

In all three versions of Douglass's life, the text's pivotal moment begins with Douglass seeking out his master, Thomas Auld, after Covey delivers a particularly brutal beating. Rationalizing Covey's behavior, Auld orders Douglass to return to Covey. Upon his return, Covey immediately rushes to beat him. Douglass runs away, hiding in the woods. There he meets another slave, Sandy, who offers Douglass a magical root that he claims will offer protection from Covey. Although Douglass is skeptical of Sandy's superstitious beliefs, the charm, at least at first, appears to work. When Douglass comes out of hiding, Covey, instead of beating him, speaks kindly to him. All is well until the next day, when Covey, no longer constrained by the Sabbath, tries to beat Douglass. It is then that Douglass suddenly resists.

As Douglass says, the moment he physically confronts Covey is "the turning point in my career as a slave" (113).[10] This moment is quite literally a turning point, turning Douglass from a slave into a Man.[11] Given that before this battle Douglass explains how Covey had succeeded in breaking him ("behold a man transformed into a brute") and that after it he declares himself a "man," it is not surprising that Douglass frames this event in quite spectacular terms (105). Lasting for nearly two hours, this battle is staged as an epic struggle between Good and Evil. Douglass designates Covey not only as the incarnation of the slave system but as a stand-in for Satan (nicknamed "the Snake," Covey "think[s] himself equal to deceiving the Almighty") as well as for the anti-Christ (Covey's "comings," in a perverse parody of Christ, "were like a thief in the night" [113, 104, 103]).[12] In turn, Douglass represents himself as an archetypal Christian hero who experiences "a glorious resurrection" (113). Since this scene is presented in such a self-consciously mythic manner, it does not seem inappropriate to approach this moment allegorically, as an event that exceeds its particulars.[13] More than a fight between two individuals, this incident – much like Rousseau's account of the origins of the social contract, Hegel's "Lordship/Bondage" narrative, or Althusser's heuristic scene of interpellation – stands as a primal scene, as the ur-moment of identity.[14]

After this act of resistance, Douglass declares that he is now unalterably and unconditionally free. As Douglass explains, from this moment on "however long I might remain a slave in form the day had passed forever when I could be a slave in fact" (113). Although Douglass claims to be free "in fact," one might imagine that Douglass remains a slave both "in fact" and "in form": his master has not emancipated him nor has he physically escaped from the slave South. The freedom he has achieved, in other words, is fundamentally abstract. Indeed, rather than corresponding to his material circumstance, his newfound freedom is defined by its discontinuity with empirical circumstance. Douglass stops being a slave not when he is emancipated in any political, legal, or social sense, but when he understands that his essential identity is fundamentally distinct from the influence of any individual, institution, or environment. This fight, in short, allows Douglass to appreciate the distance between what he is and what the law and slaveholders understand him to be.

The fight, it appears, establishes Douglass as what we would now call an abstract individual. Fundamentally disembodied and holding only a negative relation to his context, Douglass represents his freedom in terms of his ability to transcend not only his circumstance but his body and bodily markers. As Douglass will state in later descriptions of the fight, in the course of the fight "the very color of the man was forgotten" (*My Bondage*, 242; *Life and Times*, 140). After the battle with Covey, Douglass never again identifies himself as a "brute" because after this battle Douglass no longer imagines that either his identity or his freedom hinges on the question of whether he is a slave "in form."

In this sense, the fight with Covey stands in contrast to reading *The Columbian Orator*, the text's other crucial liberatory event.[15] Having learned to read, Douglass gets hold of *The Columbian Orator*, a popular primer in eloquence; he is especially affected by a "Dialogue between a Master and a Slave" – a piece in which a slave convinces his master to set him free. This text is particularly significant in Douglass's narrative because it allows Douglass to see slavery as a political institution (and thus open to rational debate) rather than as a structure ordained by Nature (and thus beyond rational debate). Reading this text leads Douglass on "the pathway from slavery to freedom" because it teaches him that slavery is not his inevitable and proper condition. (78). Rather than sanctioned by reason, slavery is revealed to be opposed to reason.

Although reading may point Douglass towards freedom and certainly makes him an unruly slave, it, unlike fighting, does not make Douglass free. What distinguishes reading from fighting, most significantly, is that reading does not show Douglass that his value and his freedom are absolute and intrinsic. Literacy, in fact, makes Douglass more miserable. "Learning to read," Douglass explains, "had been a curse rather than a blessing" (84). It is a curse because even though reading allows Douglass to understand the injustice of slavery, it also makes clear to him that he is fundamentally defined by the grip of this unjust institution. Reading, in contrast to fighting, entrenches Douglass more deeply in his material condition. Indeed, Covey can succeed in breaking Douglass precisely to the extent that Douglass understands both his freedom and his identity as contextual, as effects of where he is and how he is treated. In the end, reading not only does not emancipate Douglass, but it also carries with it a concept of freedom and identity that makes Douglass especially vulnerable to Covey's manipulations. At Covey's, Douglass explains, "I was broken in body, soul, and spirit"; the "dark night of slavery closed in upon me; and behold a man transformed into a brute!" (105).

If, rather than making Douglass permanently free, literacy perpetuates Douglass's oscillating between being a "man" and being a "brute," the battle with Covey produces an unconditional break with slavery. Having fought Covey, Douglass will no longer see his identity as subject to contingency, as transformable or wobbly. After the fight, his "personhood" is absolute. Fundamentally discontinuous from and untouched by his empirical situation, it now stands as the solid foundation that authorizes Douglass's claim that he is not a slave even when he is in slavery.

Indeed, Douglass himself identifies his battle with Covey as producing a definitive rupture between his identity as a slave and his identity as a "man"; something that reading fails to do. As he will declare in later versions of his autobiography, "I was a changed being after that fight. I was nothing before; I WAS A MAN NOW" (*My Bondage and My Freedom* 246). To the extent that Douglass's resistance to Covey *makes* him a "man," "manhood" seems to be represented as a performative identity, something produced by the act of resistance, rather than prior to or independent of it. Rather than resisting because he is a Man, Douglass becomes a Man by resisting. According to Douglass, manhood, in distinction to liberal accounts of "personhood," is an effect not a cause, an identity born at rather than antecedent to the moment of resistance. And although this event is ostensibly a moment of choice ("I resolved to fight"), the chooser, it appears, is radically absent. Douglass, in fact, suggests not simply that there is no "agent" behind the deed, but that the "agent" is itself a function of the "deed."

But as dramatically as Douglass represents the battle as producing a fundamentally new identity, he more forcefully represents this fight as producing no change at all. The fight may make Douglass a Man, but, more significantly, it expresses his "personhood," revealing the fact that he has always been a being who could never be justly enslaved ("you have seen how a man was made a slave") and making clear that this identity precedes any action or behavior he may or may not perform. According to Douglass, the fight merely allows him to fully possess what he already is: a "person" rather than a thing. The fight, Douglass explains,

> *re*kindled the few expiring embers of freedom, and *re*vived within me a sense of my own manhood. It *re*called the departed self-confidence, and *inspired me again* with a determination to be free. . .. It was a glorious *re*surrection, from the tomb of slavery, to the heaven of freedom (113, emphasis added).

By insistently using the prefix "re," Douglass defines his victory in terms of a logic of restoration. Such hyperbolic language is not simply a rhetorical ornament. It announces how completely Douglass embraces the liberal assumption that "personhood" is an antecedent identity. Unlike "manhood," "personhood" possesses an *a priori* hardness that simply needs to be reawakened, revealed, and reclaimed. And at this moment, what "the bloody arm of slavery" (literalized by Covey) has struggled to withhold, Douglass once and for all retrieves. Rather than representing a transformation, this event signals a return.

Such an understanding of slavery as the systematic repression of the slave's essential "personhood" is, of course, familiar. And this line of argument certainly is evident throughout the *Narrative*. Douglass scrupulously describes how the peculiar institution systematically works to turn "persons" into Things (separating families, feeding and ranking slaves as animals, alienating slaves from their own desires etc), but such efforts are never represented as actually turning slaves into animals. Rather such tactics are represented as proving the fundamental immorality of slavery: slavery misidentifies beings who are intrinsically "persons." Such treatment may be necessary for the slave system to perpetuate itself – slaves, as well as masters, must "be made to feel that slavery is right" – but it never succeeds in erasing the fact that slaves never can become things (135). Douglass acknowledges that slaves may often be deceived by such manipulations, as he says, "I have found that, to make a contented slave, it is necessary to make a thoughtless one. . . .and he can be brought to that only when he *ceases* to be a man" (135, emphasis added). The slave system, in other words, certainly may succeed in making slaves into brutes, and it surely can stop slaves from acting like a "man" (in the sense they no longer act with honor and self-respect) but such manipulations are always unethical because they violate what slaves fundamentally are: slaves simply are "persons" no matter how they act or how they are treated. Slaves and masters may be victims of the false consciousness that slavery imposes, but Black slaves never are, in any ontological sense, things. Or as Douglass puts it in "The Nature of Slavery," an 1850 lecture he reprinted as an appendix to *My Bondage and My Freedom*, "The slave is a man. . .It is such a being that is smitten and blasted. The first work of slavery is to mar and deface those characteristics of its victims which distinguish *men* from *things*, and *persons* from *property*."[16]

Given this line of argument, it is not surprising that Douglass represents his fight with Covey as a spectacular triumph not because he unequivocally defeats Covey (Covey eventually stops fighting, claiming a victory that Douglass disputes) but because the fight allows Douglass to finally possess the very knowledge that slavery had been intent on repressing: the fact that he is, always has been, and forever will be a "person." The fight, in this sense, stands as the quintessential expression of the liberal idiom. It testifies to how Douglass understands his "personhood" as natural and inborn, something that slavery attempts to deny but never erases, that remains inviolable, beyond and beneath the fluctuations of the social and the relational and the circumstantial.[17] Reading may give "tongue to interesting thoughts of my own soul, which had frequently flashed through my mind, and died away for want of utterance," but fighting remains the only modality for giving permanent utterance to a truth that precedes the distortions of slavery (84). Somewhat paradoxically, only fighting fully articulates Douglass's true identity because only fighting allows him to recognize what he always already is (a "person") rather than defines him wholly in terms of what he does (what Douglass calls "manhood").

Such a liberal conceptualization of identity, however, does not exhaust the story of Douglass's fight with Covey. There is, one might say, a second story contained within the overtly liberal narrative. Although Douglass, after the fight, plainly recounts his struggle with Covey as allowing him to recover what he has possessed all along (his absolute "personhood"), there seems to be a tension between Douglass's account of this event and his reflections afterwards. What is most intriguing about Douglass's representation of the fight is that Douglass never describes the experience of the fight itself as the inevitable expression of his "personhood." Indeed, an explanation of why Douglass resists Covey remains conspicuously absent.

That is, given the explicitly liberal tenor of Douglass's narrative, one might imagine that Douglass resists Covey at the moment his "personhood" finally expresses itself. According to such an account, Douglass would resist when the irrepressible truth that he is a being with inalienable rights, one who can never be justly treated like the oxen he attempts to herd, can no longer be repressed.[18] He would resist at a moment of greatest desperation, a moment when, having been subject to Covey's constant brutality, such brutality finally forces his "personhood" to surface and motivate his resistance. And this resistance would vividly demonstrate how at the very moment when the institution of slavery most directly seeks to curb, distort, and deny the innate "personhood" of the slave, such "personhood" returns with all the force of the repressed, proving once and for all that slavery can never succeed in its quest to transform "persons" into things.

Indeed, critics have often put forth precisely such a reading of this event as the moment when the repressed returns, arguing, for example that

> Douglass's foundational point in the *Narrative* is that the fundamental humanity of the enslaved cannot be denied; in removing from Douglass his own heightened awareness of his condition and confusion as one of the enslaved, Covey reduces Douglass to his fundamental humanity. . . ..When Covey reduces Douglass to a brute, he changes the nature of his ongoing struggle to dominate. No longer struggling against merely a man, having reduced that man to his essence, Covey finds himself struggling with the Almighty.[19]

Such an argument makes clear how the conceptual category of the "person" functions like a theological category, an absolute that can be "obscured by one's constructed identity, but not lost."[20]

Significantly, Douglass never offers such an explanation of his motivation. At the very instant when one might expect Douglass to acknowledge the irreducibility of his "personhood," Douglass declares that he himself is mystified as to the cause of his resistance:

> As soon as I found what he was up to, I gave a sudden spring, and as I did so, he holding to my legs, I was brought sprawling on the stable floor. Mr. Covey seemed now to think he had me, and could do what he pleased; but at this moment – *from whence came the spirit I don't know* – I resolved to fight.
>
> (112, emphasis added).

In every version of his autobiography, Douglass reiterates that the most crucial action in his life is ultimately inexplicable. In *My Bondage and My Freedom* (1855), he states that

> Whence came the daring spirit necessary to grapple with a man who, eight-and-forty hours before, could, with his slightest word have made me tremble like a leaf in a storm, *I do not know*. . .[21]

And he repeats these same words (adding only a comma) in *The Life and Times of Frederick Douglass* (1892):

> Whence came the daring spirit necessary to grapple with a man who, eight-and-forty hours before, could, with his slightest word, have made me tremble like a leaf in a storm, *I do not know*. . .[22]

There appears to be nothing inherent *in* Douglass motivating his resistance ("from whence came the spirit. . ."). He does not rise up in the name of his repressed and authentic identity as a "person." Certainly, as Douglass says, the fight makes him a "man," but, it is important to note, he does not fight because he already is a Man. Rather than compel him to resist, his manhood, as I discussed earlier, is precisely what is produced by his willingness to fight. Or to put the metaleptic logic underwriting this scene in its starkest terms, Douglass acts in the name of the very identity that his actions actually bring into being.

What is particularly striking about Douglass's resistance is that even though the significance of this resistance is never in question, the question of its source persists. Indeed, to the extent that Douglass, when describing this event, does not categorically integrate his resistance within a liberal narrative of the inevitable expression of an antecedent "personhood," the foundational moment of Douglass's story remains an effect without a cause. Disconnected from any origin in his "personhood," his resistance seems to actively unsettle the logic of liberal thought. In fact, Douglass himself appears to draw attention to the absence at the center of his narrative of resistance, going so far as to thematize the problem of identifying the root of his resistance by enveloping this event with the enigmatic story of a magic root given him by his fellow slave Sandy Jenkins.

Just before the fight with Covey, Sandy gives Douglass a "certain root" that will, he claims, protect Douglass from a whipping by any white man if worn on the right side of his body. When Covey does not whip Douglass for running away, Douglass begins to wonder if this magic token can explain Covey's unaccountable behavior:

> Now, this singular conduct of Mr. Covey really made me begin to think that there was something in the *root* which Sandy had given me; and had it been on any other day than Sunday, I could have attributed the conduct to no other cause than the influence of that *root*; and as it was, I was half inclined to think the root to be something more than I at first had taken it to be (111).

Ultimately Douglass does not accept that this artifact of African-American folk culture lies at the root of Covey's action. He declares the root powerless, little more than a "superstition. . .very common among the more ignorant slaves" (119). Distancing himself from those who foolishly attribute any consequence to this fetish object, Douglass offers a *rational* explanation for Covey's seemingly inexplicable behavior, asserting that it was Covey's hypocritical respect for religion (it was the Sabbath when Douglass returned) that restrained Covey from whipping Douglass and reasoning that it was Covey's self-interest (Covey depends upon his reputation as a "nigger-breaker" to acquire cheap labor) that inhibited him from publicly punishing Douglass for his resistance.[23]

Although Douglass demystifies the talismanic power of the root and thereby marks his entrance into Western enlightened thought, the problem of explaining the origin of remarkable behavior – the very question incarnated by the root – haunts Douglass's own description of the climactic event of his *Narrative*. Indeed, Douglass himself self-consciously puns on the resonant meanings of the word *root* in later versions of his autobiography, introducing the moment he resists Covey's beating by stating "I now forgot my *roots*" (*My Bondage and My Freedom*, 242, original emphasis).[24] This turn on the word "root" suggests that Douglass's repudiation of the power of the magical root is not simply an effort to prove his proper Enlightenment credentials.[25] The root both fascinates and must be denied because it speaks to a deeper anxiety about the referential crisis initiated by his resistance. Sandy's root, in short, *is* "something more than [Douglass] at first had taken it to be"; it is the text's primary fetish object (111).[26] Simultaneously concentrating and managing Douglass's tension over the missing foundation motivating his will to fight, the mysterious power of this root testifies to Douglass's longing for a clear root of his own. Sandy's concrete root, in essence, raises the theoretical problem of whether a slave can possess sufficient grounds for resistance.

In the end, however, Douglass seems to have no difficulty repudiating Sandy's root and affirming his own. The disavowal of the literal root suggests the extent to which Douglass acknowledges his anxiety over the root of resistance only to foreclose it. Although Douglass's fascination with roots certainly constellates significant questions about the origin of his resistance, as soon as the fight is over any potential challenge that this root poses to the liberal narrative of resistance seems to disappear. Immediately after the fight, the liberal order of things reasserts itself, and Douglass's resistance is incorporated in a liberal plot of the "person's" liberation from repression. After the fight, Douglass, as I discussed earlier, views the battle with Covey as crucial because it

> *re*kindled the few expiring embers of freedom, and *re*vived within me a sense of my own manhood. It *re*called the departed self-confidence, and *inspired me again* with a determination to be free. . .. It was a glorious *re*surrection, from the tomb of slavery, to the heaven of freedom (113, emphasis added).

In this account, any anxiety about the origin of Douglass's resistance and freedom is suppressed. At this moment the justification for both clearly lies in the slave's inherent identity as a "person." Rather than remain contingent upon or an effect of a specific action, Douglass's identity is now once again securely installed as foundational, as immunized from any historical context, beyond construction and debate.

To the extent that readers have understood the plot of Douglass's narrative in terms of the gradual unfolding of the slave's unconditional "personhood" and suppressed the story of how Douglass's identity is produced in and through action, this event is the "turning-point" of Douglass's story because it foregrounds the key question behind any slave narrative: the question of what authority legitimates a slave's inalienable right to be free. Is a pre-political notion of the "person" required? Can a slave's "personhood" be imagined as something to be produced and still be politically effective? Indeed, this event can be seen as the point at which the two narratives of Douglass's identity converge. In one, Douglass's identity is fundamentally performative, the ostensible cause of Douglass's resistance an effect of the act of resistance itself; in the other his identity is fundamentally constantive, a free-standing cause, something that always already exists and thus needs only to be acknowledged rather than produced.

The "turning-point" of Douglass's narrative, in other words, registers a turn from one narrative about identity to the other. At the moment of the fight, Douglass puts forward a narrative in which he *becomes* a "Man" by fighting, but as soon as the fight is over he represents his "personhood" as foundational, putting forth the claim that this identity in and of itself precedes, resists, and exceeds any context. If this event in general and the root in particular foregrounds the tension between the text's two narratives about the formation of the slave's subjectivity, what is striking is that the *Narrative*'s turn away from the performative account toward the liberal account occurs after the fight, after Douglass's "personhood" has become secure. This turn, in short, is symptomatic. On the one hand, it illustrates how liberal clarity about the "person" is installed retroactively, confidently cited only after the "personification" of the slave is complete. And, on the other, it suggests how powerfully liberal thought must foreclose any acknowledgment of the historical moment when a "person" is created, inciting an irreparable chasm between the moment of and the moment after "personification."

If Douglass's turn away from the mystified roots of his resistance writes small the question of what authorizes a slave's claim for the inalienable rights of "persons," it also anticipates the retroactive conversion of historical contingency into necessity that characterizes modern accounts of the antebellum debate over slavery. Our certainty that a slave self-evidently is a "person" demonstrates how such certainty is only possible after questions about the legitimacy of slavery have been resolved, only possible because competing arguments about "personhood" of the slave have been rendered illegitimate. Rather than proving how the "person" intrinsically guarantees a particular politics, such arguments prove how thoroughly the problem of slavery has ceased to be a political problem for us. In this sense, the notion of the "person" can now ground arguments against slavery because it is beside not above politics, post rather than pre-political.

Thus, if, from one viewpoint, antebellum debates over slavery seem connected to contemporary debates over reproductive rights, cloning, and stem cell research in the way each places the concept of the "person" at the center of any judgment about the legitimacy of a particular practice, these debates are dramatically different because modern accounts of slavery are no longer fractured by warring assertions of who is a "person." If we now invoke the "personhood" of the Negro slave as a hard fact, we do so only because this question is now settled in a way that debates over genetic engineering and fetal "personhood" are not. Rather than save ethics, the "person," I have been arguing, only brings a false clarity to ethical problems. Most troublingly, it transforms the present into the inevitable, representing what we know as a means to trump politics rather than to trumpet a particular form of politics.

THE COUNTERNARRATIVE

Douglass's narrative suggests that it is only after one has become a "person" that one acquires the history of having always been a "person" and thus indicates why the problem of slavery needs to be rephrased: at issue is not the danger of forsaking the anchor of any claims for social justice but how little has historically been gained by conceiving of the "person" as a self-sustaining category. Although registering an uneasiness over liberal assertions about the solidity of the "person," Douglass's text ultimately perpetuates the liberal mystification of the origin of the "person."[27] Such anxiety, however, is not peculiar to Douglass; it is rehearsed in other slave narratives. For example, William Wells Brown discusses the difficulty of understanding a slave's sudden transformation from chattel to legal subject in his introduction to his novel *Clotel*:

> I was no more a chattel, but a MAN. . ..The fact that I was a freeman – could walk, talk, eat, and sleep as a man, and no one to stand over me with the blood-clotted cowhide – *all this made me feel that I was not myself.*[28]

Brown represents his metamorphosis as fundamentally uncanny. If, on one hand, his status as a freeman is justified because it reflects what he always already is (i.e. a "person"), it, on the other hand, makes him into something he has never been. This rupture suggests the limits of liberal claims that "personhood" stands as the repressed origin of resistance – "personhood" is existentially experienced as an identity that is context-bound, not context-transcendent, an identity that is not intrinsic but produced. The question therefore is not how are "persons" finally recognized, but how are "persons" produced.

To offer a brief example of how such a question can be answered I want to turn to a lesser known slave narrative, John Brown's *Slave Life in Georgia: A Narrative of the Life, Sufferings, and Escape of John Brown, A Fugitive Slave, Now in England* (1855). Brown's narrative of his enslavement in the Deep South challenges the sufficiency of arguments that begin from the premise that slavery is immoral because it obviously misidentifies "persons" as things; persuasively disrupts the continuity between claims about the essential identity of the "person" and liberatory practices; and suggests how slavery can be opposed at the moment when the foundational concept for determining social justice (the "person") is the subject of dispute.

Brown directly addresses the problem of invoking the "person" as an unimpeachable authority above politics in the chapter "My Reflections," a chapter culminating in his horrifically detailed account of slavery's brutality. There he states that:

> Slaveholders are not sensible to moral arguments, because they believe their interests are bound up in maintaining the system of slavery. I would not advise to leave off arguing out the question on moral grounds; but I would urge them to pay a little more attention to the commercial part of the subject.. . . I do not see how the system is to be put down except by undermining it. I mean by underselling it in the markets of the world. . .*I am quite convinced that if slavery is to be put down, one of the most certain means – if it is not, indeed, the only one – is to reduce the value of its products in the markets* (emphasis added).[29]

Although Brown begins by stating he would not discontinue moral arguments about the self-evident humanity of the slave, he quickly moves to the conclusion that such arguments are ultimately inadequate. Economic arguments, he concludes, must subsume moral ones because moral arguments are inadequate when one is faced with an opponent who does not acknowledge the force of such arguments. Although many assume that slavery in and of itself violates morality and that this truth will prevail once self-interest and baser motives are overcome, Brown questions whether morality so clearly stands outside and beyond power. According to Brown, morality cannot so easily be invoked to trump self-interest because morality is itself inextricable from questions of commercial and political interest. It cannot persuade someone to stop acting immorally because morality itself hinges on a particular political and economic context. Since Brown is unwilling to put his faith in morality until the social and economic context changes, he opposes slavery by arguing for a particular kind of affiliation between morality and the market. Rather than claiming that morality can only be preserved if it is delinked from political issues such as self-interest, Brown seeks to defend the power of moral claims by linking them with politics.

That is, although Brown collapses the categories of self-interest and morality, such a line of thought does not vitiate the standing of moral arguments. It only suggests that moral arguments are not freestanding, referring to an authority independent from any politics. Indeed, rather than undermine morality, Brown simply proposes that the most powerful moral arguments about the slave are a function of self-interest. Brown challenges the sufficiency of moral arguments in and of themselves not because he does not believe in morality but because he does not see morality as existing in a vacuum, possessing an inherent power beyond the fluctuations of circumstance. In Brown's narrative, morality becomes a contingent concept, one that expresses rather than stands outside particular political and economic arrangements. Therefore, rather than citing morality to challenge slavery, Brown calls for a new economic arrangement, one that will allow new definitions of morality.

Brown suggests one reason why morality in and of itself cannot be summoned to persuade someone to stop acting immorally: the "person" – the foundation of such moralizing – itself hinges on a particular political and economic context. Indeed, one could speculate that Brown's lack of confidence in the obvious moral truth of the "person" has been deeply shaken by his own experience. The violence he was legitimately subjected to as a slave perhaps has demonstrated to him the contingency of the identity category that supposedly intrinsically authorizes an opposition to slavery. I will cite the most shocking moment that Brown represents to illustrate how he sees slavery as putting the relationship between ethics and the "person" into question.

In "gratitude" for being cured of a serious illness, Brown's master, Thomas Stevens, lends Brown to a doctor for a series of scientific experiments carried out over a period of nine months. After using Brown to research the effects of heat exhaustion (the result of which allows Hamilton to patent an enormously profitable remedy for sunstroke), Dr. Hamilton set out to ascertain how deep "black skin went" (340).[30] This work was done by

> applying blisters to my hands, legs and feet, which bear the scars to this day. He continued until he drew up the dark skin from between the upper and the under one. He used to blister me at intervals of about two weeks. He also tried other experiments upon me, which I cannot dwell upon (340).

The social significance of scientifically determining whether Black skin is more than simply a superficial marker of difference – more than an effect of climate – surely underwrote these experiments. By burning off the epidermis of a Negro, Hamilton sets out to explore whether blackness is merely skin-deep or if it is organic to the Negro race. If he can reveal a subcutaneous blackness, this scientific evidence would prove the Negro an essentially different being, rather than a white man whom the environment has accidentally darkened. Hamilton, it appears, is attempting to substantiate the widespread assumption, articulated for example by Dr. Samuel Cartwright, that the blackness of the Negro "is not confined to the skin, but pervades, in a greater or less degree, the whole inward man down to the bones themselves, giving the flesh and blood, the membranes and every organ and part of the body, except the bones, a darker hue than in the white race."[31]

That Hamilton experiments upon a living slave rather than on a Negro corpse (dissection not only would require he purchase a corpse but also was illegal in many states during the antebellum period) reflects how deeply his scientific work is already premised on the belief that the Negro is fundamentally Black and essentially not a "person." The very form of the experiment betrays the answer that he ostensibly seeks to discover. To imagine that Dr. Hamilton must, on some level, be riven by guilt is to anachronistically project a modern certainty about "persons" onto antebellum culture, a certainty that the brutality of the experiment and the numerous contemporaneous political, religious, and scientific justifications of slavery compellingly controvert. To always already know what is being repressed and what must be uncovered is not only to leave unasked how we know this to be the case but also to perpetuate the liberal idea that the "person" can guarantee ethics. Indeed, Brown's narrative suggests what a weak resister to oppression the identity category of the "person" is at the moment we confront a competing claim about who is a "person." And, in turn, Hamilton is such a troubling figure not because he can be dismissed as clearly evil but because he was an honored and respected gentleman who may actually have believed that he was helping his fellow man.[32] Thus, one might hypothesize that the reason that US slavery has proven so deeply troubling is not because it demonstrates how the United States has failed to live up to its ideals, but because it demonstrates how contingent these ideals are and how easily these ideals can (at least from our perspective) be blithely violated. Although the logic of liberal thought incites us to invoke the absoluteness of the "person," the practice of slavery suggests how little "personhood" in and of itself can do.

ETHICS AFTER THE 'PERSON'

If Brown's narrative raises fundamental questions about the liberal claim that "personhood" is a stable, pre-discursive identity, this departure from the logic of liberal representation does not mean that we are left with no secure strategy for condemning slavery. It only suggests that the strategy we have relied on is itself not as secure as liberals hope. In order to defamiliarize the logic of liberal representation, I have foregrounded the fetishistic logic of liberal thought. Rather than rehearsing the traditional claim that the horror of slavery devolves from the fundamental mistake of treating "persons" as if they were things, I have redescribed liberal thought as invoking the very term in dispute to settle its foundational ethical disputes. This redescription of liberalism, rather than forsaking the most effective argument against slavery, acknowledges the extent to which the "person" does not fulfill its primary function as the incontestable ground of social justice at the very moment when this function is most necessary, the very moment when the notion of the "person" is under debate. But again, to foreground the fetishistic logic underwriting liberal thought implies neither that an anti-slavery position, in particular, nor social justice, in general, will inevitably follow once one approaches the "person" as constructed in and relative to context. It is only to suggest that different arguments might more effectively intervene in arguments over ethics and "personhood." Such arguments would acknowledge our role in constructing "persons" rather than focus on how the "person" is repressed by certain practices and thus obscure how we are implicated in producing what a "person" is.

If the liberal Enlightenment project is to establish the truth as that which emerges in spite of context, this project has focused on the privileged referent of liberal representation to explore how the "person" fails to be the lever with which one can disrupt the limitations of historical and social conditions. Rather than consider the "person" as an identity untouched by historical change and as a means to liberate us from the limitations of perspective, it has approached the "person" as the primary register of historical change and the primary symptom of historical perspective. That is, I have foregrounded the impulse to identify the "person" as that which resists history in order to pursue two questions: firstly, whether this conceptual category can ever fulfill the office that liberal political theory has assigned it and secondly, what is gained by abandoning the goal of identifying the accuracy of a particular account of the "person" for the sake of examining the effect of a particular construction of the "person" within a particular context.

To see liberalism's foundational referent as a goal to be generated rather than a pre-existing fact to be resurrected, however, is not to lose the identity that anchors claims for social justice. Although it might seem reassuring to imagine the "person" as an identity to be expressed (rather than created), the political history of the "person" undermines any assertion that the "person" exceeds its historical context. As Sartre has dramatically put it,

> Tomorrow, after my death, certain people may decide to establish fascism, and others may be cowardly or miserable enough to let them get away with it. At that moment, fascism will be the truth of man, and so much the worse for us. In reality, things will be as much as man has decided they are.[33]

One may hope that fascism fundamentally violates universal principles of justice and truth, but this assertion, Sartre argues, is itself contingent and fundamentally political, an effect of a particular historical and social situation.[34] To question whether the truth of the "person" is intrinsic and will always shine through is not to question the possibility of ethical judgment but to foreground our responsibility for creating what a "person" is; it is to recover the politics of "personhood."

Having reached a moment when the ostensibly objective and scientific definition of the "person" has itself become the object of human intervention – a moment when we are now patenting life, fusing the human and the animal, dissolving the dichotomy of the organic and the technological – we are perhaps entering a moment when the truth of the "person" is going to be put under new kinds of pressure.[35] Indeed, it is becoming increasingly difficult to imagine the "person" as a fixed category to be unveiled as we are becoming increasingly engaged with the process of producing, manipulating, and recognizing new "persons." And at the moment when biotechnology and nanotechnology are providing us with new choices regarding the creation of new people, the current geopolitical situation is tragically demonstrating how easily certain beings (whom we consider "persons") can be deemed to be "non-persons." In such a context, the question of what a "person" is seems less crucial than the question of what we aspire "persons" to be. That is, as the problem of choosing who is a "person" is becoming more and more conspicuous, the political nature of this choice is beginning to seem more and more inescapable.

As I have argued, this choice is not unique to contemporary US culture.[36] It was violently enacted during the antebellum period. Modern readings of US slavery, however, have been predicated on forgetting the extent to which antebellum culture put the notion of the "person" into dispute, and such a reading of history has assured us that the conceptual category of the "person" can once again be summoned to resolve current arguments over fetal personhood, stem-cell research, animal rights, green politics, neural computing, and genetic patenting. But what history teaches us perhaps is that these modern debates, much like the antebellum debate over race-based slavery, cannot be resolved by appealing to the very category on which such debates turn. By invoking the "person" and thus reproducing the logic of liberal representation, we are left with no way to confront the particular problem that the Human Genome Project and recent advances in nanotechnology insistently provoke: finding a language which can engage the question of what we want a "person" to be and why.

Although undermining the liberal logic of "personhood" will not, unfortunately, guarantee social justice, it will incite us to be more attentive to our role in producing "persons." A shift in the way we frame the problem will encourage us to examine how we are bringing a certain truth into being. Rather than imagine that we can simply invoke some pre-existing, irreducible truth that wholly exceeds us, we will be compelled to approach the "person" as an identity that we are in the process of constructing and to think about how this process implicates us. Indeed, I would suggest that once these disputes have been definitively settled, they might seem as the antebellum dispute over slavery now does: as debates essentially beyond debate, as questions that have always possessed inevitable answers. And, as with race-based slavery, I would say, that those who in the future would overlook such debates and ignore such questions will have erased the substance of our political struggles.

Notes

INTRODUCTION – THE FIGURE A PERSON MAKES: ON THE AESTHETICS OF LIBERALISM

1 Winthrop D. Jordon, *White over Black: American Attitudes Toward the Negro, 1550–1812* (New York: W.W. Norton & Co., 1968), p. 341. For an exemplary account of the "inexorable" abolition of slavery instaurated by the Founding Fathers see William W. Freehling, "The Founding Fathers and Slavery," *American Historical Review* 77 (1972): 81–93.

2 Rogers M. Smith has articulated this argument in a series of articles and finally in his book *Civic Ideals: Conflicting Visions of Citizenship in US History* (New Haven: Yale University Press, 1997).

3 Garry Wills, *Lincoln at Gettysburg: The Words that Remade America* (New York: Simon & Schuster, 1992), p. 100. Similarly, it is imagined that Southern apologists were resolute in resisting such a placing of the Declaration of Independence at the beginning of US history. See for example Celeste Michelle Condit and John Louis Lucaites, *Crafting Equality: America's Anglo-African Word* (Chicago: University of Chicago Press, 1993), esp. pp. 69–98.

4 The phrase "plain words" is from David Zarefsky, *Lincoln, Douglas, and Slavery: In the Crucible of Public Debate* (Chicago: University of Chicago Press, 1990), p. 151. Although this project will focus on the interpretative problems surrounding the term "men," the term "equal" has also raised significant questions. There exists a long tradition of questioning the transparency of the Declaration's claim that all men are born equal. As John Calhoun asserted the principle that "all men are born free and equal" is a basic "error." Calhoun argued that "Taking the proposition literally (it is in that sense it is understood), there is not a word of truth in it." As he explained, men are not born (infants are and infants are not capable of freedom) and men clearly do not all possess equal mental or physical abilities, appearances, or morals. John C. Calhoun, "Speech on the Oregon Bill," June 27, 1848 in *The Works of John C. Calhoun* (New York: D. Appleton and Co., 1857), 4: 507–511.

5 See George M. Fredrickson, *The Black Image in the White Mind: The Debate on Afro-American Character and Destiny, 1817–1914* (Middletown: Wesleyan University Press, 1971), p. 323 (emphasis added).

6 This linking of the United States to an ideology of human rights was perhaps articulated most famously by Gunnar Myrdal in *The American Dilemma: The Negro Problem and Modern Democracy* (New York: Harper & Row, 1944). Myrdal has called "the American Creed" the deep commitment to the worth and moral equality of all individual human beings, the promised protection of an individual's "inalienable rights to freedom, justice, and a fair opportunity," and the principled rejection of all marks of hereditary privilege (pp. 3–4; 7–8, 25, 52).

For an account of how the Declaration has historically come to achieve its prominence see Pauline Maier, *American Scripture: the Making of the Declaration of Independence* (New York: Knopf, 1997) and Philip F. Detweiler, "The Changing Reputation of the Declaration of Independence: The First Fifty Year," *William and Mary Quarterly*, 3rd series, 19:4 (1962): 557–574.

7 Taney argued that if we abandon the original intent of this phrase and choose any "other rule of construction," we would inevitably "abrogate the judicial character of this court, and make it the mere reflex of the popular opinion or passion of the day" (*Dred Scott v. Sandford*, 60 US (19 How.) 426). All further references will be cited parenthetically.

8 In rendering the majority opinion in *Scott v. Sandford* (Sanford's name was misspelled in the style of the case), Taney chose not to focus on the specific details of the case (for example, on whether Scott remained a slave even after he resided with his master in a free state), but on what he saw as the fundamental question informing the case: whether any Negro (either slave or free) could ever claim a right to the basic rights guaranteed to the "People" by this nation's founding documents. According to Taney:

> The question is simply this: Can a Negro, whose ancestors were imported into this country, and sold as slaves, become a member of the political community formed and brought into existence by the Constitution of the United States, and as such become entitled to all the rights, and privileges, and immunities, guaranteed by that instrument to the citizen? One of which rights is the privilege of suing in a court of the United States in the cases specified in the Constitution (*Dred Scott v. Sandford*, 60 US (19 How.) 405).

Taney's answer was a resounding no. According to Taney, who claimed that "the words 'people of the United States' and 'citizens' are synonymous terms, and mean the same thing," Blacks "are not included, and were not intended to be included, under the word 'citizens' in the Constitution, and can therefore claim none of the rights and privileges which that instrument provides for and secures to citizens of the United States" (404, 405).

9 I use the superannuated term "Negro" to emphasize how thoroughly historical the subject of natural rights is. My account of liberal representation is animated by the tension between the transcendence (and thus innocence) connoted by the term "person" and the clear historicity (and thus distortion) suggested by the term "Negro."

10 The most distinguished American ethnologist, Samuel G. Morton, for example, assembled and meticulously catalogued the largest collection of crania in the world, found that the ancient crania from a given race did not differ from those of their modern descendants, and concluded that it was impossible for these differences to be explained by environmental factors given the history of the world. See Samuel George Morton, *Crania Americana; or, A Comparative View of the Skulls of Various Aboriginal Nations of North and South America: to which is Prefixed an Essay on the Varieties of the Human Species* (Philadelphia: J. Dobson, 1839). In *Types of Mankind*, a massive compilation of the scientific findings of the American School, which eventually ran through ten editions, Josiah Nott proclaimed that "the permanence of existing physical types will not be questioned by any archaeologist or Naturalist of the present day. Nor, by such competent arbitrators, can the consequent permanence of moral and intellectual peculiarities of type be denied. The intellectual man is inseparable from the physical man" (p. 50). Josiah Nott and George R. Gliddon, *Types of Mankind: or, Ethnological Researches, Based upon the Ancient Monuments, Paintings, Sculptures, and Crania of Races, and upon their Nature, Geographical, Philological, and Biblical History: Illustrated by Seclections from the Unedited Papers of Samuel George Morton, M. D., and by Additional Contributions from Prof. L. Agassiz, L. L. D; W. Usher, M. D.; and Prof. H. S. Patterson, M. D.* (Philadelphia: Lippincott, Grambo and Company, 1854).

For an account of antebellum racial theory see Fredrickson, *The Black Image in the White Mind*; William Stanton, *The Leopard's Spots: Scientific Attitudes Toward Race in America, 1815–1859* (Chicago: University of Chicago Press, 1960); Reginald Horsman, *Race and Manifest Destiny: The Origins of American Racial Anglo-Saxonism* (Cambridge: Harvard University Press, 1981), Audrey Smedley, *Race in North America: Origin and Evolution of a Worldview* (Boulder: Westview, 1993), Richard H. Popkin, "Pre-Adamism in 19th Century American Thought: 'Speculative Biology' and Racism" in *Philosophia: Philosophical Quarterly of Israel* 8:2–3 (November 1978): 205–240; William H. Tucker, *The Science and Politics of Racial Research* (Urbana: University of Illinois Press, 1994), pp. 9–36; and William Sumner Jenkins, *Pro-Slavery Thought in the Old South* (Chapel Hill: University of North Carolina Press, 1935).

11 The Arkansas Supreme Court, for example, thought the inspection of an individual's feet a reliable and objective technique for detecting "negro blood." See *Daniel v. Guy* (1857), 23 Ark. 52.

12 In an appendix to *Crania Americana*, George Combe argued that the cranial differences identified by Morton revealed not only intelligence, but also interior qualities such as "self-esteem," "benevolence," and "firmness" (272–277). See also "On the Internal Capacity of the Cranium in the Different Races of Men," in *Crania Americana*. Stephen Jay Gould, *The Mismeasure of Man* (New York: W.W. Norton & Co., 1981) esp. pp. 50–73, offers a powerful critique of these ostensibly objective measurements.

13 The argument between proponents of monogenesis and polygenesis cannot simply be graphed onto an anti-slavery vs. proslavery grid. For example, although it might seem that monogenesis would inevitably undermine the legitimacy of slavery, Southern society, for the most part, turned away from the polygenetic arguments of science in order to embrace a principally religious defense of slavery. The strongest monogenetic arguments, in fact, were formulated in the South, an occurrence perhaps made most dramatically clear in John Bachman's (a proslavery Southern minister) famous debate with Morton over the question of polygenesis. See Dana Nelson, " 'No Cold or Empty Heart': Polygenesis, Scientific Professionalization, and the Unfinished Business of Male Sentimentalism" in *Differences* 11:3 (1999/2000): 29–56, and Lester D. Stephens, *Science, Race, and Religion in the American South: John Bachman and the Charleston Circle of Naturalists, 1815–1895* (Chapel Hill: University of North Carolina Press, 2000).

14 Josiah Priest, *Slavery, As It Relates to the Negro* (Albany 1843). Although often identified as a Reverend (indeed, MA. was added to the title page of reprints), Priest was a self-educated saddle-maker. See Stephen Haynes, *Noah's Curse: The Biblical Justification of American Slavery* (New York: Oxford University Press, 2002) for an account of the influence of Priest in defenses of slavery. See also Mason Stokes, *The Color of Sex: Whiteness, Heterosexuality, and the Fictions of White Supremacy* (Durham: Duke University Press, 2001) for an intriguing discussion of nineteenth century religious accounts of the Negro's role in the Garden of Eden. One of the most popular ideas was that the serpent of "Nachash" who tempted Eve was not a snake but a "negro gardener." This interpretation was based on the fact that the Hebrew word "Nachash" meant both snake and "to be or become black."

15 Moncure D. Conway, *Autobiography, Memories and Experiences of Moncure Daniel Conway* (New York: Houghton, Mifflin and Co. 1904), vol. I, pp. 87–90. Later in his life, Conway became an ardent abolitionist. In *Testimonies Concerning Slavery*, Conway recounts the story of a kinsman who publicly declared that "Negroes are not men, in the sense in which that term is used by the Declaration of Independence. Were the slaves *men*, we should be unable to disagree with Wendell Phillips." Moncure D. Conway, *Testimonies Concerning Slavery* (London, 1964), pp. 28–30. Albert Gallatin Brown, quoted in John Ashworth, *Slavery, Capitalism, and Politics in the Antebellum Republic, vol I: Commerce and Compromise, 1820–1850* (Cambridge: Cambridge University Press, 1995), p. 216.

16 Richard Furman to Dear Sir [Rev. W. Mg.], June 29 1807. Quoted in Larry E. Tise, *Proslavery: A History of the Defense of Slavery in America, 1701–1840* (Athens: University of Georgia Press, 1987), p. 39.

17 See *Congressional Globe*, 33rd Congress, 1st Session, app., 212–214, Feb. 20, 1854; 33rd Congress, 2nd Session, app., 234–237, Feb. 23, 1855.

18 Frederick Douglass in *The North Star*, April 7, 1849.

19 Solomon Northup, *Twelve Years a Slave* [1853], Sue Eakin and Joseph Logsdon eds. (Baton Rouge: Louisiana State University Press, 1968), p. 206.

20 Frederick Douglass, "The Claims of the Negro Ethnologically Considered" in *The Life and Writings of Frederick Douglass*, 5 vols. (New York: International Publishers, 1950), vol. II, p. 210. In the same essay, Douglass declares this "vital question" the "moral battlefield to which the "scholars of America" are now called (210).

21 In this context, it is important to note that the Three-Fifths Clause of the Constitution, often cited as an example of how the Constitution declared all Negroes to be three-fifths of a white man, actually did not participate in such arguments over the nature of the Negro. The Framers were not making an argument about the nature of Black personhood. Rather they were making a statement about status and wealth. The fraction itself originated under the Articles of the Confederation as a means to use population as a surrogate for wealth in allocating taxes. In the process of making the Constitution this device was used to work out a compromise between slaveholding and non-slaveholding states. Slaves, for the purposes of representation, counted as three fifths of a person, but free Blacks (just like children and white women) were counted as whole persons (at least in terms of political representation). See Paul Finkelman, "The Founders and Slavery: Little Ventured, Little Gained," *The Yale Journal of Law of the Humanities* 13:2 (Summer 2001): 413–449. See also Don E. Fehrenbacher, completed and edited by Ward M. McAfee, *The Slaveholding Republic: An Account of the United States Government's Relations to Slavery* (New York: Oxford University Press, 2004).

22 Andrew Kull *The Color-blind Constitution* (Cambridge, M.A.: Harvard University Press, 1992); Fehrenbacher, *The Slaveholding Republic*, p. 351. Modern legal scholars have, of course, universally condemned Taney's opinion, calling it "the worst atrocity in the Supreme Court's history," a "dereliction of constitutional law," and, according to *The Oxford Companion to the Supreme Court*, "the worst [decision] ever rendered by the Supreme Court." See Christopher L. Eisgruber, "Dred Again: Originalism's Forgotten Past," 10 *Constitutional Commentary*, (1993), 37; Derrick Bell, *Race, Racism and American Law* (Boston, Little Brown, 1973), pp. 21–22; Walter Ehrlich, *Scott v. Sandford* in *The Oxford Companion to the Supreme Court of the United States*, Kermit L. Hall ed., (New York: Oxford University Press, 1992), p. 761. Indeed, it would not be an exaggeration to state that currently everyone, from Derrick Bell to Robert Bork, repudiates Taney's decision. Justice Anton Scalia, for example, invoked Justice Curtis' dissent in *Dred Scot* to legitimate his controversial dissent in *Planned Parenthood of Southeastern Pennsylvania v. Casey*, 505 US 833 (1992), 984.

23 I am following K. Anthony Appiah in distinguishing racism from racialism. For Appiah racism involves "racial prejudice," the making of harmful distinctions based upon race, while racialism is simply that view that there are heritable characteristics based upon race. According to Appiah both racialism and racism are logically flawed positions, but only racism is necessarily invidious. Appiah, *In My Father's House: Africa in the Philosophy of Culture* (New York: Oxford University Press, 1992).

24 Samuel Cartwright, "Natural History of the Prognathous Species of Mankind," *New York Day-Book,* November 10, 1857; reprinted in E. N. Elliott, *Cotton is King, and Pro-Slavery Arguments* (Augusta: Pritchard, Abbot & Loomis, 1860), p. 707.

25 I should add that I use the term "person" rather than the term "subject" in part because the term "subject" is often deployed to describe processes that are done to the pre-existing "person" or "human being." Most, following Foucault's weakest formulation of his project, have sought "to create a history of the different modes by which, in our culture, *human beings* are made subjects" ("The Subject and Power," emphasis added). According to this account, the subject is a quality added to the human being. In contrast, I am interested in how particular beings became "human" – in the sense that they are regarded as naturally deserving respect. The term "person" foregrounds that this privileged status is not restricted to or coterminous with a species category.

26 See Dictionary Act of 1871 (Act of Feb. 25, 1871, ch. 71, 2, 16 Stat. 431). The Dictionary Act gives instructions about how to read acts of Congress; it states, "In determining the meaning of any Act of Congress, unless the context indicates otherwise, the word 'person'. . .includes corporations, companies, associations, firms, partnerships, societies, and joint stock companies, as well as individuals."

Recently, eco-theorists have worked to show how the traditional markers of the "person" (reason, language, the use of tools, altruism, etc.) can be identified beyond the species barrier. As Donna Haraway has notoriously stated, "the boundary between the human and the animal is thoroughly breached. The last beachheads of uniqueness have been polluted, if not turned into amusement parks. . . . Movements for animal rights are not irrational denials of human uniqueness; they are clear-sighted recognition of connection across the discredited breach of nature and culture." "A Cyborg Manifesto: Science, Technology, and Socialist-Feminism in the Late Twentieth Century," in *Simians, Cyborgs, and Women: The Reinvention of Nature* (New York: Routledge, 1991), pp. 151–152. The classic statement of this project is *The Great Ape Project,* Paola Cavalieri and Peter Singer eds. (New York: St. Martin's Press, 1993). See also Luc Ferry, *The New Ecological Order* trans. Carol Volk (Chicago: University of Chicago Press, 1995) for a sophisticated account of what it means that rocks and trees have been granted standing in contemporary legal theory.

27 Of course, there is no term that should be deployed without scare quotes. I am, however, putting only the term "person" in quotation marks because it is the construction of this category that is my focus of study.

28 For a brilliant deconstruction of the ostensibly obvious difference between the artificial and the natural "person" see Barbara Johnson, "Anthropomorphism in Lyric and Law" in *Yale Journal of Law & the Humanities* vol. 10 (summer 1998): 549–574. Johnson argues that "the personification of the corporation ends up revealing, paradoxically enough, is that there is nothing 'natural'

about the natural person often taken as its model. The natural person, far from being a 'given,'" has, in fact, "been borrowed from the nature of the corporation" (573, 572).

29 Michel Foucault, "Nietzsche, Genealogy, History" in *Language, Counter-memory, Practice*, Donald F. Bouchard ed. (Ithaca: Cornell University Press, 1977), p. 154.

30 The antebellum crisis over how to represent the "person," of course, extended beyond the question of race-based slavery. I foreground the slavery question not because it was the only or the most significant example of how the category of the "person" was being disputed during the antebellum period, but because slavery has long been the litmus test for whether a society is liberal.

31 According to this color blind theory, "a derogation from individuality" occurs whenever there is a failure to distinguish between the individual and the merely "social," "accidental," "ascribed," or "inherited" characteristics. See, for example, Randall Kennedy, "Racial Critiques of Legal Academia," *Harvard Law Review* 102 (1989): 1745–1819. The phrase "wastebasket of the contingent" is from Stanley Fish, "Mission Impossible: Settling the Just Bounds Between Church and State," *Columbia Law Review* 97:8 (December 1997): 2319. In this account, more and more beings have been recognized as "persons" precisely to the extent that more and more markers of identity (religion, race, gender, sexuality) have been understood to be contingent, politically-charged attributes and thus separate from one's fundamental nature.

32 Editorial from *Richmond (Va.) Examiner* is quoted in *The National Era* (vol. 7, no. 317) Jan. 27, 1853, p. 14; emphasis added. Southern intellectuals developed a philosophical defense of slavery based on the fact that the slavery of Africans enabled the freedom of the white man. See, for example John C. Calhoun's "Remarks on the States Rights' Resolutions in Regard to Abolition, Jan. 12, 1838" in *The Works of John C. Calhoun* (New York: D. Appleton and Co., 1855), vol. III, p. 180.

33 One might say that since the 1950s race has been progressively severed from any secure root in biology. See Luigi Luca Cavalli-Sforze, "Race Differences: Genetic Evidence" in *Plain Talk about the Human Genome Conference*, Edward Smith and Walter Sapp eds. (Tuskegee: Tuskegee University Press, 1997). Cavalli-Sforza emphasizes that "one important conclusion of human population genetics is that races do not exist" (52–53). See also the classic article in this argument, R. L. Cann, M. Stoneking, and A. C. Wilson, "Mitochondrial DNA and Human Evolution," *Nature*, no. 325 (1982): 31–36. Some have taken this scientific proof as a sign of how race is nothing but an outmoded fiction (see Walter Benn Michaels, "Autobiographies of the Ex-White Men," *Transitions* 7:1 (1998): 122–143).

34 This assumption is made particularly clear in contemporary critiques of Black thinkers. For example, in a recent study of Black intellectual history, Mia Bay is troubled by the essentialist premises that characterized nineteenth century African-American ethnological thought. According to Bay, "what was

distinctive about black ethnology" was "its emphasis on two not always compatible themes: human sameness and racial distinctions. . .black thinkers invariably conceded that blacks and white were not quite the same, while simultaneously insisting that they were equal. These competing claims to equality and difference run through virtually all nineteenth-century black racial thought." See Mia Bay, *The White Image in the Black Mind: African-American Ideas about White People, 1830–1925* (New York: Oxford University Press, 2000), 54. Since Bay assumes that the true equality must operate according to an identitarian logic, she argues that as long as Black thinkers deployed discourse of racial essences they would remain "ensnared by the fallacy of race even as they sought to refute racism's insult against their humanity" (224). See also Patrick Rael, *Black Identity and Black Protest in the Antebellum North* (Chapel Hill: University of North Carolina Press, 2002). Rael also is troubled by the "creep toward essentialist premises" in the basic premises of Black thought (249).

35 See M. I. Finley, *Ancient Slavery and Modern Ideology* (New York: Penguin, 1980); and Michael Carrithers, Steven Collins, and Steven Lukes, *The Category of the Person: Anthropology, Philosophy, History* (Cambridge: Cambridge University Press, 1985).

36 For example, the American Declaration of the Rights and Duties of Man (1948) begins: "The American Peoples have acknowledged the dignity of the individual. . .. The American states have on repeated occasions recognized that the essential rights of man are not derived from the fact that he is a national of a certain state, but are based upon attributes of his human personality." The preamble to the American Convention on Human Rights (1978) repeats these words.

37 Hanna Fenichel Pitkin, *The Concept of Representation* (Berkeley: University of California Press, 1967).

38 It is precisely because Pitkin imagines representation as fundamentally mimetic that she has trouble discussing symbolic representation (the book's shortest chapter). Symbolic representation (in which there is an affective and ultimately arbitrary conjunction between the symbol and referent) threatens to disrupt the priority of the represented object to the act of representation that drives her account. See in particular pp. 100–101; 110–111.

39 Jacques Derrida, "Declarations of Independence," trans. Tom Keenan and Tom Pepper, *New Political Science* no. 15 (Summer 1986): 7–15.

40 There is, of course, a long tradition of scholarship that identifies liberalism as the heart of the politics of the United States. Since 1955 when Louis Hartz published *The Liberal Tradition in America*, the dominant interpretation of American culture has advanced the notion of a liberal consensus in the United States. See also Lionel Trilling, *The Liberal Imagination: Essays on Literature and Society* (New York: Viking, 1950). Trilling declared that in the United States "liberalism is not only the dominant but even the sole intellectual tradition" (ix).

Scholars, of course, have questioned Hartz's single-factor analysis of American history and have argued for the centrality of neoclassical republicanism in the formation of the United States. See, for example, Bernard Bailyn, *The Ideological Origins of the American Revolution* (Cambridge, M. A.: Belknap, 1967); J.G.A. Pocock, *The Machiavellian Moment: Florentine Political Thought and the Atlantic Republican Tradition* (Princeton: Princeton University Press, 1975); Gordon S. Wood, *The Creation of the American Republic, 1776–1787* (Chapel Hill: University of North Carolina Press, 1969); Robert E Shalhope, "Toward a Republican Synthesis: The Emergence of an Understanding of Republicanism in American Historiography," *William and Mary Quarterly* (1972); G. Edward White, "Reflections on the 'Republican Revival': Interdisciplinary Scholarship in the Legal Academy," *Yale Journal of Law and the Humanities* volume 6:1 (Winter 1994): 1–35.

41 See Will Kymlicka, *Liberalism, Community and Culture* (Oxford: Clarendon Press, 1989).

42 A similar logic explains why I see the longstanding debate within political philosophy over liberal and republican/communitarian theory as beside the point. These debates are framed in terms of a disagreement over the true nature of the "person." See, for example, Michael J. Sandel, *Liberalism and the Limits of Justice* (Cambridge: Cambridge University Press, 1982).

43 In addition to Pitkin, see F. R. Ankersmit, *Aesthetic Politics: Political Philosophy beyond Fact and Value* (Stanford: Stanford University Press, 1996). See also Gayatri Spivak, "Can the Subaltern Speak?" in *Marxism and the Interpretation of Culture*, Cary Nelson and Lawrence Grossberg eds. (Urbana: University of Illinois Press, 1988), pp. 271–313. A revised version appears in the chapter "History" of Spivak's *A Critique of Postcolonial Reason* (Cambridge, MA: Harvard University Press, 1999), pp. 198–312.

44 Joan Hedrick, *Harriet Beecher Stowe: A Life* (New York: Oxford University Press, 1994), vii. This quotation is sometimes cited as "So this is the little lady who made this big war." See Ann Douglas, "Introduction: The Art of Controversy," in Harriet Beecher Stowe, *Uncle Tom's Cabin* (New York: Penguin, 1986), p. 19. Douglas cites the year as 1863.

45 For a discussion of the politicians, novelists, and scientists who felt compelled to respond to Stowe, see Thomas F. Gosset, *Uncle Tom's Cabin and American Culture* (Dallas: Southern University Press, 1985).

46 For an overview of this "absence" see Jean Fagan Yellin, "Hawthorne and the American National Sin," in *The Green American Tradition: Essays and Poems for Sherman Paul*, ed. by H. Daniel Peck ed. (Baton Rouge: Louisiana State University Press, 1989), pp. 75–97. This essay has recently been revised, see Yellin, "Hawthorne and the Slavery Question," in *A Historical Guide to Nathaniel Hawthorne*, Larry J. Reynolds ed. (New York: Oxford University Press, 2001), pp. 135–164. See also Jennifer Fleischner, "Hawthorne and the Politics of Slavery," *Studies in the Novel* 23:1 (Spring 1991): 96–106; Eric Cheyfitz, "The Irresistibleness of Great Literature: Reconstructing

Hawthorne's Politics," *American Literary History* 6 (1994): 539–558. See also Deborah L. Madsen, "'A for Abolition': Hawthorne's Bond-Servant and the Shadow of Slavery," *The Journal of American Studies* 25:2 (August 1991): 255–269.

For a contemporaneous articulation of this "notorious" absence see George William Curtis, "The Works of Nathaniel Hawthorne," *North American Review* October 1864 (99): 539–557.

47 Nathaniel Hawthorne, *Life of Franklin Pierce* in *The Works of Nathaniel Hawthorne* vol. 12 (Boston, Riverside Books, 1883), p. 417. Although it is sometimes asserted that Hawthorne wrote Pierce's campaign biography only because Pierce asked him to, Hawthorne himself offered to do so (albeit with a characteristically displaced sense of agency) in his congratulatory letter to Pierce: "It has occurred to me that you might have some thought of getting me to write the necessary biography. Whatever service I can do you, I need not say, would be at your command; but I do not believe that I should succeed in this matter so well as many other men." Hawthorne, in fact, arranged for his publishers Ticknor and Fields to publish the book, something the prestigious Northern publishing house would probably not have done otherwise. *The Letters: 1843–1853, The Centenary Edition of the Works of Nathaniel Hawthorne vol. 16* (Columbus: Ohio University State Press, 1985), p. 545.

48 *The Letters: 1843–1853, The Centenary Edition of the Works of Nathaniel Hawthorne vol. 16* (Columbus: Ohio University State Press, 1985), p. 605. See also Hawthorne's letter to Burchmore, *Letters*, 456.

49 See, for example, Jonathan Arac, "The Politics of *The Scarlet Letter*," *Ideology and Classic American Literature*, Sacvan Bercovitch and Myra Jehlen eds. (Cambridge: Cambridge University Press, 1986), pp. 247–263; Cheyfitz, "The Irresistibleness of Great Literature"; Sacvan Bercovitch, *The Office of The Scarlet Letter* (Baltimore: Johns Hopkins University Press, 1991; Jay Grossman, "'A' is for Abolition?: Race, Authorship, *The Scarlet Letter*," *Textual Practice* 7:1 (Spring 1993): 13–30; David Anthony, "Class, Culture, and the Trouble with White Skin in Hawthorne's *The House of the Seven Gables*," *The Yale Journal of Criticism* 12 (1999): 249–268; Shawn Michelle Smith, *American Archives: Gender, Race, and Class in Visual Culture* (Princeton: Princeton University Press, 1999); Paul Gilmore, *The Genuine Article: Race, Mass Culture, and American Literary Manhood* (Durham: Duke University Press, 2001); Leland S. Person, "The Dark Labyrinth of Mind: Hawthorne, Hester, and the Ironies of Racial Mothering," *Studies in American Fiction* 29:1 (Spring 2001): 33–48; Teresa A. Goddu, "Letters Turned to Gold: Hawthorne, Authorship, and Slavery," *Studies in American Fiction* 29:1 (Spring 2001): 49–76.

For a powerful example of an argument designed to redeem Hawthorne's understanding of slavery see Larry Reynolds, " 'Strangely Ajar with the Human Race': Hawthorne, Slavery, and the Question of Moral Responsibility", *Hawthorne and the Real: Bicentennial Essays*, Millicent Bell, ed. (Columbus, OH: Ohio State University Press, 2005), pp. 40–69.

50 See Jane Tompkins, *Sensational Designs: The Cultural Work of American Fiction, 1790–1860* (New York: Oxford University Press, 1985); Nina Baym, "Melodramas of Beset Manhood: How Theories of American Fiction Exclude Women Authors," *American Quarterly* 33 (1981): 123–139; reprinted in Nina Baym, *Feminism and American Literary History* (New Brunswick: Rutgers University Press, 1992), pp. 3–18. See also Eric Cheyfitz, "Matthiessen's *American Renaissance*: Circumscribing the Revolution," *American Quarterly* 41 (1989): 341–361; Jonathan Arac, "F. O. Matthiessen: Authorizing an American Renaissance," *The American Renaissance Reconsidered: Selected Papers from the English Institute, 1982–1983*, Walter Michaels and Donald Pease eds. (Baltimore: Johns Hopkins University Press, 1985), pp. 90–112.

51 See, for example, Arac who contrasts the anti-slavery project of *Uncle Tom's Cabin* to *The Scarlet Letter*, a text he classifies as propaganda "*not* to change your life" (Politics of *The Scarlet Letter*, 251).

52 Ed Piacentino, "Stowe's *Uncle Tom's Cabin*," *Explicator*, 58:3 (Spring 2000), p. 135.

53 Richard Yarborough, "Strategies of Black Characterization in *Uncle Tom's Cabin* and the Early Afro-American Novel," in *New Essays on Uncle Tom's Cabin*, Eric Sundquist, ed. (New York: Cambridge University Press, 1986), p. 47.

54 Charles Swann, *Nathaniel Hawthorne: Tradition and Revolution*, (Cambridge University Press, 1991), p. 5.

55 Tzvetan Todorov, *Literature and its Theorists* (Ithaca: Cornell University Press, 1987), 190. See also Richard Wolin, "Antihumanism in the Discourse of French Postwar Theory" in *Labyrinths: Explorations in the Critical History of an Idea* (Amherst: University of Massachusetts Press, 1995), pp. 175–209. Wolin expresses this fear that one cannot construct a powerful politics of human rights if one loses the philosophical grounds of support – Wolin, for all intents and purposes, equates human rights with metaphysics.

56 Norman Geras, "Language, Truth, and Justice," *New Left Review* 209 (January-February 1995): 110.

57 Clifford Geertz, "Distinguished Lecture: Anti-Anti Relativism," *American Anthropologist* 86 (June 1984): 264. The critique of anti-foundationalism has been most notoriously articulated by Alan Sokal in his infamous hoax. See Alan Sokal, "Transgressing the Boundaries: Towards a Transformative Hermeneutics of Quantum Gravity," *Social Text* 46–47 (Spring-Summer 1996): 217–252. See also *The Sokal Hoax: The Sham That Shook the Academy*, ed. the Editors of *Lingua Franca* (Lincoln: Nebraska, 2000).

58 Michael Freeman declares that the loss of a "universal concept of reason" is "good news for tyrants." See Freeman, "The Philosophical Foundations of Human Rights," *Human Rights Quarterly* 16:3 (1994): 512. Although Geertz would not call himself a relativist, he notes the anti-relativist hysteria, and citing Paul Johnson's *Modern Times: The World from the Twenties to the Eighties* (New York: Harper and Row, 1983), Geertz mocks how relativism has been considered responsible "for the whole modern disaster – Lenin

and Hitler, Amin, Bokasso, Sukarno, Mao, Nasser, and Hammarskjold, Structuralism, and the New Deal, the Holocaust, both world wars, 1968, inflation, Shinto militarism, OPEC, and the independence of India" ("Anti Anti-Relativism," 267). See also Jeffrey Stout who asks "What, then, can the pragmatist say when the torturers come?" Jeffrey Stout, *Ethics After Babel* (Boston: Beacon Press, 1988), p. 256.

59 For a powerful articulation of this line of argument see Jurgen Habermas, "Richard Rorty's Pragmatic Turn" in *Rorty and his Critics* ed. Robert B. Brandom (Oxford: Blackwell, 2000), pp. 31–55.

60 See Richard Rorty, "Hilary Putnam and the Relativist Menace" in *Truth and Progress, Philosophical Papers*, vol. 3 (Cambridge University Press, 1998), pp. 43–62.

61 See, for example, *Roe v. Wade*, 410 US 113 (1973). *Weaks v. Mounter*, 493 P. 2d 1307 (Nev. 1972). In *Roe v. Wade* it was decided that a fetus was not a "person" until the second trimester and in *Weaks v. Mounter* it was decided that a fetus was a "person" and thus had the standing – once born – to sue for intra-uterine injuries.

See also Michael D. Rivard, "Toward a General Theory of Constitutional Personhood: A Theory of Constitutional Personhood for Transgenic Humanoid Species," 39 *UCLA Law Review* (1992), 1425–1510, and Francis Fukuyama, *Our Posthuman Future: Consequences of the Biotechnology Revolution* (New York: Farrar, Strauss and Giroux, 2002).

62 It is precisely such arguments, which cite the very notion that they are arguing over (the "person") as the only legitimate means to definitively end the argument, that are irresolvable in the terms formulated. For an example of how the analogy between slavery and debates over choice can be misunderstood see Edwin Armstrong, "The Parallels between Slavery and Abortion," *National Minority Politics*, May 1994 (6:5): 25–26.

SLAVES AND PERSONS

1 The Louisiana slave code of 1824, for example, reads as if it were a point by point inversion of the liberal rights guaranteed by the Bill of Rights: the slave cannot make contracts, own property, hold public office, appeal to the judicial system, assemble voluntarily, marry, assert any natal claims, be educated, speak or move freely.

2 John Locke, *Two Treatises of Government* (Cambridge: Cambridge University Press, 1963), 1.1. Locke's remarks, of course, are directed at Sir Robert Filmer's defense of absolutism in *Patriarchia* not, it is important to note, explicitly at the issue of chattel slavery.

3 James Farr, " 'So Vile and Miserable an Estate:' The Problem of Slavery in Locke's Political Thought," *Political Theory* 14:2 (May 1986): 263–289. See Wayne Glausser, "Three Approaches to Locke and the Slave Trade," *Journal of the History of Ideas* 51:2 (April/June 1990): 199–216.

4 David Brion Davis, *The Problem of Slavery in Western Culture* (Ithaca: Cornell University Press, 1966), p. 119.

5 David Theo Goldberg, *Racist Culture* (Oxford: Blackwell Publishers, 1993), p. 4. Susan Buck-Morss continues this line of thought, asking how could 'enlightened' thinkers not see the "glaring discrepancy" between freedom and the presence of slavery. See Susan Buck-Morss, "Hegel and Haiti", *Critical Inquiry* 26:4 (Summer 2000): 821–865). In contrast to Buck-Morss, who seeks to recover the "discordant facts" that have been ignored, I am interested in how these facts emerge (822). Thus, rather than indict Rousseau for failing to "put two and two together" when he "declared all men equal" without discussing French slavery, I focus on how the notion of "man" is not historically solid enough to ground such a statement (831).

See also Naomi Zack, *Race and Mixed Race* (Philadelphia: Temple University Press, 1993) and Zack, *Bachelors of Science: Seventeenth-Century Identity, Then and Now* (Philadelphia: Temple University Press, 1996).

6 Louis Hartz, *The Liberal Tradition in America* (New York: Harcourt, Brace & World, Inc., 1955), p. 140.

7 According to Gunnar Myrdal's *An American Dilemma: The Negro Problem and Modern Democracy* (New York: Harper and Brothers, 1944), the statue of Blacks is "an anomaly in the very structure of American society" (lxix). In addition to Myrdal, quotations from Edmund S. Morgan, *American Slavery, American Freedom* (New York: Norton, 1975), p. 75; John Hope Franklin, "Slavery and the Constitution," in *Encyclopedia of American Constitution*, L. Levy ed., (1986), p. 1695. Nathan Huggins, "The Deforming Mirror of Truth: Slavery and the Master Narrative of American History" in *Radical History* 49 (winter 1991): 25. See also Chapter 1 of Jennifer L. Hochschild, *The New American Dilemma: Liberal Democracy and School Desegregation* (New Haven: Yale University Press, 1984) for a discussion of this anomaly thesis.

8 Winthrop D. Jordan, *White over Black: American Attitudes Toward the Negro, 1550–1812* (New York: W. W. Norton & Co., 1968).

9 See, for example, Morgan, *American Slavery, American Freedom* and Theodore W. Allen, *The Invention of the White Race*, Volumes I and II (New York: Verso, 1994, 1997).

Morgan's text offers a compelling materialist account of how liberal freedom and race-based slavery were mutually constitutive in Colonial Virginia but it ultimately remains committed to the assumption that slavery and liberal ideals should be antithetical. As Morgan asks in the closing lines of his study:

> But were the two [race-based slavery and liberal conceptions of freedom] more closely linked than . . . [this nation] could admit? Was the vision of a nation of equals flawed at the source by contempt for both the poor and the black? Is America still colonial Virginia writ large? More than a century after Appomattox the questions linger (387).

10 See, for example, Rogers M. Smith, *Civic Ideals: Conflicting Visions of Citizenship in US History* (New Haven: Yale University Press, 1997).

11 See, for example, Conor Cruise O'Brien, *The Long Affair: Thomas Jefferson and the French Revolution* (Chicago: University of Chicago Press, 1996). According to Winthrop Jordan, it is hypocritical that "[w]hile Americans were claiming liberty for themselves they were denying it to a group of men in their midst" (Jordan, *White Over Black*, p. 289). This claim of hypocrisy is, of course, longstanding, instantiated perhaps most memorably by Samuel Johnson's quip: "How is it that we hear the loudest yelps for liberty among the drivers of negroes?" See also Barbara J. Fields, "Ideology and Race in American History," in *Region, Race, and Reconstruction*, J. Morgan Kousser and James M. McPherson eds., (New York: Oxford University Press, 1982).

12 See, for example, Samuel Huntington, *American Politics: The Promise of Disharmony* (Cambridge: Harvard University Press, 1981).

13 See, for example, Herman Belz, "Equality Before the Law: The Civil War Amendments," *Center Magazine* 20:6 (Nov-Dec, 1987): 4–19. Belz states that "Truly or properly understood, slavery always violated the natural rights principles on which republican institutions rested. In 1776, however, when the Constitution was written, this fact was not sufficiently understood, or if understood was not seen as the basis of action by a sufficient number of people to cause it to be expressed in American public law" (5). The other quotation is from Judith Shklar, "Redeeming American Political Theory," *American Political Science Review* 85:1 (March 1991): 15. See also Judith Shklar, *American Citizenship* (Cambridge: Harvard University Press, 1991).

See also Clarence Thomas, "Toward a 'Plain Reading' of the Constitution– The Declaration of Independence in Constitutional Interpretation," *Howard Law Journal* 30:4 (1987): 983–995; and Stephen Holmes, *The Anatomy of Antiliberalism* (Cambridge, MA: Harvard University Press, 1993), esp. pp. 107–108.

14 For a prominent example of the claim that "abstract equality is utterly enmeshed in the narrative of black subjection" and that the "stipulation of abstract equality produces white entitlement and black subjection" see Saidiya V. Hartman *Scenes of Subjection: Terror, Slavery, and Self-Making in Nineteenth-Century America* (New York: Oxford University Press, 1997), p. 116. See also Christopher Newfield's *The Emerson Effect: Individualism and Submission in America* (Chicago: University of Chicago Press, 1996).

15 Some have argued that the identitarian formula upon which liberal equality requires that all difference be denigrated as inferior, immoral, and deviant. See, for example, William Connelly, "Liberalism and Difference," in *Identity/Difference: Democratic Negotiations of Political Paradox* (Ithaca: Cornell University Press, 1991); and essays collected in *Democracy and Difference*, Seyla Benhabib ed. (Princeton: Princeton University Press, 1996). See also Iris Young, *Justice and the Politics of Difference* (Princeton: Princeton University Press, 1990).

16 Matthew Frye Jacobson, *Whiteness of a Different Color: European Immigrants and the Alchemy of Race* (Cambridge, MA: Harvard University Press, 1998), p. 12. Richard Delgado, "Rodrigo's Seventh Chronicle: *Race, Democracy, and*

the State" in Delgado, *The Rodrigo Chronicles: Conversations about America and Race* (New York: New York University Press, 1995), pp. 135–163.

17 For a sophisticated articulation of the symbiotic relationship between slavery and liberalism see Samira Kawash, *Dislocating the Color Line* (Stanford: Stanford University Press, 1997). According to Kawash slavery, is not "an aberrant violation" of liberal thought but "animating" of it (39–40).

18 Patricia Williams says, "'Rights' feels new in the mouths of most black people. It is still too deliciously empowering to say. It is the magic wand of visibility and invisibility, of inclusion and exclusion, of power and no power. The concept of rights, both positive and negative, is the marker of our citizenship, our relation to others" (164). In a similar vein, Kimberle Crenshaw explores the way in which many critical legal scholars deeply suspicious of rights discourse underestimate the transformative potential that liberalism offers. Kimberle Williams Crenshaw, "Race, Reform, and Retrenchment: Transformation and Legitimation in Antidiscrimination Law" reprinted in *Critical Race Theory*, Kimberle Crenshaw, Neil Gotanda, Gary Peller, Kendall Thomas eds. (New York: The New Press, 1995), p. 118.

19 This is very different from Claude Lefort's discussion of liberalism. Claude Lefort, *Democracy and Political Theory* (trans. David Macey) (Minneapolis: University of Minnesota Press, 1988). Lefort claims that liberal democracy is always only a formal link between abstract subjects and that as soon as we try to fill it out with concrete human content we risk falling into totalitarianism. I am not claiming that liberalism demands an "empty subject" but rather that it always fills the subject position with a content – a content that in the case of modern liberalism is "empty."

20 David Potter, *The Impending Crisis, 1848–1861* (New York: Harper & Row, 1976), p. 331.

21 Douglas to the editor of the *Concord, N.H., State Capitol Reporter*, February 16, 1854, Robert W. Johannsen, ed., *The Letters of Stephen A. Douglas* (Urban: University of Illinois Press, 1961), p. 288.

22 Douglas does leave open the possibility that white male voters in individual states can, if they chose to, bestow upon the Negro certain rights. Indeed, he claims that, at least as a political question, he is neutral as to whether slavery is "voted up or voted down." Of course, as Lincoln repeatedly points out, Douglas only seeks to bracket the substantial issue at hand because he does not consider slavery an absolute evil in the first place. Douglas' pose of neutrality, in short, is anything but neutral.

23 Speech on the Kansas-Nebraska Act, Peoria, October 16, 1854 in Lincoln, *Selected Speeches and Writings: 1832–1858*, ed. Don Fehrenbacher (New York: Library of America, 1989), pp. 315, 328.

24 David Brion Davis, *The Problem of Slavery in Western Culture.* All further references will be cited parenthetically in the text.

25 Stanley Cavell, *The Claim of Reason: Wittgenstein, Skepticism, Morality, and Tragedy* (New York: Oxford University Press).

26 Wilbur J. Cash, *The Mind of the South* (New York: Knopf, 1941); Charles G. Sellars, Jr., "The Travail of Slavery," in Charles G. Sellars, Jr. (ed.), The *Southerner as American*, Charles G. Sellers, Jr. ed. (Chapel Hill: University of North Carolina Press, 1960), pp. 40–71. See also Bell Wiley and C. Vann Woodward who argue that the defeat of the Confederacy could be partly attributed to guilt. This line of argument culminated in Richard E. Beringer, Herman Hattaway, Archer Jones, and William N. Still, Jr. *Why the South Lost the Civil War* (Athens, Ga.: University of Georgia Press, 1986). For an overview of this line of argument see Gaines M. Foster, "Guilt Over Slavery: A Historiographical Analysis," *Journal of Southern History* 56:4 (Nov. 1990): 665–694. For an opposing view, see Drew Gilpin Faust, *The Ideology of Slavery: Proslavery Thought in the Antebellum South, 1830–1860* (edited with an introduction by Drew Gilpin Faust) (Baton Rouge: Louisiana State University Press, 1981). Faust argues that "southerners may have felt far less guilty and ambivalent" than is commonly argued (*The Ideology of Slavery*, p. 4). See also James Oakes, *The Ruling Race: A History of American Slaveholders* (New York: Knopf, 1982).

27 John Ashworth offers an extensive argument against the claim that masters were consumed by guilt, stating that:

> slaveholders were convinced that the slave was indeed quite suited to his condition. . . Again and again they insisted that their bondsmen and bondswomen were happy and contented and that both masters and slaves were simply acting in accordance with the divine plan.

John Ashworth, *Slavery, Capitalism, and Politics in the Antebellum Republic, Vol I: Commerce and Compromise, 1820–1850* (Cambridge: Cambridge University Press, 1995), pp. 8–9. For an idiosyncratic critique of the guilt thesis see David Donald, "The Proslavery Argument Reconsidered," *Journal of Southern History*, 37:1 (Feb. 1971): 3–18.

28 For a concise articulation of the "ineradicable contradiction" argument see Kenneth Stampp, *The Peculiar Institution* (New York: Knopf, 1956). Stampp declares "the slave's status as property was incompatible with his status as a person" (193).

29 Eugene D. Genovese, *Roll, Jordan, Roll: The World the Slaves Made* (New York: Pantheon Books, 1974), p. 30. All further references to this work will be cited parenthetically in the text. See also Reuel E. Schiller, "Conflicting Obligations: Slave Law and the Late Antebellum North Carolina Supreme Court," *Virginia Law Review* 78 (August 1992): 1243.

30 See also Mark Tushnet, *American Law of Slavery, 1810–1860: Considerations of Humanity and Interest* (Princeton: Princeton University Press, 1981); A. E. Keir Nash, "Reason of Slavery: Understanding the Judicial Role in the Peculiar Institution," *Vanderbilt Law Review* 32 (1979): 7–218; and William W. Fisher III, "Ideology and Imagery in the Law of Slavery," *Chicago-Kent Law Review* 68 (1993): 1051–1086.

31 *State v. Mann,* 13 N.C. 170 (1829). James Oakes, *Slavery and Freedom: An Interpretation of the Old South* (New York: Alfred A. Knopf, 1990) offers a version of the argument that any limits on master's power implicitly granted rights to slaves:

> any action that forced the legal system to recognize the slave as in any way independent of the master represented an implicit threat to the principle of total subordination. Grounded in the presumption of universal rights, the American political system at once defined the slaves as rightless and yet risked undermining slavery every time it recognized the legal personality of the slave (155–159).

Rather than exposing slavery as dangerously incoherent, regulating the relationship between master and slave did not give slaves rights as much as restrict the rights of owners.

32 See, for example, A. Leon Higginbotham, Jr. and Barbara K. Kopytoff, "Property First, Humanity Second: The Recognition of the Slave's Human Nature in Virginia Civil Law" in *Ohio State Law Journal* 50 (Summer 1989): 511–540.

33 See Jenny Bourne Wahl, *The Bondsman's Burden: An Economic Analysis of the Common Law of Southern Slavery* (Cambridge: Cambridge University Press, 1998). Slave law, according to Wahl, recognized the humanness of the slave in order to create a new legal category: that of human property. Indeed, when the law limited rights of slave-owners to punish slaves, judges argued that such restrictions were required for the sake of maintaining the humanity of the master not the slave. Cruelty degrades the master and threatens his identity.

Thomas Morris also argues that Southern laws regarding slaves as human beings principally made slavery work better not worse. Thomas D. Morris, *Southern Slavery and the Law, 1619–1860* (Chapel Hill: University of North Carolina Press, 1996), p. 247. According to Morris, "Southern judges and lawmakers wove humanness into slavery jurisprudence without creating rights in slaves" (435). Or, as the abolitionist William Goodell asserted in 1853, the slave becomes "*'a person'* whenever he is to be *punished*!. . . He is under the *control* of law, though *unprotected by* law, and can know law only as an enemy, and not as a friend." William Goodell, *American Slave Code in Theory and Practice* (New York: American and Foreign Antislavery Society, 1853), p. 309. See also, William E. Wiethoff, *A Peculiar Humanism: The Judicial Advocacy of Slavery in High Courts of the Old South, 1820–1850* (Athens: University of Georgia Press, 1996). For an account of how humanitarianism was inspired by slave-holders' concern for their own character and thus offered a "comfortable mesh with a system of human bondage," see Joyce E. Chapin, "Slavery and the Principle of Humanity: A Modern Idea in the Early Lower South," in *The Journal of Southern History* 24:2 (winter 1990): 299–316.

34 As Judge John W. Green stated in *Allen v. Freeland,* "Slaves are a peculiar species of property. They have moral qualities, and confidence and attachment grow up between master and servant; the value of which cannot be estimated by a jury" (3 Rand. 170, 176 (Va. 1825).

35 *Summers v. Bean*, 13 Grattan, 411 (Va., 1856).

36 Judge Nathan Green, in *Ford v. Ford*, 7 Humphreys 91, at 95 (Tenn. 1846).

37 A. E. Keir Nash, "Reason of Slavery," p. 205.

38 Priscilla Wald, *Constituting Americans: Cultural Anxiety and Narrative Form* (Durham, N. C.: Duke University Press, 1995).

39 For a similar argument see Kawash, *Dislocating the Color Line*. Like Wald, Kawash argues that the success of slavery depended on "its power to suppress the tension between person and property embodied in the slave" (46–47). See also Hortense Spillers classic, "Mama's Baby, Papa's Maybe: An American Grammar Book" in *diacritics* 17:2 (1987): 65–81. Spillers' deconstructive reading of slavery's warring strands of signification presumes that the tensions of slavery are inherent in its grammar.

40 See in particular her account of the Dred Scott decision (40–47).

41 Cassuto's explicit argument concerns the nearly impossible project of turning human slaves into nonhuman chattels, but given his theory of the ineluctably anthropomorphic dynamics of human perception, one could use Cassuto's scientific evidence to support the claim that humanity does not inhere in the object of perception but in the perceiving subject. Leonard Cassuto, *The Inhuman Race: The Racial Grotesque in American Literature* (New York: Columbia University Press, 1997).

42 See most famously Toni Morrison, *Beloved* (New York: Penguin, 1987). See also Teresa A. Goddu, *Gothic America: Narrative, History, and Nation* (New York: Columbia University Press, 1997) and Julia A. Stern, *The Plight of Feeling* (Chicago: University of Chicago Press, 1997). Rather than registering cultural contradictions, the gothic, I am suggesting, produces these contradictions.

43 Orlando Patterson, *Slavery and Social Death* (Cambridge, M. A. Harvard University Press, 1982). Crucially, in the US slavery did not serve as a substitute for death during war. In this sense US slavery should not be seen as "social death" because the US never acknowledged that the slave was ever "alive." The US slave was never a "person" and thus never forfeited any rights.

44 See, for example, the philosopher Lewis Gordon's discussion of racism as bad faith. Gordon invokes the obviousness of the humanity of the Black people. "How is it possible," Gordon asks, "that some human beings are able to regard some members of their species as fundamentally nonhuman?" Gordon's answer is that the racist is stubborn; he is not only able to "resist types of evidence" but also to "deceive himself." See Lewis R. Gordon, *Bad Faith and Antiblack Racism* (Atlantic Highlands, N. J.: Humanities Press, 1995), pp. 6, 75.

45 Many would now agree that the classic theorists of liberalism held a distinctive view of the human virtues that was grounded in a definite conception of human nature. Indeed, it is commonly argued that classic political philosophy is inseparable from a theory of human nature, from claims that are advertised as applying to people at all times and in all places. See, for example, *Human Nature in Politics*, J. Roland Pennock and John W. Chapman eds. (New York: New York University Press, 1977); *Ethics, Politics, and Human Nature*,

Ellen Frankel Paul, Fred D. Miller Jr., Jeffrey Paul eds. (Oxford: Basil Blackwell, 1991).

46 John Rawls, *Political Liberalism* (New York: Columbia University Press, 1993), p. 8. All further references to this work will be cited parenthetically in the text.

47 John Rawls, *A Theory of Justice* (Cambridge, MA: Harvard University Press, 1971) and "Introduction to the Paperback Edition" in *Political Liberalism* (New York: Columbia University Press, 1996), p. xlii.

48 Richard Rorty, "The priority of democracy to philosophy" rpt. in *Objectivity, Relativism, and Truth, Philosophical Papers*, volume 1 (Cambridge: Cambridge University Press, 1991), pp. 180, 185, 183.

49 Rawls does not address the extent to which decisions about who deserves to be represented in the OP is itself inseparable from a particular political decision. For example, in a slave society, the question of whether slaves are to be represented in the OP would itself be a fundamentally political and deeply contested claim.

50 I owe this point, among others, to discussions with Robert Gunn.

51 In this sense, Rawls invocation of Shakespeare's *Macbeth* is particularly revealing. Just as an actor follows script, the "person" in the OP is entering a scenario that he has not written and whose end is already set. Indeed, if one really presses on Rawls' analogy, the reference to Shakespeare is far from innocent; Shakespeare, after all, is the one author whose words we dare not rewrite.

52 Numerous political philosophers have criticized *Political Liberalism* for disabling politics. See, for example, Chantal Mouffe, *The Democratic Paradox* (London: Verso, 2000), esp. pp. 22–34.

53 Saidiya V. Hartman, *Scenes of Subjection*, pp. 22, 134. All further references will be cited parenthetically in the text.

54 Hartman describes conscience as "discipline internalized and lauded as virtue" and discusses individuality as a "burdened" and burdening concept (126). It remains unclear, however, whether individuality or conscience is in the end any more burdening for Blacks than whites. As she asks, "[i]s not the free will of the individual measured precisely through the exercise of constraint and autonomy determined by the capacity to participate in relations of exchange that only fetter and bind the subject?" (124). Hartman's ultimate object of critique in other words, seems to transcend race altogether; it is liberal subjectivity itself.

55 Judith Butler, *The Psychic Life of Power* (Stanford: Stanford University Press, 1997).

56 Judith Butler, *Excitable Speech: A Politics of the Performative* (New York: Routledge, 1997), p.40. Since these books were published almost simultaneously, one is tempted to treat them as companion works.

57 In "Power and Strategies," Foucault states, "one should not assume a massive and primal condition of domination, a binary structure with 'dominators' on one side and 'dominated' on the other, but rather a multiform production of relations of domination which are partially susceptible of integration into overall strategies." Michel Foucault, *Power/Knowledge: Selected Interviews and Other Writings 1972–1977* ed. Colin Gordon (New York: Pantheon, 1980), p. 142.

58 Butler's suspicion of deliberate agency becomes clear in the way she imagines performativity as detaching resistance from intentional agency. Performativity "eclipses power with power" because iterations of dominant identities produce unintentional slippages that expose the contingency of their construction (15). See especially "Gender is Burning: Questions of Appropriation and Subversion" in *Bodies that Matter: On the Discursive Limits of "Sex"* (New York: Routledge, 1993), pp. 121–140.

59 *The Lincoln-Douglas Debates: The First Complete Unexpurgated Text,* ed. Harold Holzer (New York: Harper Collins, 1993), p. 63.

60 See, for example, LaWanda Cox, "Lincoln and Black Freedom" in *The Historian's Lincoln,* Gabor S. Boritt ed. (Champagne-Urbana: University of Illinois Press, 1988), p. 175.

For a striking instance of the claim that to be against slavery one needed to be *for* racial equality see Lerone Bennett, Jr., "Was Abe Lincoln a White Supremacist?" *Ebony* 23 (February, 1968): 35–38, 40, 42; this argument has been expanded into, *Forced into Glory: Abraham Lincoln's White Dream* (New York: Johnson Publishing Co., 2000); see also Herbert Mitgang, "Was Lincoln Just a Honkie?" *New York Times Magazine* 11 February 1968, 34–35, 100–107. Also see George M. Fredrickson, "A Man but Not a Brother" in *The Arrogance of Race: Historical Perspectives on Slavery, Racism, and Social Inequality* (Middletown, CT: Wesleyan University Press, 1988), pp. 54–72. Arvarh E. Strickland, "The Illinois Background of Lincoln's Attitude Toward Slavery and the Negro," *Journal of the Illinois State Historical Society* 56 (Autumn 1963): 474–494. For a good overview, see Stephen B. Oates, *Abraham Lincoln: The Man Behind the Myths* (New York: Harper and Row, 1984), esp. pp. 21–30.

61 For an example of Delany's essentialist logic see "The Political Destiny of the Colored Race on the American Continent" in Frank A. Rollin [Frances A. Rollin], *Life and Public Services of Martin R. Delany* (1868; rpt. Boston: Lee and Shephard, 1883), in *Two Biographies by African American Women,* ed. William L. Andrews (New York: Oxford University Press, 1991). For a powerful discussion of Delany's complex racial politics see Robert S. Levine, *Martin Delany, Frederick Douglass, and the Politics of Representative Identity* (Chapel Hill: University of North Carolina Press, 1997).

62 For a discussion of the ascendance of a colorblind reading of the Constitution after the Civil War see Paul Moreno, "Racial Classifications and Reconstruction Legislation," *The Journal of Southern History* 61: 2 (May 1995): 271–304. The colorblind argument, Moreno argues, was deployed by conservatives to disguise their abiding efforts to deny civil rights to Blacks.

FAMILY VALUES AND RACIAL ESSENTIALISM IN *UNCLE TOM'S CABIN*

1 Harriet Beecher Stowe, *Uncle Tom's Cabin; or Life Among the Lowly* (1852), ed. Alfred Kazin (New York: Bantam, 1981), p. 20. All further references to the novel will be from this edition and will be cited parenthetically in the text.

2 For example, Walt Whitman patriotically announces in a contemporary editorial that Washington's portrait "hangs from every wall, and he is almost canonized in the affections of our people". Whitman, *I Sit and Look Out: Editorials from the Brooklyn Daily Times*, ed. Emory Holloway and Vernolian Schwarz (New York: Columbia University Press, 1932), p. 59.

3 Nineteenth-century Washington hagiography emphasized above all else Washington's love of "domestic felicity," his commitment to the family and to Christian virtue; it continually placed Washington's devotion to peace above his success in war. See, for example, Edward Everett, *Orations and Speeches on Various Occasions* in 4 vols (Boston: Little, Brown and Co., 1850–1868), 4:20–40. See also, George Forgie, *Patricide in a House Divided* (New York: Norton, 1979), esp. pp. 159–200. See also Garry Wills, *Cincinnatus: George Washington and the Enlightenment* (Garden City, N. Y., 1984).

4 By the novel's conclusion, Tom, as if he were following in Washington's footsteps, comes to be called Father Tom by his fellow slaves.

5 Unlike in the case of Jefferson, there is no evidence that Washington took a slave mistress. See Nathan I. Huggins, "The Deforming Mirror of Truth: Slavery and the Master Narrative of American History" in *Radical History Review* 49 (Winter 1991): 25–49; on the way that African-Americans have used the illicit sexual unions between white slaveholders and Black slaves, such as the one between Thomas Jefferson and Sally Hemmings, to legitimate their claims to the birthright of national citizenship.

6 I am following K. Anthony Appiah, in distinguishing between *racialism* and *racism.* According to Appiah, racialism is the view that human beings are defined by heritable characteristics that justify the categorization of races; in effect, it is simply the belief in the biological notion of race. Racism, in contrast, uses racialism for socially pernicious ends, such as the legitimation of invidious social hierarchies. See Kwame Anthony Appiah, *My Father's House: Africa in the Philosophy of Culture* (New York: Oxford, 1992).

7 In addition to the works discussed later in the text, see for example, Richard Yarborough, "Strategies of Black Characterization in *Uncle Tom's Cabin* and the Early Afro-American Novel," in *New Essays on Uncle Tom's Cabin* ed. Eric Sundquist (Cambridge: Cambridge University Press, 1986), pp. 45–84. Yarborough states "although Stowe unquestionably sympathized with the slaves, her commitment to challenging the claim of black inferiority was frequently undermined by her own endorsement of racial stereotypes" (46). Yarborough sees Stowe's interest in racial difference as a "tragic failure of imagination" (65). See also Thomas Graham, "Harriet Beecher Stowe and the Question of Race," *The New England Quarterly* 46 (December 1973): 614–622, for one of the few defenses of Stowe's understanding of race and "inborn temperament." See also, Moody E. Prior, "Mrs. Stowe's Uncle Tom," *Critical Inquiry* 5 (1970): 651–662.

8 J. C. Furnas, *Goodbye to Uncle Tom* (New York: William Sloane, 1956), p. 50. All further references to this work will be cited parenthetically in the text.

Furnas's argument expands on the claims of James Baldwin in "Everybody's Protest Novel," rpt. in James Baldwin, *Notes of a Native Son* (Boston: Beacon Press, 1955), pp. 13–23.

9 See Hortense J. Spillers, "Changing the Letter," *Slavery and the Literary Imagination*, Deborah E. McDowell and Arnold Rampersad eds. (Baltimore: The Johns Hopkins University Press, 1989) on the question of the "muting of 'race' in this [style] of cultural analysis" (58–59). Tompkins' influential recuperation of *Uncle Tom's Cabin*, for example, blatantly subordinates the novel's racial politics to its gender politics. Tompkins' focus on Eva's rather than Tom's death is emblematic of how critics have set out to represent the novel's deepest political aspirations as expressed only secondarily in its attack on the slave system precisely because they are uncomfortable with the novel's racial politics. See Jane Tompkins, *Sensational Designs: The Cultural Work of American Fiction, 1790–1860* (New York: Oxford University Press, 1985).

10 Gillian Brown, *Domestic Individualism* (Berkeley: University of California Press, 1990), p. 41. See also Lori Merish, *Sentimental Materialism* (Durham: Duke University Press, 1999).

11 Brook Thomas, *Cross-Examinations of Law and Literature* (New York: Cambridge University Press, 1987), p. 130.

12 See also Eric Sundquist's introduction to *New Essays on Uncle Tom's Cabin* in which he argues that Stowe's investment in racial stereotypes marks the "limits of abolitionist idealism"; *New Essays on Uncle Tom's Cabin* ed. Eric Sundquist (Cambridge: Cambridge University Press, 1986), p. 32.

13 Timothy Powell, *Ruthless Democracy: A Multicultural Interpretation of the American Renaissance* (Princeton: Princeton University Press, 2000). All further references to this text will be cited parenthetically.

14 See Eugene H. Berwanger, "Negrophobia in Northern Proslavery and Antislavery Thought," *Phylon* 33 (Fall 1972): 266–275, for an example of how racism provides an inadequate standard for distinguishing pro- and antislavery discourse. For an example of the way in which racism and anti-slavery were at times powerfully congruent, see Hinton Rowan Helper, *The Impending Crisis* (New York: Burdick Brothers, 1857).

15 Harriet Beecher Stowe, *The Key to Uncle Tom's Cabin* (1853; New York: Arno Press, 1968), v. All further references will be to this edition and will be cited parenthetically in the text.

16 See also Alexander Kinmont, *Twelve Lectures on the Natural History of Man* (Cincinnati, 1839) and William Ellery Channing, "Emancipation" (1840), *The Works of William E. Channing, D.D.* (Boston, 1867), for other examples of the way in which anti-slavery advocates summoned the essential character to demonstrate the fundamental immorality of slavery. It is interesting to note that Channing moves away from his claim in *Slavery* (Boston, 1836) that slavery violates universal human rights (i.e. liberal rights) toward the essentialist view that slavery is a sin against the Christianity inherent in the African race.

17 Although instinctive Christianity is clearly the race's most redeeming characteristic, Stowe also notes some of the race's more mundane traits: "they are not naturally daring and enterprising, but home-loving and affectionate," they possess "an indigenous talent" for cooking, and because he holds "deep in his heart" "a passion for all that is splendid, rich, and fanciful," the Negro is enchanted by bright colors and ornate displays (*Key*, 93, 205, 161).

18 The Negroes' natural gift for Christianity is evidenced most clearly in their susceptibility to evangelical fervor. Stowe describes how sometimes "in their religious meetings they will spring from the floor many times in succession, with a violence and rapidity which is perfectly astonishing. They will laugh, weep, and embrace each other convulsively, and sometimes become entirely paralysed and cataleptic." (*Key*, 45). The reason for such "extravagances" is the Negro's "sensitive and exceedingly vivacious temperament" (*Key*, 45). Also see Alice C. Crozier, *The Novels of Harriet Beecher Stowe* (New York: Oxford University Press, 1969) for a discussion of Stowe's affectional religion.

19 The term "romantic racialism" is George Fredrickson's. See *The Black Image in the White Mind* (Middletown, CT: Wesleyan University Press, 1971), pp. 97–129. See also John L. Thomas, "Romantic Reform in America, 1815–1865," *American Quarterly*, 17 (Winter 1965): 656–681. My discussion of *Uncle Tom's Cabin* is indebted to Fredrickson, but rather than view such romantic racialism with suspicion, I am interested in the way that racialism can effect a progressive social movement.

20 Thomas Wentworth Higginson, "The Maroons of Surinam" *The Atlantic Monthly* (May, 1860), pp. 549–557.

21 William Gilmore Simms, *Southern Quarterly Review* 24 (July 1853): 234.

22 Nehemiah Adams, *The Sable Clould: A Southern Tale, with Northern Comments* (Boston: Ticknor and Fields, 1861), p. 135; quoted in Yarborough, "Strategies of Black Characterization," 81.

23 Reginald Horsman, *Race and Manifest Destiny* (Cambridge, MA: Harvard University Press, 1981), p. 157. See also, Thomas F. Gossett, *Race: The History of an Idea in America* (Dallas: Southern Methodist University Press, 1963) rpt. New York: Schocken Books, 1965; and see also Fredrickson, *The Black Image in the White Mind*, esp. pp. 43–130.

24 Josiah C. Nott and George R. Gliddon, *Types of Mankind* (Philadelphia: Lippincott, Grambo and Company, 1854), 49.

25 E. G. Squier, "American Ethnology," *American Whig Review* 9 (April 1849): 386.

26 In *Pro-Slavery Thought in the Old South* (Chapel Hill: North Carolina University Press, 1935), Jenkins cites Josiah Nott's letters to James Hammond in which Nott regularly referred to ethnology as "niggerology" or the "nigger business" (2578–260).

27 Samuel G. Morton, *Crania Americana; or, A Comparative View of the Skulls of Various Aboriginal Nations of North and South America; to which is Prefixed An Essay on the Varieties of the Human Species* (Philadelphia: John Pennington, 1839).

28 See Stanton, 24–53. For a critique see Gould.

29 For a discussion of the racialist thought of antebellum historians see David Levin, *History as Romantic Art: Bancroft, Prescott, Motley, and Parkman* (Stanford: Stanford University Press, 1959) esp. pp. 74–92; 126–159.

30 See in particular Francis Lieber, *On Civil Liberty and Self-Government* (Philadelphia: J. B. Lippincott and Co., 1859).

31 Robert Knox, *Races of Men: A Fragment* (Philadelphia, 1850), p. 7.

32 Ralph Waldo Emerson, *English Traits* (1856) in *The Library of America, Emerson: Essays and Lectures* Joel Porte ed. (New York: Library of America, 1983), p. 791. All references to Emerson's works will refer to this edition and will be cited parenthetically in the text. See also Emerson's essay "Fate," where he repeats this assessment of Knox whom he calls "a rash and unsatisfactory writer, but charged with pungent and unforgettable truths" (950).

33 See Philip L. Nicoloff, *Emerson on Race and History* (New York: Columbia University Press, 1961) for an example of the energy critics expend in an attempt to excuse Emerson's racist hierarchy of human essences.

34 William Ellery Channing, "Emancipation" (1840) in *The Works of William E. Channing, D.D.*, vol. VI (Boston: American Unitarian Association, 1867), p. 88. See also Alexander Kinmont's claim that "All the sweeter graces of the Christian religion appear almost too tropical and tender plants to grow in soil of the Caucasian mind; they require a character of human nature, of which you can see the rude lineaments in the Ethiopian, to be implanted in, and grow naturally and beautifully withal," *Twelve Lectures on the Natural History of Man* (Cincinnati, 1839), p. 218.

35 Louisiana law derives from the French Napoleonic code while the rest of United States' law derives from English Common Law.

36 Philip Fisher, *Hard Facts* (New York: Oxford University Press, 1987); future references will be cited parenthetically in the text.

37 For a powerful discussion of how the debate over the concept of the family was one of the primary ideological subjects for the antebellum United States see Lora Romero, *Home Fronts: Domesticity and Its Critics in the Antebellum United States* (Durham: Duke University Press, 1997); Amy Kaplan, "Manifest Domesticity," *American Literature* 70:3 (September 1998): 581–606. For a discussion of the family that foregrounds the ideological centrality of the family but incompletely historicizes the question of who can be related to whom see Elizabeth Barnes, *States of Sympathy: Seduction and Democracy in the American Novel* (New York: Columbia University Press, 1997).

38 This tradition of reading *Uncle Tom's Cabin* as a pro-family novel is not recent. Ever since George Sand noted in her 1852 review that "this book is essentially domestic and of the family," critics have emphasized the absolutely domestic character of the book. George Sand, "Review of *Uncle Tom's Cabin*," *La Presse*, 17 Dec. 1852). See, for instance, the essays collected in *Critical Essays on Harriet Beecher Stowe*, Elizabeth Ammons ed. (Boston: G. K. Hall, 1980).

39 Robert Hayne, quoted in William W. Freehling, *Prelude to Civil War* (New York: Harper and Row, 1966), p. 41.

40 C. G. Memminger, *Lecture Delivered Before the Young Men's Library Association of Augusta, April 10, 1851, Showing African Slavery to be Consistent with the Moral and Physical Progress of a Nation* (Augusta, W. S. Jones Newspaper, Book, and Job Printer, 1851), p. 14. See also Stephanie McCurry, "The Two Faces of Republicanism: Gender and Proslavery Politics in Antebellum South Carolina," *The Journal of American History* 78 (March 1992): 1245–1264; for a discussion of the ways Southerners imagined slavery as continuous with the power relations within the family, particularly the submission of the wife to the husband.

41 Ibid., 15.

42 This claim, of course, was most forcefully presented by John Calhoun. Although Calhoun did not place the family at the center of his defense of slavery, he did emphasize the communal nature of rights and often pointed to the family as a model of natural subjection. See, for example, John C. Calhoun, "Speech on the Reception of Abolition Papers (1837); "Speech on the Importance of Domestic Slavery" (1838). Both are reprinted in Eric L. McKitrick. *Slavery Defended: The Views of the Old South* (Englewood Cliffs, N.J.: Prentice Hall, 1963).

43 It is for this reason that although Fitzhugh expressed distrust for any book on moral science less than 400 years old, he made Robert Filmer's *Patriarcha* (1634) an exception.

44 George Fitzhugh, *Sociology for the South, or the Failure of Free Society* (Richmond: A Morris Publisher, 1854), p. 46.

45 George Fitzhugh, *Cannibals All! or Slaves Without Masters* (Richmond: A. Morris, 1857); rpt. 1960 C. Vann Woodward ed. (Cambridge, MA: Harvard University Press, 1960), p. 36.

46 One writer in the *Southern Quarterly Review*, in fact, refused to call the Southern system slavery. Slavery, he argued, existed only in Europe, in the South there existed "patriarchal government," the "same form of government to which the abolitionists subject their wives and children." Samuel A. Cartwright, "Canaan Identified with the Ethopian," *Southern Quarterly Review* 2 (October 1842): 364–365.

47 Fitzhugh, *Cannibals All!*, pp. 205–206. According to Fitzhugh, abolitionists have forgotten that the slave holder considers the slave a part of the domestic circle and by doing so becomes obligated to his slaves:

> Infant negroes, sick, helpless, aged and infirm negroes, are simply a charge to their master; he has no property in them in the common sense of the term, for they are of no value for the time, but they have the most invaluable property in him. He is bound to support them, to supply all their wants, and relieve them of all care for the present or future. . . . What a glorious thing to man is slavery, when want, misfortune, old age, debility, and sickness overtake him (*Sociology*, 68).

By arguing that slaves have as much property in the master as he has in them, Fitzhugh is able to contrast the antagonism between worker and employer that characterizes Northern capitalism to the organic reciprocity of slavery. See also Eugene D. Genovese, *The World the Slaveholders Made: Two Essays in Interpretation* (New York: Random House, 1969), pp. 118–244.

48 Fitzhugh, "Popular Institutions," *De Bow's Review*, 28 (December 1860): 523.

49 Fitzhugh was the first writer in the United States to foreground Auguste Comte's recently coined term "sociology" in a title; Henry Hughes published *A Treatise on Sociology* (Philadelphia, 1854) later the same year.

50 Later in life Fitzhugh did accept racialist premises. See Fredrickson, *The Black Image in the White Mind*, 60–68. But Fitzhugh appreciated that the anti-materialist logic of the familial defense of slavery required that he not depend on race to legitimate the system. See also Henry Hughes, *Treatise on Sociology* (1854) who argued that the "ethnical qualification" of the South's labor system was, in his words, "accidental" (42).

51 Fitzhugh, "Southern Thought," *De Bow's Review* 23 (May 1857): 337–384; quotation on 347.

52 George Fitzhugh, "Origin of Civilization – What is Property? – Which is the Best Slave Race," *De Bow's Review*, XXV (1858): 653–664.

53 This is not to deny miscegenation but only to argue that Fitzhugh does not see biology as determining the relations between master and slave.

54 Unlike Severn Duvall, "*Uncle Tom's Cabin*: The Sinister Side of Patriarchy" in *Images of the Negro in American Literature*, Seymour L. Gross and John Edward Hardy eds. (Chicago: University of Chicago Press, 1966), pp. 163–180, I am not arguing that Southern representations of the family were false or that Stowe merely "exposed the legend," because before Stowe could argue for the "hypocrisy" of the Southern model, she needed to propose a persuasive alternative model of the family. That is, rather than revealing the "basic inconsistencies" or the "crushing paradoxes" of the patriarchal model of slavery, Stowe conjured these contradictions (171, 168).

55 See Orlando Patterson, *Slavery and Social Death* (Cambridge, MA: Harvard University Press, 1982); and M.I. Finley, *Ancient Slavery and Modern Ideology* (New York: Penguin Books, 1980) for a discussion of the ways in which slavery cannot *only* be defined as a property relation since there are numerous human relations that involve property claims in others that fall short of slavery.

56 See Marc Shell, *The End of Kinship* (Stanford: Stanford University Press, 1988), esp. pp. 3–25, for a discussion of the problem of determining the "true" family.

57 For an interesting discussion of the centrality of choice at this moment see Susan M. Ryan, "Charity Begins at Home: Stowe's Antislavery Novels and the Forms of Benevolent Citizenship," *American Literature* 72:4 (December 2000): 751–782. But whereas Ryan seeks to redeem benevolent citizenship by exploring how "volitional arrangements"(what one chooses) stand as an "alternative" to race, my argument asks whether, for Stowe, volition can ever

be distinguished from the essential categories of race and gender, i.e. the things that make one a chooser in the first place (772).

58 This, of course, is not to say that racial essentialism is always progressive, only to suggest that such essentialism cannot be axiomatically designated as pernicious.

59 Appiah, *In My Father's House*, 13.

60 See *Race and Representation: Affirmative Action*, Robert Post and Michael Rogin eds. (New York: Zone Books, 1998) and Allan David Freeman, "Legitimizing Racial Discrimination through Antidiscrimination Law: A Critical Review of Supreme Court Doctrine." See also Gary Peller "Race Consciousness," and Kimberle Williams Crenshaw, "Race, Reform, and Retrenchment: Transformation and Legitimation in Anti-Discrimination Law." The Freeman, Peller, and Crenshaw articles are collected in *Critical Race Theory*.

61 This emphasis on the biased effect of an ostensibly neutral policy cannot simply be divided into a Left and Right binary. Milton Friedman, for example, has noted that U. S. anti-drug laws have led to a higher rate of incarceration for Blacks in the United States than in apartheid-era South Africa and then asks: "can any policy, however, high-minded, be moral if it . . .has so racist an effect?" See Milton Friedman, "There's No Justice in the War on Drugs," *New York Times* (January 11, 1998): sec. 4, p. 19.

62 See, for example, Robert Post, "Prejudicial Appearances: The Logic of American Antidiscrimination Law," 88 *California Law Review* (January 2000): 1–40; see also Reva Siegel's response "Discrimination in the Eyes of the Law," 88 *California Law Review* (January 2000): 77–93.

EVA'S HAIR AND THE SENTIMENTS OF RACE

1 See Eric Sundquist, "The Literature of Slavery and African American Culture," *The Cambridge History of American Literature*, vol. 2 1820–1865, Sacvan Bercovitch ed. (Cambridge: Cambridge University Press, 1995), p. 292. This, of course, is not to say that Stowe is advocating violence: Dred – supposedly a son of Denmark Vesey, whom Stowe deliberately also links to Nat Turner – after all, never leads his rebellion because Stowe kills him off. Nor is it to say that the novel presents an unconflicted account of racial amalgamation: the interracial families it presents are Black parents who sacrifice themselves for poor white children and Edward Clayton, Stowe is careful to say, marries a white woman. Thus critics have observed that Stowe concludes this ostensibly integrationist novel "with a careful disavowal" of interracial sex. See Susan M. Ryan, "Charity Begins at Home: Stowe's Antislavery Novels and the Forms of Benevolent Citizenship," *American Literature* 72:4 (December 2000): 773.

2 Robert S. Levine, *Martin Delany, Frederick Douglass, and the Politics of Representative Identity* (Chapel Hill: University of North Carolina Press, 1997), p. 146. Further references will be cited parenthetically in the text.

It is important to note that Black leaders, such as Delany, often initiated their own plans for the emigration of former slaves and free Blacks to Africa or to other communities outside the borders of the United States. That is, what African-American intellectuals often opposed was not necessarily the idea of emigration it and of itself, but the particulars of the white-sponsored plans of the American Colonization Society.

3 Harriet Beecher Stowe, *Dred: A Tale of the Great Dismal Swamp* [1856] (New York: Penguin Books, 2000), pp.328, 306. It is important to note that these sentiments are articulated by Anne and Edward Clayton, the characters whom Stowe presents as the novel's most admirable reformers.

4 Cynthia S. Hamilton, "*Dred*: Intemperate Slavery," *Journal of American Studies* 34:2 (2000): 275.

5 Lori Merish, *Sentimental Materialism: Gender, Commodity Culture, and Nineteenth-Century American Literature* (Durham: Duke University Press, 2000), p. 163.

6 Harriet Beecher Stowe, "A Brilliant Success," *Independent* 10 (September 30, 1858): 1.

7 For an alternative reading of this passage see Levine, *Martin Delany, Frederick Douglass*, 150–151.

8 Elizabeth Barnes, *States of Sympathy: Seduction and Democracy in the American Novel* (New York: Columbia University Press, 1997), p. 4.

9 Stowe in the Introduction she wrote for the 1879 edition which renewed the copyright explained that *Uncle Tom's Cabin* began with a vision. Referring to herself in the third person, as if she were merely a medium for God's word, she states:

> The first part of the book ever committed to writing was the death of Uncle Tom. This Scene presented itself almost as a tangible vision to her mind while sitting at the communion table in the little church in Brunswick. She was perfectly overcome by it, and could scarcely restrain the convulsion of tears and sobbings that shook her frame. She hastened home, and wrote it; . . . From that time the story can less be said to have been composed by her than imposed upon her. Scenes, incidents, conversations, rushed upon her with a vividness and importunity that would not be denied. The book insisted upon getting itself into being, and would take no denial (*Uncle Tom's Cabin* [Boston, 1879], xiii-xiv).

Despite Stowe's extraordinary and somewhat questionable account about the power of Tom's death, it should not be forgotten that Stowe, who as a rule was very reliable about meeting her deadlines, missed the next installment in the novel's serialization after writing Eva's death. See E. Bruce Kirkham, *The Building of Uncle Tom's Cabin* (Knoxville: University of Tennessee Press, 1977), p. 130.

10 The scene's power extended beyond the reading audience. This scene was also the centerpiece of the melodramatic and tremendously successful "Tom Shows." See Stephen A. Hirsch, "Uncle Tomitudes: The Popular Reaction to *Uncle Tom's Cabin*," in *Studies in the American Renaissance* (1978).

11 Ann Douglas, *The Feminization of American Culture* [1977] (New York: Anchor Press, 1988); Jane Tompkins, *Sensational Designs: The Cultural Work of American Fiction, 1790–1860* (New York: Oxford University Press, 1985).

12 Sentimentality, according to this account, represents "the political sense obfuscated or gone rancid"; the genre exists only to offer "distraction" and "for the sake of titillation" (*Feminization*, 254).

13 Although Douglas is the most notorious anti-sentimentalist, she simply culminates a long tradition in which it was argued that the genre allowed its readers to "escape rather than. . . challenge" the world (Herbert Ross Brown, *The Sentimental Novel in America 1789–1860* (Durham, N.C.: Duke University Press, 1940), p. 369). According to this account, the sentimental allows readers to indulge their feelings without doing what should be done. See Mark Jefferson, "What's Wrong with Sentimentality?'" *Mind* 92 (1983): 519–527; Mary Midgley, "Brutality and Sentimentality," *Philosophy* 54 (1979).

14 Philip Fisher, *Hard Facts* (New York, Oxford University Press, 1985). All further references to this work will be cited parenthetically in the text.

15 See Shirley Samuels ed., *The Culture of Sentiment: Race, Gender, and Sentimentality in Nineteenth-Century America* (New York: Oxford University Press, 1992). See also Nancy Armstrong, "The Racial Logic of American Sentimentalism," in *The Yale Journal of Criticism* 7:2 (Fall 1994):1–24.

16 Michelle Burnham, *Captivity and Sentiment* (Hanover, NH: University Press of New England, 1997).

17 Glenn Hendler, "The Limits of Sympathy: Louisa May Alcott and the Sentimental Novel," *American Literary History* 3:4 (Winter 1991): 685–706. See also Glenn Hendler, *Public Sentiments: Structures of Feeling in Nineteenth-Century American Literature* (Chapel Hill: University of North Carolina Press, 2001).

18 Karen Sanchez-Eppler, *Touching Liberty: Abolition, Feminism, and the Politics of the Body* (Berkeley: University of California Press, 1993) all further references to this text will be cited parenthetically in the text. See also Michael Ryan, *Politics and Culture* (Baltimore: Johns Hopkins University Press, 1989); esp. pp. 134–148; who applies the structure of metaphor to liberal theory.

19 For a complementary critique see Laura Wexler, "Tender Violence: Literary Eavesdropping, Domestic Fiction, and Educational Reform," in *The Yale Journal of Criticism* 5:1 (Fall 1991): 151–187; rpt in Samuels' *The Culture of Sentiment.* Implicit in Wexler's critique of sentimentalism is the belief that there are fundamental physical differences between races and genders that sentimental narratives seek to dissolve.

20 Dana Nelson, *The Word in Black and White: Reading "Race" in American Literature, 1638–1867* (New York: Oxford University Press, 1993), p. 142 (original emphasis).

21 For some examples of the large archive on the link between disembodiment and liberal citizenship, see Lauren Berlant, *The Queen of America Goes to Washington City* (Durham: Duke University Press, 1997); Michael Warner, "The Mass Public and the Mass Subject," *Habermas and the Public Sphere*, Craig Calhoun ed. (Cambridge, MA: MIT Press, 1992), pp. 377–401; and Russ Castronovo, *Necro Citizenship: Death, Eroticism, and the Public Sphere in the Nineteenth-Century United States* (Durham: Duke University Press, 2001).

22 Berlant's argument builds on Wendy Brown's work on the problem of building identity around pain and ressentiment, see *States of Injury: Power and Freedom in Late Modernity* (Princeton: Princeton University Press, 1995).

23 Lauren Berlant, "The Subject of True Feeling" in *Cultural Studies and Political Theory*, Jodi Dean, ed. (Ithaca: Cornell University Press, 2000), pp. 44, 50. It is important to note that in this revised version of the essay Berlant adds the word "liberal"; see version in *Cultural Pluralism, Identity Politics, and the Law*, Sarat and Kearns eds. (Ann Arbor: University of Michigan Press, 1999), p. 53.

24 Given this linkage, it is perhaps unsurprising that Marianne Noble attempts to redeem the sentimental by detaching it from liberalism. According to Noble, the sentimental promotes "embodied, affective personhood" against the disembodied, abstract, and "repressive legal definitions of personhood" of liberalism. Marianne Noble, "The Ecstasies of Sentimental Wounding in *Uncle Tom's Cabin*," *Yale Journal of Criticism* 10 (Fall 1997): 302.

25 Any discussion of humanitarian reform begins with the magisterial work of David Brion Davis. See in addition, Thomas L. Haskell, "Capitalism and the Origins of the Humanitarian Sensibility, Parts 1 and 2" reprinted in *The Anti-Slavery Debate: Capitalism and Abolitionism as a Problem in Historical Interpretation*, Thomas Bender ed. (Berkeley: University of California Press, 1992), pp. 107–160; and Karen Halttunen, "Humanitarianism and the Pornography of Pain in Anglo-American Culture" *The American Historical Review*, vol. 100:2 (April, 1995): 303–334.

26 Judith Shklar, *Ordinary Vices* (Cambridge, MA: The Belknap Press of Harvard University Press, 1984), Chapter I, passim. Richard Rorty borrows Shklar's definition in *Contingency, Irony, and Solidarity* (Cambridge: Cambridge University Press, 1989), xv, 74, 146.

27 Stowe's claim that Blacks feel more is intended to counter the widespread assumption that the African race inherently feels less than the Anglo-Saxon. See, for example, Samuel Cartwright's "Report on the Diseases and Physical Peculiarities of the Negro Race. . .," *New Orleans Medical and Surgical Journal*, VII (1851): 691–715.

28 P. Tidyman, "Sketch of the most remarkable diseases of the Negroes of the Southern States with an account of the method of treating them, accompanied by physiological observations," *Philadelphia Journal of Medical and Physical Sciences*, vol. 12 (1826), p. 315. Such a line of argument was expressed most vividly by Mrs. Henry Schoolcraft, who in a pro-slavery response to *Uncle Tom's Cabin*, explains that Negroes could not be overworked and that it was physically impossible for a master to knock a slave "senseless to the ground" – as anti-slavery writers so often claimed – because the Negro skull was so thick and solid that the white man's fist would inevitably be broken if such a blow was attempted. See Mrs. Henry R. Schoolcraft, *The Black Gauntlet: A Tale of Plantation Life in South Carolina* [1860] (New York: Negro Universities Press, 1969), pp. 49, 61.

29 Thomas R. R. Cobb, *An Inquiry into the Law of Negro Slavery in the United States of America* [1858] rpt. (New York: Negro Universities Press, 1968), p. 39.

30 George S. Sawyer, *Southern Institutes; or, an Inquiry into the Origin and Early Prevalence of Slavery and the Slave-Trade* (Philadelphia, J. B. Lippincott & Co., 1858), 223, 222. In a similar vein, Hammond claims that "Negroes are themselves both perverse and comparatively indifferent about" the keeping their family together and therefore "almost invariably prefer forming connexions [sic] with slaves belonging to other masters, and at some distance." James Henry Hammond, *Letter to an English Abolitionist* [1845] in *The Ideology of Slavery: Proslavery Thought in the Antebellun South*, Drew Gilpin Faust ed. (Baton Rouge: Louisiana State University Press, 1981), 192.

31 Wendell Phillips, "Against Idolatry" [October 4, 1859] in *Wendell Phillips on Civil Rights and Freeedom*, Louis Filler ed. (New York: Hill and Wang: 1965), p. 82.

32 See Douglas, *Feminization*, 200–226.

33 Thomas Baldwin Thayer, *Over the River; or Pleasant Walks into the Valley of Shadows, and Beyond. . .* (Boston: Tompkins and Company, 1864), p. 249.

34 See, for example, Dolf Sternberger, *Panorama of the 19th Century*, trans. Joachim Neugroschel (New York: Urizen Books, 1977).

35 As Eva states, "I can understand why Jesus *wanted* to die for us. . . .Because I've felt so, too" (274).

36 This scene, like most of the novel, does not unequivocally invoke a disembodied Christian community. Indeed, rarely does Stowe imagine salvation without reference to the fact of bodily difference. For example when Topsy explains that she could never be good unless "I could be skinned, and come white," Eva replies that Jesus will help her to be good, to go to Heaven, and finally be "an angel forever, *just as much as if you were white*" (280, 281 emphasis added). At best, the differences between Anglo-Saxons and African's are not reconciled as much as Blackness is simply erased as a category, and, at worst, as Blacks are "skinned" and thus rendered "white."

37 For a sociological account of hair see Anthony Synnott, *The Social Body: Symbolism, Self, and Society* (London: Routledge, 1993), pp. 103–127.

38 The circularity of Browne's experiment is spectacular: he presumes the very difference he sets out to test.

39 It had been thought, particularly during the 18th century that the pigmentation of Africans was a secondary characteristic, contingent rather than determining of the race's identity. For example, Benjamin Rush argued that "the Black Color (as it is called) of Negroes is derived from LEPROSY" and therefore he believed that race, like any other "disease," could be cured. See Benjamin Rush, "Observations intended to favour a supposition that the Black Color (as it is called) of the Negroes is derived from LEPROSY. Read at a Special Meeting July 14, 1797," *Transactions*, American Philosophical Society, IV (1799), 289–297. In a similar vein, Reverend Samuel Stanhope Smith who argued that dark skins might well "be considered as a universal freckle," a product of climate signfying nothing essential. See *An Essay on the Causes of the*

Variety of Complexion and Figure in the Human Species (rev. edn.; Philadelphia, 1788, 13.

40 Peter A. Browne, "A Microscopic Examination and description of some of the Piles of the Head of Albinos," *Proceedings*, AAAS,III (1850), 108–114. I owe much to William Stanton, *The Leopard's Spots: Scientific Attitudes toward Race in America 1815–1859* (Chicago: University of Chicago Press, 1960), pp. 149–154.

41 Peter A. Browne, *The Classification of Mankind by the Hair and Wool of their Heads, with the Nomenclature of Human Hybirds* (Philadelphia: J. H. Jones, 1852).

42 In the eighteenth century Johann Friedrich Blumenbach, one of the founders of anthropology, attempted to classify races by the structure of their hair. Later, Bory de Saint-Vincent and Franz Pruner-Bey, following the suggestions of George Buffon, did extensive independent work on the difference between the straight and woolly-haired species of man.

43 See James C. Prichard, *Researches into the Physical History of Man* (London: John and Arthur Arch, 1813); *The Natural History of Man: Comprising Inquiries into the Modifying Influence of Physical and Moral Agencies on the Different Tribes of the Human Family* (London: H. Bailliere, 1843). It is important to note that even though Prichard believed that mankind was a single species, he believed that racial difference was biologically permanent and determined temperament and character.

44 Prichard argued that even if the:

> cuticular excrescence of the Negro were really not hair, but a fine wool,–if it were precisely analogous to the finest wool,–still this would by no means prove the Negro to be of a peculiar and separate stock, since we know that some tribes of animals bear wool, while others of the same species are covered with hair. It is true that some instances this peculiarity depends immediately on the climate, and is subject to vary when the climate is changed; but in others, it is deeply fixed in the breed, and almost amounts to a permanent variety (*The Natural History of Man* volume I, 97).

45 Peter A. Browne, *Trichologia mammalium; or, A treatise on the organization, properties and uses of hair and wool, together with an eassay upon the raising and breeding of Sheep* (Philadelphia: J. H. Jones, 1853).

46 *Proceedings*, Academy of Natural Sciences of Philadelphia, V (1851), pp. 145–146.

47 Although it is tempting especially since Browne was by training a lawyer.

48 John Campbell, *Negromania: Being an Examination of the Falsely Assumed Equality of the Various Races of Men; Demonstrated by the Investigations of Champollion, Wilkinson, Rosellini, Van-Amringe, Gliddon, Young, Morton, Knox, Lawrence, Gen. J. H. Hammond, Murray, Smith, W. Gilmore Simms, English, Conrad, Elder, Prichard, Blumenbach, Cuvier, Brown, Le Vaillant, Carlyle, Cardinal Wiseman, Burckhardt, and Jefferson* (Philadelphia: Campbell & Power, 1851), pp. 339–364.

49 See, for example, "The Hair and Wool of the Different Species of Man," an unsigned review in *The United States Magazine, and Democratic Review,* 24 (1850): 451–456. J. H. Baxter, *Statistics, Medical and Anthropological, of the Provost Marshal-General's Bureau, Derived from Records of the Examination for Military Service in the Armies of the United States during the Late War of the Rebellion, of over a Million Recruits, Drafted Men, Substitutes, and Enrolled Men,* 2 vols. (Washington, D.C., 1875), I, 61. For an example of Browne's support among the pro-slavery thinkers see J. H. Van Evrie, M. D., *White Supremacy and Negro Subordination,* (New York: Van Evrie, Horton and Co., 1868), esp. 98–104). See also John Haller, *Outcasts from Evolution* (Chicago: University of Illinois Press, 1970).

50 See Thomas F. Gossett, *Race: The History of an Idea in America* (New York: Schocken Books, 1963), p. 81.

51 Henry Box Brown, *Narrative of the Life of Henry Box Brown, Written by Himself* (Manchester: Lee and Glynn, 1851), p. 6.

52 William Van Amringe, *An Investigation of the Theories of the Natural History of Man* (New York, 1848), p. 397. Amringe cites this story in the course of arguing for the separation of the white and Negro. He bases his argument, however, not on the fact that the Negro has wool, but on the fact that Negro hair is "wholly different in every respect" from the hair of Europeans (402).

53 In *The Color Complex* (New York: Harcourt Brace Jovanovich, 1992), Kathy Russell, Midge Wilson, and Ronald Hall quote the story of a Black woman in a restroom who remarks, as she is fixing her hair, "what is this mass of sheep's wool that so prominently atop our heads? What did Black people do to deserve this bad-ass hair from hell?" (81).

54 Frederick Douglass, "The Claims of the Negro Ethnologically Considered: An Address Delivered in Hudson, Ohio, on 12 July 1854," in *The Frederick Douglass Papers* Ser.1, Vol.2, *Speeches, Debates, and Interviews, 1847–1854,* John Blassingame et al., eds. (New Haven: Yale University Press, 1982), p. 508.

55 Malcolm X, *The Autobiography of Malcolm X* (New York: Ballantine Books, 1964), p. 54.

56 Dialogue from *School Daze* in Spike Lee and L. Jones, *Uplift the Race: The Construction of School Daze* (New York: Simon and Schuster, 1988), p. 157.

57 See Paulette M. Caldwell, "A Hair Piece: Perspectives on the Intersections of Race and Gender" in *Duke Law Journal* vol. 1991:2 (1991): 365–398.

58 Kobena Mercer, "Black Hair/Style Politics," *Out There: Marginalization and Contemporary Cultures,* Russell Ferguson, Martha Gever, Trinh T. Minh-ha, Cornel West eds. (Cambridge, MA: MIT Press, 1990), pp. 251–252. Reprinted in Kobena Mercer, *Welcome to the Jungle: New Positions in Black Cultural Studies* (New York: Routledge, 1994).

59 See James T. Smith, "Review of Dr. Cartwright's Report on the Diseases and Physical Peculiarities of the Negro Race," *New Orleans Medical and Surgical Journal* vol. 8 (1851): 230.

60 The court's confidence on the reliability of hair as a stable racial marker is quite striking. According to Judge Tucker:

> Suppose three persons, a black or mulatto man or woman with a flat nose and woolly head; a copper-coloured person with long jetty black, straight hair; and one with a fair complexion, brown hair, not woolly nor inclining thereto, with a prominent Roman nose, were brought together before a Judge upon a write of Habeas Corpus, on the ground of false imprisonment and detention in slavery: that the only evidence which the person detaining them in his custody could produce was an authenticated bill of sale from another person, and that the parties themselves were unable to produce any evidence concerning themselves, whence they came &c. &c. How must a Judge act in such a case? I answer he must judge from his own view. He must discharge the white person and the Indian out of custody, . . . and he must deliver the black or mulatto person, with the flat nose and woolly hair to the person claiming to hold him or her as a slave (11. Va at 19–140).

Tucker, in short, presumes that difference in hair proved differences in equality.

61 See Walter Johnson, "The Slave Trader, the White Slave, and the Politics of Racial Determination in the 1850s" in *The Journal of American History* (June 2000): 13–38. Johnson examines in detail this case. I have relied on his account.

62 See Lynn Wardley, "Relic, Fetish, Femmage: The Aesthetics of Sentiment in the Work of Stowe," *Yale Journal of Criticism* 5:3 (fall 1992): 165–191.

63 Charles Loring Brace, *The Races of the Old World: A Manual of Ethnology* (New York: Scribner, 1863), p. 14.

64 Sacvan Bercovitch, *The Office of The Scarlet Letter* (Baltimore: Johns Hopkins University Press, 1991).

A IS FOR ANYTHING: US LIBERALISM AND THE MAKING OF *THE SCARLET LETTER*

1 This truth, of course, was not always so clear. Contemporaneous readers of *The Scarlet Letter* did not emphasize the ambiguity of the letter, but rather stressed the objectivity and subtlety of Hawthorne's representation of sin and passion. See, for example, Bertha Faust, *Hawthorne's Contemporaneous Reputation: A Study of Literary Opinion in America and England, 1828–1864* (New York: Octagon Books, 1977), pp. 67–87.

2 See, for example, Michael Colacurcio "Footsteps of Anne Hutchinson: The context of *The Scarlet Letter*," *ELH*. 39 (1972): 457–494 who argues that the A stands for Antinomianism, and Amy Schrager Lang, *Prophetic Women: Anne Hutchinson and the problem of Dissent in the Literature of New England* (Berkeley: University of California Press, 1987), pp. 161–192. who sees the A designating Anne Hutchinson, Millicent Bell, *Hawthorne's View of the Artist* (Albany: State University of New York Press, 1962). who sees A representing the Artist, and Jonathan Arac who sees the A representing Apathy. See also Jay Grossman, " 'A' is for Abolition?: Race, Authorship, *The Scarlet Letter*," *Textual Practice* 7:1 (Spring 1993): 13–30.

3 Charles Feidelson, *Symbolism and American Literature* (Chicago: University of Chicago Press, 1953), p. 15. John Irwin, *American Hieroglyphics: The Symbol of*

Egyptian Hieroglyphics in the American Renaissance (New Haven: Yale University Press, 1980), p. 245.

4 Although New Critics focused on the ways in which the symbol could mediate and resolve conflicting meanings, and post-modernist critics, such as Norman Bryson "Hawthorne's Illegible Letter," in *Teaching the Text*, Susanne Kappeler and Norman Bryson eds. (London: Routledge, 1983) and Kenneth Dauber, in *Rediscovering Howthorne* (Princeton: Princeton University Press, 1977) investigate the ways in which the *A* exposes the instability of signification, both remain remarkably consistent in their belief that the scarlet letter is a sign that exceeds any single interpretation. One continues to see this understanding of the Romance's central symbol in New Historicist readings. For example, Jonathan Arac argues that *The Scarlet Letter* mystifies action by means of ambiguity.

5 Lauren Berlant offers a graphic example of how this anti-literalist style of reading *The Scarlet Letter* translates into a critique of liberal disembodiment. See *The Anatomy of National Fantasy: Hawthorne, Utopia, and Everyday Life* (Chicago: University of Chicago Press, 1991).

6 Sacvan Bercovitch, *The Office of The Scarlet Letter* (Baltimore: Johns Hopkins University Press, 1991). All future references to this text will be cited parenthetically.

7 Frank Kermode, *The Classic: Literary Images of Permanence and Change* (Cambridge, MA: Harvard University Press, 1983), p. 114. See also Kermode's "Hawthorne's Modernity," *Partisan Review* 41 (1974): 428–441, where he makes an even stronger claim for Hawthorne's modernity being the result of Hawthorne's refusal to give his materials any secure interpretation.

In another essay, Bercovitch discusses his recasting of Kermode's argument:

> Frank Kermode's claim for Hawthorne's modernity – 'his texts. . .are meant as invitations to co-production on the part of the reader' – is accurate in a sense quite different from that which he intended. Kermode speaks of 'a virtually infinite set of questions': *The Scarlet Letter* holds out that mystifying prospect. . .in order to implicate us as co-producers of meaning in a single, coherent moral-political-aesthetic design.

Bercovitch, *Rites of Assent: Transformation in the Symbolic Construction of America* (New York: Routledge, 1993), 212.

8 By identifying the symbol as the characteristic figure of American literary history, Bercovitch follows classic accounts of Hawthorne's style such as Ivor Winter's characterization of Hawthorne's "formula of alternative possibilities" and F. O. Matthiessen's discussion of Hawthorne's symbol as a "device of multiple choice." Ivor Winters, *Maule's Curse* (Norfolk, CT: New Directions, 1938), p. 18; F. O. Matthiessen, *American Renaissance* (New York: Oxford, 1941), p. 276.

9 Some critical accounts have taken race-based slavery as the implicit subtext of *The Scarlet Letter*. Assuming that race-based slavery must – on some level – have preoccupied Hawthorne, critics have, quite compellingly, read through

the manifest content of Hawthorne's texts to identify race-based slavery as the ultimate subject of his fiction. In addition to Arac and Grossman, see, for example, Deborah L. Madsen, "'A is for Abolition': Hawthorne's Bond-servant and the Shadow of Slavery," *The Journal of American Studies* 25 (1991): 255–259; Leland S. Person, "The Dark Labyrinth of Mind: Hawthorne, Hester, and the Ironies of Racial Mothering," *Studies in American Fiction* 31:2 (Spring 2003): 33–48.

Other critics represent *The Scarlet Letter* as fundamentally uninterested in the issue of slavery. For example, Russ Castronovo has argued that *The Scarlet Letter* "despite its publication at the height of heated compromise debates on slavery" is not "an analysis of race in the United States" because the novel enacts the "individualization and privatization of blackness as Hester's [sexual] sin (67). Russ Castronovo, *Necro Citizenship: Death, Eroticism, and the Public Sphere in the Nineteenth-Century United States* (Durham: Duke University Press, 2001). See also Laura Hanft Korobkin, "The *Scarlet Letter* of the Law: Hawthorne and Criminal Justice," *Novel* 30:2 (Winter 1997): 193–218. Korobin argues that Hawthorne "eliminated whatever would have suggested a resemblance between her [Hester's] situation and that of the slave" (195).

10 I am following Bercovitch in using the term America to distinguish the ideological fiction (America) from the material history and practices of the United States.

11 For a critique of this tradition of reading Hawthorne see Sharon Cameron, *The Corporeal Self: Allegories of the Body in Melville and Hawthorne* (Baltimore: Johns Hopkins University Press, 1981), p. 2.

12 That is, since "[n]ot doing its office almost comes to define the function of the symbol," Hawthorne, according to Bercovitch, is able to "rescue the symbol" from its own negative momentum by having Hester's return but keeping the explicit reasons for Hester's conversion to the letter unexpressed (*Office*, 90, 91). In doing so, Hawthorne "invites us [the reader] to participate in a free enterprise democracy of symbol making" (*Office*, 92).

13 This change in the meaning of compromise is, of course, clearest in contemporaneous accounts of Daniel Webster's notorious compromise with Calhoun and Clay (1850).

14 This claim, of course, resembles the argument of Hartz's *Liberal Tradition in America*, which in turn revives the argument Tocqueville proposed in *Democracy in America.*

15 Bercovitch acknowledges Feidelson as offering the best reading of *The Scarlet Letter.* See Barbara Foley, "From New Criticism to Deconstruction: The Example of Charles Feidelson's *Symbolism in American Literature*," *American Quarterly* 36 (Spring 1984): 44–64, for an account of Feidelson's influence.

16 In this sense, even Paul de Man's apparently revisionary reading of allegory retains liberal premises. For de Man, allegory rather than the symbol represents the impossibility of fixing definite meaning. De Man, in other words, keeps the same liberal values, simply transferring the term to which they apply.

17 See Cleanth Brooks, "The Heresy of Paraphrase" in *The Well Wrought Urn* (New York: Harcourt, Brace and Co., 1947), pp. 192–214; as well as his "Irony as a Principle of Structure." See also John Crowe Ransom, "Criticism as Pure Speculation," in *Critical Theory Since Plato*, Hazard Adams, ed. (New York: Harcourt, Brace, and Jovanovitch, 1971), pp. 881–890. Ransom describes the poem's historicity as the accumulation of "irrelevant *local* substance or texture" (887).

18 The term "intelligible" is crucial because New Critics did posit an essence to a poem, but this essence was incommunicable. See Paul de Man's "The Dead-End of Formalist Criticism" in *Blindness and Insight: Essays in the Rhetoric of Contemporary Criticism*, second edn. revised (Minneapolis: University of Minnesota Press, 1983), pp. 229–245.

19 Cleanth Brooks, "What Does Poetry Communicate" in *The Well Wrought Urn*, 73.

20 For another account of the interpretative fiction instaurated by America, see Philip Fisher, Introduction to *The New American Studies: Essays from Representations* (Berkeley: University of California Press, 1991) pp. vii–xxii.

21 Indeed, one might conclude that the post-modern privileging of allegory continues the liberal demonizing of specificity, simply inverting the term in the binary that imposes fixed meaning. Whereas romantic readers repudiate allegory for enforcing a particular meaning, deconstructive readers champion allegory by redefining it as contentless, as embodying the formal logic of signification rather than any meaning in and of itself.

22 John Rawls, *A Theory of Justice* (Cambridge, MA: Harvard University Press, 1971). I focus on this text because *Political Liberalism* was not yet published when *Office* was published (although individual chapters were).

23 Rawls, "Justice as Fairness: Political not Metaphysical" [1985] in John Rawls, *Collected Papers*, ed. Samuel Freeman (Cambridge, MA: Harvard University Press, 1999), p. 388.

24 Several critics have noted the connections between Bercovitch's work and Tocqueville. See, for example, Daniel Walker Howe, "Descendants of Perry Miller" *American Quarterly* 34 (Spring 1982); David Harlan, "A People Blinded from Birth: American History according to Sacvan Bercovitch" *Journal of American History* 78:3 (December 1991): 949–971, esp. 962–963. An expanded version of this argument appears in Harlan's *The Degradation of American History* (Chicago: University of Chicago Press, 1997). Bercovitch alludes to himself as a modern day Tocqueville, a foreign observer of the nation, when he describes his journey from Canada to the United States. See *Rites of Assent*.

25 Alexis de Tocqueville, *Democracy in America*, George Lawrence trans.; J. P. Mayer ed. (New York: Anchor Books, 1969), p. 12. All quotations from this edition.

26 On November 15, 1839, Tocqueville wrote to his translator, "I am writing in a country and for a country where the cause of equality is from now on won – without the possibility of a return toward aristocracy. In this state of affairs

I felt it my duty to stress particularly the bad tendencies which equality may bring about in order to prevent my contemporaries surrendering to them."

27 Tocqueville states Indians do not want to accept white civilization 326ff.

28 See Marc Shell, who in *Children of the Earth: Literature, Politics and Nationhood* (New York: Oxford University Press, 1993), argues that Christian universalism ("all men are my brothers") can too easily be turned into the notion that "only my brothers are men and all others are animals."

29 Indeed, Tocqueville declares that race prejudice against the Negro seems "to increase in proportion to their emancipation . . . inequality cuts deep into mores as it is effaced from the laws" (344).

30 Later in *Democracy in America* one learns that not only race, but also gender, remains materially recalcitrant to the figural logic of equivalence. The differences between men and women will not dissolve because Americans, according to Tocqueville, "think that nature, which created such great differences between the physical and moral constitution of men and women, clearly intended to give their diverse faculties a diverse employment. . . . In America, more than anywhere else in the world, care has been taken constantly to trace clearly distinct spheres of action for the two sexes" (601).

31 The pernicious abstraction of liberal political theory has been most frequently critiqued by feminist political theorists (such as Carol Pateman) and critical race theorists (such as Cheryl Harris), who argue that modern liberalism has been founded on a political and legal universalism that forgets its dependence upon a particular figure, the bourgeois white European male.

32 Sophia Hawthorne to Mary Mann, February 4, 1850 in *Nathaniel Hawthorne: The Letters, 1843–1853*, ed. Thomas Woodson et al. (Columbus: Ohio State University Press, 1985), p. 313.

33 In *The Scarlet Letter*, Hawthorne offers intriguing comments about how the A is the mark of the Black Man. When impatient about Pearl's demand for a story about the Black Man, Hester exclaims that "once in my life I met the Black Man!. . .This letter is his mark!" (*Scarlet Letter*, 148). And later in the text, Mistress Hibbard chides Hester for not admitting that the Black Man has also inscribed Dimmesdale's identity:

> Thou wearest it openly; so there need be no question about that. But this minister! Let me tell thee in thine ear! When the Black Man sees one of his own servants, signed and sealed, so shy of owning to the bond as is the Reverend Mr. Dimmesdale, he hath a way of ordering matter so that the mark shall be disclosed in open daylight to the eyes of all the world! (*Scarlet Letter*, 186).

Such moments, however, have typically been read in terms of the history of witchcraft rather than of race. See, for example, the footnote on the Black Man in the Norton Third Edition. According to the Norton, "The Black Man, in folklore, the devil or his emissary, is associated with the witch Sabbath in the forest, where the witches gathered to worship evil" p. 55. The Norton, as one might expect, underplays how such worship took place: witches had sex with the Devil.

The way that critics divide interpretations of the Black Man as the Devil and as an allusion to the Negro question, however, is in itself in need of scrutiny. For, as Timothy McMillan has pointed out, "Blacks in New England were viewed by Whites as true witches in the anthropological sense – they were inherently evil creatures, unable to control their connection to satanic wickedness" (112). Timothy J. McMillan, "Black Magic: Witchcraft, Race, and Resistance in Colonial New England" in *Journal of Black Studies* 25:1 (September, 1994): 99–117.

34 Bryson, "Hawthorne's Illegible Letter", p. 105.

35 Brook Thomas, "*The Scarlet Letter* as Civic Myth" in *American Literary History* 13: (2001): 181–211.

36 See also Brook Thomas, "Stigmas, Badges, and Brands: Discriminating Marks in Legal History" in *History, Memory, and the Law*, Austin Sarat and Thomas R. Kearns eds. (Ann Arbor: University of Michigan Press, 1999), pp. 249–282. See also Colette Guillaumin's discussion of the invention of race as a biological/natural mark. "Race and Nature: the System of Marks" in Colette Guillaumin, *Racism, Sexism, Power and Ideology* (New York: Routledge, 1995), pp. 133–152.

37 For a brilliant account of the ideological forces that contributed to making *The Scarlet Letter* hypercanonical see Jonathan Arac, "Narrative Forms," in *The Cambridge History of American Literature*, volume 2, Sacvan Bercovitch ed. (New York: Cambridge University Press, 1995), pp. 605–777.

THE ART OF DISCRIMINATION: *THE MARBLE FAUN*, "CHIEFLY ABOUT WAR MATTERS," AND THE AESTHETICS OF ANTI-BLACK RACISM

1 Nathaniel Hawthorne, *The Marble Faun: or The Romance of Monte Beni* ([1860] New York: Penguin, 1990), p. 463. All further references to this novel will be from this edition and will be cited parenthetically in the text. The text of the Penguin edition is that of the *Centenary Edition of the Works of Nathaniel Hawthorne* vol. IV (Columbus: Ohio State University Press, 1968).

2 Nathaniel Hawthorne, "Chiefly About War Matters," in *Tales, Sketches, and Other Papers* (Cambridge, MA: Riverside Press, 1883), p. 318, emphasis added. All further references will be from this edition and will be cited parenthetically in the text.

3 The idea that Hawthorne was detached from his own age characterizes some of the best historicist work on Hawthorne, see David Levin, "Shadows of Doubt: Specter Evidence in Hawthorne's 'Young Goodman Brown'," *American Literature* 34 (1964): 344–352, Michael D. Bell, *Hawthorne and the Historical Romance of New England* (Princeton: Princeton University Press, 1971), and Michael J. Colacurcio, *The Province of Piety: Moral History in Hawthorne's Early Tales* (Cambridge, MA: Harvard University Press, 1984).

4 Jonathan Arac, "The Politics of *The Scarlet Letter*" in Sacvan Bercovitch and Myra Jehlan eds, *Ideology and Classic American Literature* (Cambridge:

Cambridge University Press, 1986); pp. 247–266. Hawthorne writes, as Arac felicitously puts it, "propaganda – *not* to change your life" (251).

5 Nancy Bentley, *The Ethnography of Manners: Hawthorne, James, Wharton* (Cambridge: Cambridge University Press, 1995); Evan Carton, *The Marble Faun: Hawthorne's Transformations* (New York: Twayne Publishers, 1992). See also Mark A. R. Kemp, "*The Marble Faun* and American Postcolonial Ambivalence," in *Modern Fiction Studies* 43:1 (1997): 209–236. Kemp follows Bentley in claiming that Hawthorne's "recurring uses of the faun suggests its use as a safe metaphor, harmless, because fanciful" (218). Eric Cheyfitz, " The Irresistibleness of Great Literature: Reconstructing Hawthorne's Politics," *American Literary History* 6: 4 (Winter 1994): 539–558.

6 Indeed, it is precisely such a line of argument that conventionally guides discussions of Hawthorne's understanding of slavery in his explicitly political writing, most notoriously, of course, his biography of Franklin Pierce. The *Life of Franklin Pierce* is usually read as an effort to defer the problem of slavery (to make a real problem seem less real). In contrast, I am suggesting that the *Life of Pierce* needs to be approached not in terms of the logic of avoidance (a logic that reifies the problem of slavery) but in terms of how the text uses the aesthetic defines the problem of slavery in a particular way.

7 This potential citizenship, of course, is a theoretical not a legal possibility since the Dred Scott decision declared US citizenship for the Negro unconstitutional.

8 Hawthorne, as was his habit, was notoriously ambivalent about any title for his romances. And although he strenuously protested the title *The Transformation* in some letters, he also suggested this title (*Letters 1857–1864*, 222, 226).

9 Thus, unlike Evan Carton, I am not arguing that "Chiefly About War Matters" expresses what *The Marble Faun* attempted to repress: the problem of race-based slavery. See Carton, *The Marble Faun: Hawthorne's Transformations*, esp. 109–116. Like Carton, I read backwards, using "Chiefly About War Matters" to establish the centrality of race and slavery in *The Marble Faun*. But, unlike Carton, I do not argue that the resurrection of this image from *The Marble Faun* reveals how racial slavery is "the repressed element of the novel" (110).

10 Jean Fagan Yellin, "Hawthorne and the Slavery Question" in *A Historical Guide to Nathaniel Hawthorne*, Larry Reynolds ed. (New York: Oxford University Press, 2001), pp. 157. This essay is a revised version of Yellin's 1989 essay.

11 When traveling through Connecticut in 1838 Hawthorne came across a Negro in the Temperance Hotel in Hartford. When he overhears another man discussing how he wished he had "a thousand such fellows," Hawthorne writes that this statement made a "queer impression on me – *the Negro was really so human* – and to talk of owning a thousand like him" (emphasis added). The Negro, although not quite human, nonetheless strikes Hawthorne as a remarkable simulacrum of the human. *American Notebooks, Centenary Edition*, VIII, 151.

12 Although Donatello is not an artist, he is named after an artist.

13 See Evan Carton, "Practicing Theory, Theorizing Practice: Critical Transformations of *The Marble Faun*" in *Teaching Contemporary Theory to Undergraduates,* Dianne F. Sadoff and William E. Cain eds. (New York: Modern Language Association of America, 1994), pp. 141–153.

14 Bentley, Kemp, and Blythe Ann Tellefsen also discuss the racialization of Donatello and Miriam. Blythe Ann Tellefsen, "The case with my dear native land": Nathaniel Hawthorne's Vision of America in *The Marble Faun,*" *Nineteenth-Century Literature* 54:4 (Mar. 2000): 455–479.

15 See, for example, Lindley Spring, *The Negro at Home: An Inquiry after his capacity for self-Government and the Government of Whites for Controlling, Leading, Directing, or Co-operating in; the Civilization of the Age; its Material, Intellectual, Moral, Religious, Social and Political Interests; the Objects of Society and Government, the Business and Duties of our Race; the Offenses of Legislation* (New York: the author, 1868).

16 For a historical description of accounts of Blackness and Africans in the German aesthetic tradition see Sander Gilman, *On Blackness without Blacks: Essays on the Image of the Black in Germany* (Boston: G. K. Hall and Co., 1982).

17 See Frantz Fanon, *Black Skin, White Masks* (New York: Grove Press, 1967), esp. pp. 77–99, for a powerful theoretical discussion of ways in which values of beauty and ugliness are racially defined and instituted. See also Patricia Hill Collins, *Black Feminist Thought: Knowledge, Consciousness, and the Politics of Empowerment [1990]* (New York: Routledge, 2000).

18 Hawthorne, *The French and Italian Notebooks,* ed. Thomas Woodson, vol. 14 Centenary Edition (Columbus: Ohio State University Press, 1980), pp. 173–174 (emphasis added).

19 It was thought by some that the Negro race was born when a white woman was "*frightened*" (perhaps a euphemism) by "some hideous black monster of the antediluvian woods" most likely an orang-outang. Thus, "as some have supposed, the negro race was produced, forming an entire new class of human beings, and distinguished from the nature, color, and character of the parents, by a fright of the mother." See Josiah Priest, *Bible Defense of Slavery* (Glasgow, KY: 1852), pp. iii-iv.

20 John Blair Dabney, "The 'Whisker' Order," *Southern Literary Messenger* 8:2 (Feb. 1842). 131.

21 Jefferson observes that the Anglo-Saxon's superior ability to blush is profoundly "preferable to the eternal monotony,–that immovable veil of black which covers the emotions of the other race?" Jefferson continues

> the flowing hair, a more elegant symetry of form, their own judgment in favour of the whites, declared by their preference of them, as uniformly as is the preference of the Oran-ootan for the black women over those of his own species. . . . Besides those of colour, figure, and hair, there are other physical distinctions proving a different race. . . . [for example] Negroes secrete less by the kidnies, and more by the glands of the skin, which gives them a very strong and disagreeable ordour. (138–139).

Jefferson concludes quite logically given his assumptions, that since "[t]he circumstance of superior beauty is thought worth attention in the propagation of our horses, dogs, and other domestic animals, why not in that of men?"

22 William Harper, *Memoir on Slavery* [1838] in *The Ideology of Slavery: Proslavery Thought in the Antebellum South, 1830–1860*, Drew Gilpin Faust, ed. (Baton Rouge: Louisiana State University Press, 1981), p. 131.

23 John Campbell, *Negromania: Being an Examination of the Falsely Assumed Equality of the Various Race of Men; Demonstrated by the Investigations of Champollion, Wilkinson, Rosellini, Van-Amringe, Gliddon, Young, Morton, Knox, Lawrence, Gen. J. H. Hammond, Murray, Smith, W. Gilmore Simms, English, Conrad, Elder, Prichard, Blumenbach, Cuvier, Brown, Le Vaillant, Carlyle, Cardinal Wiseman, Burckhardt, and Jefferson* (Philadelphia: Campbell & Power, 1851).

24 Campbell's de-aestheticizing of Black women must be considered in the context of the numerous white slave owners who raped their Black slaves– one suspects that at least part of the motivation behind Campbell's account of the ugliness of the African woman is to convince his audience both that such intercourse is wrong and, perhaps, more importantly, that sexual violations simply do not occur.

25 In contrast, abolitionists, intent on establishing the personhood of the Negro, repeatedly foregrounded the beauty of Negro women and the sexual desires of white masters.

26 Both Nott and Cartwright, for example, discuss the aesthetic appearance of the African.

27 William Frederick Van Amringe, *An Investigation of the Theories of the Natural History of Man* (New York: Baker and Scribner, 1848), p. 642. Chapter on beauty 640–740.

28 Quoted in Stephen Jay Gould, *The Mismeasure of Man* (New York: W.W. Norton & Co., 1981), p. 45.

29 Calvin Colton, *The Americans, by an American in London* (F. Westley and A. H. Davis, 1833), p. 382.

30 See, for example, Thomas R. Dew, *Review of the Debate in the Virginia Legislature, 1831–32*; reprinted in *The Pro-Slavery Argument; as Maintained by the Most Distinguished Writers of the Southern States* (Charleston: Walker, Richards & Co., 1852), p. 447.

31 Perhaps most notoriously even body lice were seriously considered as a possible way to determine racial difference. In 1861, Andrew Murray, collected lice from the inhabitants of various countries. Finding that these lice differed in color and structure, he concluded that the body lice of some races could not live on the bodies of other races. This study is reported in Thomas F. Gosset, *Race: The History of an Idea in America* (New York: Schocken Books, 1965), p. 81.

32 For an example of these caricatures see Gary Nash, *Forging Freedom: The Formation of Philadelphia's Black Community, 1720–1840* (Cambridge, MA: Harvard University Press, 1988).

33 One could argue that during the antebellum period, Black was indeed threatening to become white. As Frederick Douglass contended, "if the lineal descendants of Ham are alone to be scriptually enslaved, it is certain that slavery at the south must soon become unscriptural" [*Narrative of the Life of Frederick Douglass, an American Slave,* Houston A. Baker ed. (New York: Penguin Books, 1982), p. 50]. Thus, the problem of "passing" became a topic of increasing anxiety in both the South and the North. The stories, written by both Black and white authors, about men and women who thought themselves white only to discover that they were actually Black developed into a genre of the period. See, for example, Richard Hildreth, *The Slave; or Memoirs of Archy Moore* (1836; rpt. 1852). See also work of E. D. E. N. Southworth, Rebecca Harding Davis, Epes Sargent, Gustave de Beaumont, Harriet Jacobs, and William Wells Brown who presented Tragic Mulattoes or Mulattas who discovered they were white.

34 Hawthorne, of course, was not alone in analogizing the transition from slavery to freedom in terms of clothes. On the other end of this spectrum see Samuel G. Howe who argued "Men going from slavery to freedom cannot change their habits as they change their garments." See Samuel Gridley Howe, *The Refugees from Slavery in Canada West: Report to the Freedmen's Inquiry Commission* (Boston: Wright and Potter, 1864), p. 86.

35 William Wells Brown, *A Description of William Wells Brown's Original Panoramic Views of the Scenes in the Life of an American Slave, From His Birth in Slavery to His Death or His Escape to His First Home of Freedom on British Soil* (London: Charles Gilpin, n.d.), p. 7. See also William Wells Brown, *Narrative of William Wells Brown, A Fugitive Slave* (1847) in *I Was Born a Slave: An Anthology of Classic Slave Narratives,* Yuval Taylor ed. (Chicago: Lawrence Hill Books, 1999) in which Brown describes a "beautiful girl, apparently about twenty years of age, *perfectly white*" who is being sold into slavery (690, emphasis added).

36 *Liberator,* March 12, 1858. Reprinted in *A Documentary History of the Negro People of the United States* Vol. 1 *From Colonial Times through the Civil War,* Herbert Aptheker ed. (New York: Citadel Press, 1968), pp. 402–405, quote on p. 405.

37 William Wilson, *Frederick Douglass' Paper,* March 11, 1853.

38 Frederick Douglass, *The North Star,* April 7, 1849.

39 See Henry Sussman, "*The Marble Faun* and the Space of American Letters," in *Demarcating the Disciplines: Glyph Textual Studies* 1 (Minneapolis: University of Minnesota Press, 1986), pp. 129–152; reprinted in Sussman, *High Resolution* (New York: Oxford University Press, 1989); Jonathan Auerbach, "Executing the Model: Painting, Sculpture, and Romance-Writing in Hawthorne's *The Marble Faun,*" *ELH* 47: 1 (1980): 103–120; and John Michaels, "History and Romance, Sympathy and Uncertainty: The Moral of the Stones in Hawthorne's *Marble Faun,*" *PMLA* 103:2 (March 1988): 150–161.

40 Wendy Steiner offers a brilliant reader-response interpretation of *The Marble Faun*. See *Pictures of Romance* (Chicago: University of Chicago Press, 1988), pp. 91–120.

41 It is important to note that Donatello and Miriam think that this statue will take Kenyon's mind off Hilda.

42 Hawthorne's idealization of incomplete form comes closest to reconciling the novel's opposing of the individual and the aesthetic. Indeed, as many critics have noted, the fragment governs the design of *The Marble Faun* itself. The fragment structures not only the Romance's unwillingness to provide the reader with answers to the questions it explicitly raises (what is Miriam's reputed crime? is Donatello a faun? where does Hilda go when she disappears?, who is the mysterious "model" who torments Miriam? etc), but also why the unfinished bust of Donatello is presented as the Romance's ideal art object. The fragment allows viewers the interpretative space to write their own story.

43 Because Hawthorne refuses to entertain the possibility that the literal and the figurative, the particular and the universal can be reconciled, it is appropriate to call *The Marble Faun* a fundamentally anti-Catholic text, a repudiation of incarnation.

44 For a discussion of this Romance tradition, see Richard Brodhead, *The School of Hawthorne* (New York: Oxford University Press, 1986).; John P. McWilliams Jr., "The Rationale for 'The American Romance,'" in *Revisionary Interventions into the Americanist Canon*, Donald E. Pease ed. (Durham: 1994): 71–82. Article originally appeared in *Boundary2*, vol. 17: 1 (1990): 71–82.; and George Dekker, "Once More: Hawthorne and the Genealogy of American Romance in *ESQ* 35 1989: 69–83. The Romance tradition of American literature, of course, has been articulated most influentially by Richard Chase, *The American Novel and Its Tradition* (New York: Anchor Books, 1957). See also Lionel Trilling, "Reality in America" in *The Liberal Imagination* (New York: Anchor Books, 1953), pp. 1– 19.

45 The notion that the Romance exists between the Real and the Imaginary is, of course, the definition Hawthorne establishes in The Custom-House Introduction to *The Scarlet Letter* and in the Preface to *The House of the Seven Gables.*

46 The Roman atmosphere is literally unhealthy: it is malarial.

47 For one of the most strident condemnations of Hilda see Milton R. Stern, *Contexts for Hawthorne: The Marble Faun and the Politics of Openness and Closure in American Literature* (Urbana: University of Illinois Press, 1991). Stern calls Hilda a "moral fungus" (106).

48 Richard H. Brodhead, *The School of Hawthorne*, 77.

49 Mud-sill theory became notorious after James Henry Hammonds's, "Speech in the Senate, March 4 1858," *Congressional Globe*, 35th Congress, 1st Sess., App., 71.

50 Thomas R. Dew, *Review of the Debate in the Virginia Legislature, 1831–32*; reprinted in *The Pro-Slavery Argument; as Maintained by the Most Distinguished Writers of the Southern States* (Charleston: Walker, Richards & Co., 1852), pp. 287–490. Quotation is on pp. 449–450.

FREEDOM, ETHICS, AND THE NECESSITY OF PERSONS: FREDERICK DOUGLASS AND THE SCENE OF RESISTANCE

1 For an elaboration of the problem at the heart of any debate over human rights–why do we invoke the "person" as the guarantee of human rights when it is precisely this figure that is under dispute?– see *Human Rights in Political Transitions: Gettysburg to Bosnia*, Carla Hesse and Robert Post eds., (New York: Zone Books, 1999).

2 For a powerful articulation of this liberal logic see Bernard R. Boxhill, "Radical Implications of Locke's Moral Theory: The Views of Frederick Douglass" *in Subjugation & Bondage: Critical Essays on Slavery and Social Philosophy*, Tommy L. Lott (ed.) (Lanham, MD: Rowman & Littlefield Publishers, Inc. 1998), pp. 29–48. Boxhill argues that even though slaves were:

> morally corrupted by slavery, they still possessed within themselves a sort of fail-safe mechanism that could lead to their moral rebirth and that slavery itself would trigger that mechanism. The most important part of this mechanism was their inextinguishable desire for freedom. Although suppressed and forgotten, it was the hidden cause of slave rebellions. . . (44).

I am questioning Boxhill's account of "personhood" as an inherent mechanism that slavery can never successfully repress.

3 See, for example, the positions sketched in the Introduction.

4 Frederick Douglass, *Narrative of the Life of Frederick Douglass, An American Slave* [1845] (New York: Penguin, 1986), 107. All further references will be quoted parenthetically in the text. See Russell Reising, *The Unusable Past: Theory and the Study of American Literature* (New York: Methuen, 1986), pp. 256–272.

5 For a compelling alternative reading of Douglass's narrative as an effort (albeit unsuccessful) to oppose Enlightenment liberalism see Ronald A. T. Judy, *(Dis)Forming the American Canon: African-Arabic Slave Narratives and the Vernacular* (Minneapolis: University of Minnesota Press, 1993).

6 Henry Louis Gates, "Introduction: The Language of Slavery" in *The Slave's Narrative*, Charles H. Davis and Henry Louis Gates, Jr. eds. (New York: Oxford University Press, 1985), xxiii, original emphasis.

7 Henry Louis Gates, Jr., *Figures in Black: Words, Signs, and the "Racial" self* (New York: Oxford University Press, 1987).

8 See Gates, Figures, and Stepto, *From Behind the Veil: A Study of Afro-American Narrative* (Urbana: University of Illinois Press, 1979) on the *Narrative's* linguistic complexity.

9 The term "brutification" is from Frederick Douglass, *My Bondage and My Freedom* [1855], ed. Philip S. Foner (New York: Dover, 1969), p. 247. Quotation is from Houston A. Baker, Jr., "Autobiographical Acts and the Voice of the Southern Slave" in *The Slave's Narrative*, Charles H. Davis and Henry Louis Gates, Jr. eds. (New York: Oxford University Press, 1985), p. 245, emphasis added.

10 Interestingly, Douglass revises this phrase in later versions of his autobiography, putting it in scare quotes. In *My Bondage and My Freedom*, he writes that the battle with Covey "was the turning point in my '*life as a slave*' " (246, original emphasis). In the *Life and Times of Frederick Douglass*, he writes that the battle "was the turning-point in my 'life as a slave' " (143). Such emphasis suggests how deliberately Douglass seeks to distinguish his life as a "person" from his life as a slave.

11 Since Douglass makes statements such as "A man without force is without the essential dignity of humanity," there exists a substantial body of work on Douglass's conceptions of masculinity (*My Bondage and My Freedom*, 246–247). For a sense of how wide ranging discussion has been see David Leverenz, *Manhood and the American Renaissance* (Ithaca: Cornell University Press, 1989), pp. 108–134; Maurice Wallace, "Constructing the Black Masculine: Frederick Douglass, Booker T. Washington, and the Sublimits of African American Autobiography" in *Subjects and Citizens: Nation, Race, and Gender from Oroonoko to Anita Hill*, Michael Moon and Cathy Davidson eds. (Durham: Duke University Press, 1995), pp. 245–270; *Representing Black Men*, Marcellus Blount and George P. Cunningham eds. (New York: Routledge, 1996).

Although it is often argued that Douglass stakes his "personhood" on his maleness, Douglass's privileging of the masculine needs to be distinguished from his discussion of "personhood." Douglass's account of the masculine is linked to specific behaviors (in particular honor), while he imagines "personhood" as an *a priori* condition. In this sense, Douglass's conception of masculinity competes with his conception of the "person." Although beyond the scope of this study, it would be interesting to trace this implicit rivalry between masculinity and "personhood" through the various versions of Douglass's autobiography. Such a project would examine how Douglass's increasing preoccupation with masculinity is tied to his increasing disenchantment with liberal premises. That is, as Douglass came to see all rights as produced rather than natural, he came to foreground behavior (masculinity and, in particular, violence); to de-emphasize absolute arguments; and to increasingly privilege the performative ("manhood") rather than the categorical ("personhood"). In doing so, Douglass suggests that masculinity is social and relational, as opposed to an ontological and absolute, an identity that depends upon how one acts and only exists when it is acknowledged by others. In this context, Sojourner Truth's famous comment upon hearing Douglass speak on the necessity of violent struggle – "is God dead?" – is particularly suggestive: Douglass comes to increasingly accept the death of absolutes, to construct a liberal counter-narrative only implicit in the *Narrative*.

12 Covey stands as a parody of Christ. For a discussion of the Christian structure of this battle see David Van Leer, "Reading Slavery: The Anxiety of Ethnicity in Douglass's *Narrative*" in *Frederick Douglass: New Literary and Historical Essays*, ed. Eric Sundquist (Cambridge: Cambridge University Press, 1990), pp. 118–140. See also Donald B. Gibson who declares that this "literal conflict

between them, in Douglass' eyes, is a microcosmic conflict between all true religions and false ones, all slavery and freedom, all fathers and sons, all black and white, all authority and liberty, all truth and error." Gibson, "Faith, Doubt, and Apostasy: Evidence of Things Unseen in Frederick Douglass' *Narrative*," in *Frederick Douglass: New Literary and Historical Essays*, ed. Eric J. Sundquist (New York: Cambridge University Press, 1991), p. 89.

13 The centrality of this episode is suggested by Douglass' increasing focus on this incident. In the *Narrative* the episode occupies roughly thirteen pages; in *My Bondage*, ten years later, it occupies approximately twice the number of pages. For an interesting discussion of these revisions see Peter A. Dorsey, "The Mimesis of Metaphor in Douglass's My Bondage and My Freedom," *PMLA* 111:3 (May 1996): 435–450.

14 See Leonard Cassuto, *The Inhuman Race: The Racial Grotesque in American Literature and Culture* (New York: Columbia University Press, 1997), esp. pp. 75–125, for a compelling discussion of the *Narrative's* relationship to Hegel's Lordship/Bondage narrative. See also Paul Gilroy, *The Black Atlantic: Modernity and Double Consciousness* (Cambridge: Harvard University Press, 1993), esp. pp. 41–71. For a powerful contrasting of Douglass's and Hegel's conception of slavery and the fear of death.

15 Caleb Bingham, *The Columbian Orator: Containing a Variety of Original and Selected Pieces; together with Rules; calculated to improve Youth and Others in the Ornamental and Useful Art of Eloquence* (Boston: Manning & Loring, 1804).

16 Douglass, *My Bondage and My Freedom*, p. 431 (original emphasis).

17 Given such claims, it is not surprising that Douglass is often regarded as an exemplary liberal, a Black Ben Franklin. See, for example, Robert Reid-Pharr, *Conjugal Union: The Body, the House, and the Black American* (New York: Oxford University Press, 1999) and Samira Kawash, *Dislocating the Color Line* (Stanford: Stanford University Press, 1997).

18 In future versions of his life, Douglass makes explicit the way in which his treatment is analogous to that of the oxen that Covey sends him out to tame:

> I now saw, in my situation, several points of similarity with that of the oxen. They were property, so was I; they were to be broken, so was I. Covey was to break me, I was to break them; break and be broken – such is life (*MBMF*, 212).

This analogy is pushed even further when Douglass describes how Covey whips him using a branch of a black-gum tree, an object that is "generally used for *ox goads*" (*MBMF*, 214 original emphasis).

19 John Ernest, *Resistance and Reformation in Nineteenth-Century African-American Literature: Brown, Wilson, Jacobs, Delany, Douglass, and Harper* (Jackson: University of Mississippi Press, 1995), p. 161.

20 Ernest, *Resistance*, 146.

21 Frederick Douglass, *My Bondage and My Freedom*, p. 242, emphasis added.

22 Frederick Douglass, *Life and Times of Frederick Douglass* (New York: Collier Books, 1962), p. 140, emphasis added.

23 Surprised that Covey never has him arrested, Douglass explains:

> Mr. Covey enjoyed the most unbounded reputation for being a first-rate overseer and negro-breaker. It was of considerable importance to him. That reputation was at stake; and had he sent me – a boy about sixteen years old – to the public whipping-post, his reputation would have been lost; so, to save his reputation, he suffered me to go unpunished (114).

24 In *Life and Times*, Douglass downplays the pun, recasting it (without italics) as "I now forgot all about my roots" (139).

25 One could speculate that Douglass's representation of Sandy as the one who betrays Douglass's escape attempt is itself a consequence of Douglass's need to distance himself from Sandy's root.

26 Paul Gilroy suggests that this root expresses the text's unconscious.

27 Douglass remained somewhat suspicious about the magical powers of the conceptual category of the "person," unsure whether this concept in itself could force slaveholders and defenders of the institution to accept the immorality of slavery. Thus, when discussing the issue of the "personhood" of the Negro he often approached "personhood" as an effect rather than a source of power. For example, in "The Claims of the Negro Ethnologically Considered," his 1854 Commencement Address at Western Reserve College, Douglass addresses what he sees as the crucial premise of the slave system: the "denial of the Negro's manhood" (501). Douglass explains that the fact that the Negro is a man is a truth that he cannot argue for but simply "must assert" (501). Similarly, in "What to the Slave is the Fourth of July," Douglass again declares that slaves simply are "persons." As he sarcastically asks his audience, "Must I undertake to prove that the slave is a man? That point is conceded already. Nobody doubts it" (II, 369). Although Douglass claims that this issue has been settled, it clearly has not been. The intrinsic power of the "person" in moral matters, in other words, is itself a symptom of rhetorical force.

28 William Wells Brown, *Clotel; or, The President's Daughter: A Narrative of Slave Life in the United States* [1853] (New York: Carol, 1969), p. 34, emphasis added.

29 John Brown, *Slave Life in Georgia: A Narrative of the Life, Sufferings, and Escape of John Brown, A Fugitive Slave, Now in England* [1855] in *I Was Born a Slave* vol. 2, Yuval Taylor ed. (Chicago: Lawrence Hill Books, 1999), pp. 393–394.

30 The Negro, of course, was ideally suited for such experiments since the race was understood as possessing a higher natural tolerance for heat. Thus, John H. Van Evrie offered both a religious and scientific explanation for the Negro's resistance to heat:

> God has adapted him, both in his physical and mental structure, to the tropics. . . .His head is protected from the rays of a vertical sun by a dense mat of wooly hair, wholly impervious to its fiercest heats, while his entire surface, studded with innumerable sebaceous glands, forming a complete excretory system, relieves him from all those climatic influences so fatal, under the same circumstances, to the sensitive and highly organized white man. Instead of seeking shelter himself from the burning sun of the tropics, he courts it, enjoys it, delights in its fiercest heats. Van Evrie, *Negroes and Negro Slavery* (New York, 1861), 251, 256.

That the Negro was naturally more tolerant of heat stress than the white suggests that Hamilton may have imagined that he was doing nothing wrong by performing these experiments.

For a discussion of widespread use of Negroes for medical experimentation see Todd L. Savitt, "The Use of Blacks for Medical Experimentation and Demonstration in the Old South," in *The Journal of Southern History* 48:3 (August 1982): 331–348.

31 Samuel Cartwright, "The Prognathous Species of Mankind" [1857] excerpted in *Slavery Defended: the Views of the Old South,* Eric L. McKitrick (Englewood Cliffs: Prentice Hall, 1963), p. 143.

32 See F. Nash Boney, "Doctor Thomas Hamilton: Two Views of a Gentleman of the Old South," in *Phylon,* XXVIII (Fall 1967): 288–292.

33 Jean Paul Sartre, "Is Existentialism a Humanism," *Essays in Existentialism* (New York: Citadel, 1993), p. 47.

34 Richard Rorty often cites this quotation. See, for example, Richard Rorty, *Consequences of Pragmatism* (Minneapolis: University of Minnesota Press, 1982), xliii; Richard Rorty, "Hilary Putnam and the Relativist Menace" in Richard Rorty, *Truth and Progress,* Philosophical Papers, volume 3 (Cambridge: Cambridge University Press, 1998), p. 53.

35 See for example Gina Kolata, "In Rush to Patent Genes, The Claims Get Smaller," *New York Times* September 24, 1992, p. 1 and by Nicholas Wade "Comparing Mouse Genes to Man's and Finding a World of Similarity," *New York Times* December 5, 2002, p. 1 on the way that advances in biotechnology disrupt notions of the human being.

36 Peter Sloterdijk has drawn attention to the correspondence of Enlightenment accounts of education and the work of genetic engineers, arguing that such genetic interventions simply extend what we have been doing for centuries: shape the identity of children. Humans, according to Sloterdijk, have always been made in culture. See Andrew Piper, "Project Ubermensch: German Intellectuals Confront Genetic Engineering, "*Lingua Franca* 9:9 (2000): 73–77. See also Sloterdijk, "Operable Man: On the Ethical State of Gene Technology" delivered at Goethe Institute May 21, 2000, accessed at http://www.goethe.de/uk/bos/enpslot2.m.

Index

abstraction
  as a racial trait 69–70, 159–62
  liberalism and 128–31, 162–3
  sentimentality and 92–4
  see also liberalism, person, sentimentality
affirmative action 80
  as "reverse racism" 85
  see also colorblind policies
African American
  see Negro
Agassiz, Louis 144
American School of Ethnology 2–3, 7, 66, 99, 141, 144
Animal Rights 25, 95, 184
anti-slavery argument 2, 168–9
  distinct from belief in racial equality 56–7, 62–3
  role of literature in 15–16
  see also Stowe, personhood
Appiah, Kwame Anthony, 81, 190 (note 23)
Arac, Jonathan 17

Baker, Houston 168
Bentley, Nancy 138
Berlant, Lauren 93–4, 220 (note 5)
Bercovitch, Sacvan
  The Office of The Scarlet Letter see chapter 4
    allegory and 121
    ambiguity and 115–16
    conception of person and 113, 123–7
    irony and 116–17
    liberalism and 112–15, 118
    New Criticism and 119–21
    paradox and 118
    race and 130–1
    symbol and 113–15, 117–18
Bible, slavery and 3
Brace, Charles Loring 109
Brown, Albert Gallatin 3
Brown, Gillian 61
Brown, Henry "Box" 102
Brown, John
  Slave Life in Georgia: A Narrative of the Life, Sufferings, and Escape of John Brown, A Fugitive Slave, Now in England 179–82
Brown, William Wells 102, 148, 179
Browne, Peter A. 98–101
Butler, Judith
  Psychic Life of Power 52–4

Campbell, John
  Negromania 102, 143–4
Cannibals All!
  see Fitzhugh, George
Carton, Evan 138, 225 (note 9)
Cash, W.J. 38
Cartwright, Samuel 7, 102, 182
Cassuto, Leonard 41–2
Cavell, Stanley 37–8
Cheyfitz, Eric 137
Child, Lydia Maria 4, 11
Cobb, Thomas 95
Coleridge, Samuel Taylor 154
color-blind policies 192 (note 31)
  false equality of 56–7, 81–2
  see also race
Colton, Calvin 145
Conway, Moncure 3
Constitution
  Three-fifths clause of 190 (note 21)

Dabney, John Blair 142
Davis, David Brion 36–7
Declaration of Independence 33, 73
  debate over self-evident anti-slavery meaning of 1–4, 35
  Derrida on 13–14
  see also Lincoln, Douglas, Taney
Delany, Martin 10, 55, 84
Delgado, Richard 29
Democracy in America see Tocqueville
Derrida, Jacques 13–14

Dew, Thomas R. 163
Douglas, Ann 89
Douglas, Stephen
  on Kansas-Nebraska Act 32–3
  on the Negro 32–3
Douglass, Frederick 4, 11, 84, 103, 149
  manhood and 4, 171–2, 231 (note 11)
  works:
    The Claims of the Negro Ethnologically Considered 190 (note 20), 218 (note 49), 233 (note 27)
    The Life and Times of Frederick Douglass 175
    My Bondage and My Freedom 171, 173, 175
    Narrative of the Life of Frederick Douglass, an American Slave 167–78; as quintessential liberal narrative 177–8; fight with Covey 168–70, 171–5; *Columbian Orator* in 170–1
    "The Nature of Slavery" 173
Dred Scott case
  see *Scott v. Sandford*

Emerson, Ralph Waldo
  English Traits 67–8

Feidelson, Charles 119–20, 121–2
Fisher, Philip 71, 89–92
Fitzhugh, George 3, 72–5
Foucault, Michel 8–9, 52
Frankenstein 163
Furnas, J.C.
  Goodbye to Uncle Tom 60

Garrison, William Lloyd 4
Gates, Henry Louis 168
Geertz, Clifford 22
Genovese, Eugene 39
Geras, Norman 22
Gibbes, R.W. 104
gothic, logic of the 42

Harper, William 143
Hartman, Saidiya
  Scenes of Subjection 50–1
Hawthorne, Nathaniel
  aesthetic theory 137–8, 149–55
  Negro problem and 146–8, 159–61
  opposed to Stowe 17–20
  personification and 138–9
  racism of 17–18, 19, 149
  Romance 155–6
  slavery and 16–17, 137–40
  works of:
  "Chiefly About War Matters" 136–7, 146–7
  Life of Franklin Pierce 195 (note 47), 225 (note 6)
  The Marble Faun see Chapter Five
  Fall of Man in 157–9
  The Scarlet Letter see Chapter Four
  anti-literalist interpretation of 111–12, 127
  see also racial markers, Bercovitch
Hawthorne, Sophia 132
Higginson, Thomas Wentworth 65
Hudgins v. Wright 104–5

Jacobson, Matthew Frye 29
Jefferson, Thomas
  Notes on the State of Virginia and racial aesthetics 142–3
Jordan, Winthrop 1

Kansas-Nebraska Act
  see Lincoln and Douglas
Kant, Immanuel 154
Kermode, Frank 112
Knox, Robert
  Races of Men 66
Kurzweil, Ray 7

Lee, Spike 103
Lefort, Claude 200 (note 18)
Levine, Robert S. 84–5
liberalism
  abstract formalism of 121–3
  as a theory of representation and 15, 43–5, 164
  person as foundation of 11–12, 30–1, 43–4
  racism and 29
  sentimentality and 93–4
  slavery and 34
  US political tradition and 14–15, 30
  see also slavery, Bercovitch, Declaration of Independence, personhood, Rawls, sentimentality
Lincoln, Abraham
  Emancipation Proclamation 139
  Kansas-Nebraska Act 33–4
  on the Negro 33–4, 55
  racism of 55–7
  Stowe and 16
  slavery and 2
  Declaration of Independence and 54–5
Locke, John
  and slavery 27–8

Malcolm X 103
Memminger, C.C. 72
Mercer, Kobena 104

Moncure, Richard 40
Moravec, Hans 7
Morton, Samuel G. 66

Negroes (see also African American and Black and slave)
  aesthetics and 141–5, 148–9
  concept of Man and 2–5
  feeling and 95
  inferiority of 2
  personification of 9–10, 138–9
  Stowe's representation of 63–5, 69, 84–7
  use of term 187 (note 9)
  see also Douglass, Hawthorne, Jefferson, Lincoln, personhood, Stowe
Nelson, Dana 92
Nott, Josiah 66, 102
Northup, Solomon 4

Patterson, Orlando 42
Person/Personhood
  abstract 162–3
  ancient world and 12
  as foundation of ethical thought 6, 21, 30, 42, 50, 57, 165–6
  concept of Man and 5–7
  corporation and 7, 191 (note 28)
  decontextualizing of 20, 26, 164–5
  depoliticizing of 30, 45, 179
  fetal 25, 178, 184
  foundationalist accounts of 36–43, 85, 164–6
  human being and 7
  human rights and 23–6, 35–6
  Negro and 8–9
  pragmatic account of 14, 20–1, 23–4, 182–5
  repression of 18, 20, 39–43
  retroactivity of 25, 165, 178–9
  technological production of 184–5
  use of term 7–8, 191 (note 26)
  see also abstraction, Declaration of Independence, Douglass, Hawthorne, Kansas-Nebraska Act, liberalism, Rawls, relativism, sentimentality, slavery, Stowe
Pettit, John 4
Phillips, Wendell 4, 11, 96
Pierce, Franklin 16–17
  see also Hawthorne
Pitkin, Hanna
  The Concept of Representation 12–13
Plessy v. Ferguson 145
Poe, Edgar Allan 142
Political Liberalism, see John Rawls
Polygenesis 2, 3, 189 (note 13), 66, 99
Powell, Timothy 61–2
Prichard, James Cowles 99
Priest, Josiah 3, 226 (note 19)
Putnam, Hilary 23
Psychic Life of Power, see Butler, Judith

race (see also American School of Ethnology, Stowe, Hawthorne, Lincoln, Douglas)
  antebellum theories of 65–70
  as contingent attribute 7, 9, 10
  consciousness of 57
  colorblind ideal and 56–7, 80
  essences and 55–6
racial markers 2, 145
  clothes 146–7
  feet 188 (note 11)
  hair 97–105
  lice 66, 104
  scarlet letter as 112–13, 124, 127, 132–5
  skin color, limits of 98, 105
  skull 188 (note 10), 66, 102
racial science
  see American School of Ethnology
racism 5–6, 9–11
  difference from racialism 81–3, 190 (note 26)
  see also Affirmative Action, colorblind policy, Hawthorne, liberalism, Lincoln, Stowe
Rawls
  Political Liberalism 45–50
  Theory of Justice 122–3
Relativism
  anti-foundationalism and the problem of 21–3, 166
Reynolds, Larry 195 (note 49)
Rock, John S. 148
romantic racialism 64
Rorty, Richard I. 23, 47, 95, 234 (note 34)

Sanchez-Eppler, Karen 91–2
Sartre, Jean Paul 184
Scenes of Subjection (see Saidiya Hartman)
Scott v. Sandford 2, 5
  Lincoln on 54
  see also Taney, Roger B.
Sellars, Charles 38
sentimentality
  abstraction and 90–3, 95–6
  liberalism and 88, 94–5
  personification and 15, 59, 87, 110
  as progressive 60–1, 71, 91
  as regressive 91–4
  racialism and 108–10, Chapter Two
  see also Stowe

Shklar, Judith 28, 94
Simms, William Gilmore 65
slaves (see also Douglass, Negro, personhood, slavery)
  absolute humanity of 39–40
slavery
  defenses of 35
  hypocrisy and 5, 28
  guilt and 38–9, 182
  law and 39–40
  liberalism and 27–30
  see also Douglass, Hawthorne, Kansas-Nebraska Act, Liberalism, Locke, personhood, relativism, Stowe
Smith, Rogers 1
Stowe, Harriet Beecher
  colonization and 83, 84–6
  opposed to Hawthorne 17–20
  racism of 19, 59–61, 62, 82
  racial essences and 59, 62–3, 68–70
  slavery and 15–16
  personification of the Negro slave and 59–60, 62–3, 64–5, 82–3, 88, 95
  vs. modern liberalism 81, 106
  works: *Dred* 84–6
  Uncle Tom's Cabin 58–66, 68–70
    debate over family in 70–80
    Eva St. Claire's Death 87–90, 96–7
    Eva's hair 106–8
  Key to Uncle Tom's Cabin 63–4
State v. Mann 39
Summers v. Bean 39
Sumner, William Graham 145
Symbolism and American Literature see Feidelson

Taney, Roger B. 2, 5, 134, 187 (note 8)
Thomas, Brook, 61, 133–4
Tidyman, P. 95
Tocqueville, Alexis de 127–30
Todorov, Tzvetan 22

Wald, Priscilla 40–2
Weld, Theodore 4
Wills, Garry 1
Wilson, William 148

Printed in Dunstable, United Kingdom

70606553R10143